Good Furniture
You Can Make Yourself

Good Furniture
You Can Make Yourself

F. E. HOARD AND A. W. MARLOW

COLLIER BOOKS
A Division of Macmillan Publishing Co., Inc.
NEW YORK

COLLIER MACMILLAN PUBLISHERS
LONDON

Macmillan Publishing Co., Inc.
866 Third Avenue, New York, N.Y. 10022
Collier Macmillan Canada, Ltd.

Good Furniture You Can Make Yourself was originally published in a hardcover edition as *The Cabinetmaker's Treasury*.

Library of Congress Catalog Card Number: 52-12393

First Collier Books Edition 1972
Fourth Printing 1977

Printed in the United States of America

PREFACE

This book is a practical guide to the reproduction of fine period furniture. It is especially designed to serve equally well the home-workshop enthusiast, the expert craftsman, and the lover of antiques.

For the craftsman, amateur or skilled, there are abundant working drawings, including cross sections and detail enlargements of unusual or difficult features. The accompanying text explains the required procedures, step by step, and there is a special "how to do it" section on working processes, including joinery, moldings, carving, inlaying, finishing, and the other "secrets" of good cabinet-making.

For all who are interested in fine furniture of authentic design, the book will provide a valuable guide: what to look for in "dating" old furniture, period and style characteristics, construction details, hardware, decorative features, and so forth.

Historical notes are included in the text, and are also arranged for quick reference in a special section, Chapter XI.

The individual pieces shown and described in these pages are authentic antiques of outstanding quality. Their choice was governed by three factors: beauty of design, fine workmanship, and authentic representation of period styles.

CONTENTS

Good Furniture
You Can Make Yourself

CHAPTER I

ESSENTIAL PROCESSES
IN CABINETMAKING

Everyone with a hobby knows that the amount of pleasure it gives him is in direct proportion to the effort and skill he puts into it. This is particularly true when the hobby is cabinetmaking. The creation of a fine piece of furniture is not only fun in itself; it pays an extra dividend of pleasure in each admiring glance it earns, through all the years to come. It is, moreover, a worth-while legacy for children and grandchildren—tomorrow's heirloom. It is not only worth doing, but worth doing very well indeed.

The reader who is already an expert cabinetmaker may prefer to skip this chapter, turn at once to the particular design he wishes to create, and follow the text and working drawings. This first chapter is primarily for the reader with less experience, who nevertheless wishes to do expert work. The procedures described are those used by one of the foremost custom cabinetmakers in the country. By following them accurately, the nonprofessional may obtain professional results without waste of time and effort.

We assume that our readers already know how to handle their tools, and have available at least a minimum of these. Elaborate equipment is not required. Although our text recommends the use of woodworking machines, where these are best suited to the work, hand tools may be substituted wherever necessary. With the exception of the lathe, few machines were available to the master cabinetmakers who originated our designs. These fine antiques were made with

1

hand tools, and can be reproduced in the same manner. Electric machines will, of course, save time and labor when available.

While elaborate equipment is not required, the authors strongly recommend good tools, kept in good condition. A handsaw may do the work of a bandsaw, but neither the handsaw nor the bandsaw will do good work unless it is strong and sharp. Success will depend, therefore, on having the workshop well kept, regardless of how well it is equipped.

The balance of this chapter is devoted to explanation of the fundamental processes in furniture making. For the amateur cabinetmaker some preliminary study of the processes involved will make easier reading of the later descriptions and working drawings. He should also, during the construction of any piece of furniture, refer as frequently as necessary to the appropriate sections of this chapter.

JOINERY *

In early times, a man skilled in making furniture was called a "joiner," to signify that he could assemble parts with a mortise-and-tenon joint. While crude furniture was sometimes put together with pegs and other makeshift means, the mortise-and-tenon joint was used almost exclusively in fine furniture. It is still the strongest and best joint for most furniture uses.

The mortise and tenon consists of two parts: a tongue, or "tenon," of wood on one piece, and a shaped opening, or "mortise," on another piece, into which the tenon fits to join the two pieces. The position, angle, and exact size of both mortise and tenon are carefully calculated, so as to provide a tight joint at the proper angle. For example, if a stretcher is to be joined to a chair leg, the tenon is cut at the end of the stretcher, and the mortise is cut into the chair leg at the proper height, and in the exact position on the circumference of the leg which will give the joint the required angle.

Since the tenon is the more easily reshaped, when necessary to adjust the fit, the best procedure is to cut the mortise first. Its exact size and location should be carefully measured and marked on the proper surface. Then, if a machine mortiser, or a drill press fitted with a hollow chisel mortising bit, is available, it is a simple matter to punch out the mortise. Lacking this equipment, a brace and bit may be used to bore a series of holes inside the area to be cut out. A sharp chisel is then used to remove excess stock and shape the mortise. If the shape of the piece allows it, the mortise is usually rectangular, but if necessary it may be square or even round.

---

* It is understood throughout this book that, except where otherwise indicated, all joints will be reinforced with glue.

The next step is to mark off the depth, length, and width of the tenon which is to fit into the mortise. The excess wood is then sawed away, on the *outside* of the marking lines. A tenon which is cut too large may be shaped down with a chisel, but if cut too small the joint will not hold. When shaping is completed to assure a tight fit, both mortise and tenon are coated with glue, and the assembled joint is clamped until the glue is thoroughly set.

A number of methods are used to strengthen this joint when necessary. The simplest is to bore a hole through the completed joint and drive in a wooden tenon pin. Greater strength, however, will result from the drawbore method. The holes, carefully measured for position, are bored through the mortise and tenon separately, before the joint is assembled. By placing the hole in the tenon 1/32″ nearer the tenon shoulder than the corresponding hole through the mortise, the pin will draw the tenon tightly into the mortise as it is driven through the joint. This eliminates the need of clamping while the glue sets.

A third method of providing extra strength is the wedged tenon. A saw cut is made in the end of the tenon, and a small wedge is entered. As the tenon is driven into the mortise, the wedge is forced into the saw cut, spreading the end of the tenon and causing it to fit more tightly. A slight widening of the mortise at its deepest part will allow greater spread and, consequently, a more secure joint.

Dowel joint. In many cases a joint does not require the strength of the mortise and tenon, or the angle of the grain may make this impractical. The two pieces may then be joined with dowels. These are small round hardwood sticks which may be either made or purchased ready-made in various sizes. The best dowels are grooved spirally, to allow the escape of air and excess glue as they are driven into place.

After determining the exact position and angle of the joint, the two pieces to be joined are both marked and bored with holes. The diameter and combined depth of the holes must correspond exactly with the diameter and length of the dowel. Make a trial assembly, without glue, to be sure the fit is accurate. The dowel should be completely embedded so that the two pieces come together tightly. Then coat the dowel, the holes, and the surrounding surface with glue, insert the dowel, and clamp the joint until the glue has set. This makes a blind dowel joint.

Dowels may also be used to make a visible joint, where this is desirable as decoration. This effect is most frequently employed on such pieces as Welsh cupboards, pine corner cupboards, and similar rustic furniture. In this case the surface panel is first temporarily attached to the frame with brads while the dowel holes are bored. The dowels are then glued in place. After the glue has dried, the dowels are sanded even with the surrounding surface, and the temporary brads are removed.

Lap joints and rabbet joints.   When two pieces are to be joined to form a continuous flat surface, the upper half of the stock may be cut away from one piece, and the lower half from the second piece, measuring carefully so that each lap exactly fits the piece it is to receive. The two lapped pieces may then be fitted together with the upper and lower surfaces perfectly even. This is a simple lap joint. When two boards are joined along their length in this way, the joint is called a rabbet joint.

Tongue-and-groove joints.   When two boards are to be joined along their entire length with a more secure joint than the simple rabbet, a groove is cut along the center of one edge, and a corresponding tongue on the other. The groove may be milled out with a shaper, a router, or plane fitted with a gouge blade, or by several trips across a circular saw set to give the correct depth of cut. The tongue may be formed by cutting a rabbet on each side.

Dado grooves and joints.   A dado is a groove cut across the grain of the wood. Such grooves are commonly cut in the inside surfaces of bookcases or cabinets to support shelves. Narrow, shallow dadoes are also cut to form channels for line or banding inlay. Extra care is required, in making the cut, to keep the wood from splintering. A circular saw may be used on large pieces. For fine work a sharp, thin-bladed knife, guided by a straightedge clamped to either side of the channel, may be more satisfactory.

The spline joint   bears the same relationship to the tongue and groove that a dowel bears to a mortise and tenon. A groove is milled in the edge of each piece, and the spline is made to fit both grooves, thus joining the two pieces.

Butt joints.   Two pieces attached to a framework with ends meeting so as to form one apparently continuous piece, without rabbets or other shaped joints, are said to be butt-joined.

Miter joints.   Picture frames, bracket feet, moldings, and various other members frequently require miter joints. The ends of the pieces are cut diagonally so as to fit together with no end grain exposed. For sawing flat pieces, a miter box is useful to assure a perfect fit. A simple box may be made with two hardwood sides fastened to a board bottom. Measure carefully and make a saw cut through both side boards at a 45-degree angle. Then make a second cut through both sides at exactly the same angle, but facing in the opposite direction. Work placed in the box can then be mitered in either direction by using the appropriate pair of cuts to guide the saw.

Miter joints are often reinforced with a hardwood spline, inserted with the grain running diagonally. The groove for the spline is cut across the corner after the miters are cut. If the corner is exposed so that a spline would be unsightly, the glued miter joint may be reinforced with finishing nails.

Finger joint. Two boards which are to be joined at right angles to form a corner may be cut in "fingers" which will fit together. This method is also used to make a wooden hinge. The ends of the board are first marked off in equal sections across the entire end. On the first board the sections cut out are the first, third, fifth, and so on. On the second board, the second, fourth, sixth, and so forth, are cut out. If the measuring and cutting is accurate, the fingers will fit together to make a perfect joint. A half-blind finger joint is one in which the open sections are cut only part way through one piece, leaving the surface undisturbed.

Dovetail joints are of various types. The name refers to the shape of the joint rather than to its function. It may be similar to a lap joint, a finger joint, or a tongue and groove (sliding dovetail). It may be open (exposed on both surfaces), or blind (cut only part way through one piece, leaving the surface undisturbed).

The dovetail joint is shaped, as its name suggests, like a dove's tail. It is always made with the narrowest part facing the angle of the joint: that is, the direction from which "pull" may be expected in normal wear. The wide flare is thus firmly embedded in the wood to resist the strain. Both the dovetail tenon and the hole cut to receive it must be accurately shaped for a perfect fit. For this reason, a template should first be made (*Figure O in Plate 1*). This may be cut from any thin metal with tin snips. The number, size, and spacing of the cutouts will vary according to use. A thin needlepoint scriber should be used to mark the outline on the wood, so as to leave no space between the template and the marked line.

Figures A, B, and *C, Plate 1,* show the front and side panels of a lift-lid chest or similar piece. *Figure A* is a section of the front panel in which the openings are cut. *Figure B* is an end view of the side panel, on which the dovetails are cut neatly to fit the cutouts of the front panel. *Figure C* is a surface view of this side panel. The outline represents the wide ends of the tails; the narrow ends are indicated by double lines in the center of each tail. The cutouts of the template for this piece are spaced about two inches apart and, since this is an open dovetail joint, the depth of the cutouts equals the thickness of the wood to be used. A bevel gauge set to about a 75-degree angle may be used to determine the angle of the cutouts.

When marking the front panel (*Figure A*), the template is laid on the flat surface, and the wood is marked with a thin needlepoint scriber. It is usually

Plate 1

DOVETAILING

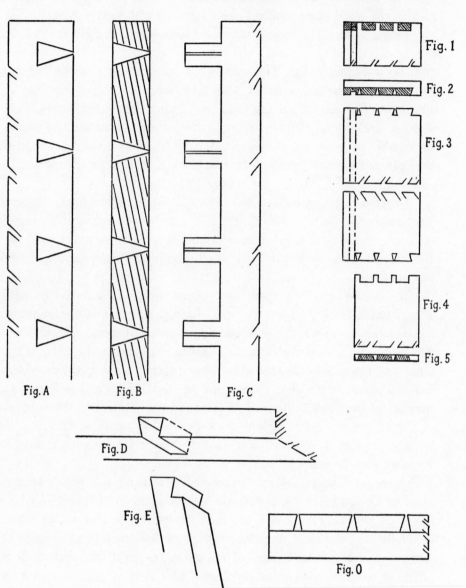

Fig. A   Fig. B   Fig. C

Fig. 1

Fig. 2

Fig. 3

Fig. 4

Fig. 5

Fig. D

Fig. E

Fig. O

the custom to work from bottom to top. The side panel then is placed in a vise, end up (*Figure B*), and the dovetail markings are made on the end surface, using the same template. Care should be taken to place the template so that the position of the marks is identical on both pieces.

The next step is to measure the exact thickness of the panel wood, and make a line parallel to the edge, marking off this measurement on both flat surfaces of each panel. Use a scratch gauge to measure and mark the line accurately. This determines the exact depth of the cuts. A small backsaw or dovetail saw is used to cut along the marked lines. On the cutout panel (*Figure A*), additional saw cuts may be made inside the cutouts to assist removal of the waste stock with a chisel. In cutting the dovetails (*Figure B*), care should be taken to saw on the waste side of the marked line. Excess stock may then be carefully removed for a perfect fit, whereas if the dovetails are cut too small a good fit is impossible.

Figures D and *E* show a blind dovetail joint, used in the stretchers of a chair. The side stretcher is cut out to within ¼″ of the top and outside edges. *Figure D* shows the bottom view. The center stretcher, *Figure E,* has the dovetail cut to match. In making the cutout for a blind dovetail, a small hole may be bored in the wood to be removed, using a bit gauge to regulate the depth. The loosened stock may then be removed with a sharp chisel.

Figures 1 to *5* are various views of the dovetailing for a drawer. For this work a template is made as in *Figure O,* with the dovetails small and closely spaced. Care must be taken in placing the template so that the lower cutout, on the side piece, will not conflict with the groove milled for the bottom of the drawer.

Use a scratch gauge to mark the end of the drawer front (from back toward front) to a depth equal to the thickness of the side piece, for the blind cutouts, as in *Figure 2*. Then mark both sides of the side piece for the matching dovetails. *Figure 1* is a back view of the drawer front. *Figure 2* is an end view of the drawer front. *Figure 3* shows both ends of the drawer side, and *Figures 4* and *5* show the inside and end views of the drawer back, respectively. The dovetails in the drawer back may be open rather than blind.

To rough out the dovetail on a drawer front, the backsaw, of course, cannot be used. It is customary, in this case, to place the drawer front face down on the workbench, clamping it securely. Mark the sections to be cut out in pencil on the back surface. Using a ½″ flat chisel and mallet, chop down vertically to the desired depth, and horizontally, from the end of the drawer front, to the thickness of the drawer side. Chop in small bites (about ⅛″) to avoid splintering the wood.

JOINING TRIPOD TABLE LEGS
(SLIDING DOVETAIL)

The tripod table has three legs which are joined to a central pedestal. The legs may curve outward below the joint in many different shapes according to the style of the table, but all are alike in that the upper end is vertical at least on the inside, and shaped to fit snugly against the pedestal. For added strength, the grain of the wood should always follow a straight line from hip to toe. In shaping the hip joint, a wide dovetail-shaped tongue is left, running the full length of the vertical section. This tongue at the apex is about one-quarter the thickness of the leg, with approximately ⅛″ widening taper at each side. The tongue is carefully shaped and smoothed.

The lower end of the pedestal is then marked for the grooves which are to receive the tongues. After locating three equidistant points on the circumference of the pedestal, a scratch awl is used to mark the exact pattern of each tongue end on the bottom of the pedestal, and the length and width of the narrow apex of the tongue on the vertical side of the pedestal. The stock inside the markings is then removed, and the groove carefully shaped with a sharp chisel, to make a tight fit for the tongue. After the tongues and grooves for this sliding dovetail joint have been prepared, each leg is then separately joined to the pedestal by gluing and sliding the tongue upward from the base of the pedestal into the glued groove. If the joint fits tightly no clamping is necessary, but the glue should be given time to set thoroughly before further handling. This leg assembly is illustrated in *Plate 49*.

If an unusually large tripod is constructed, it is well to reinforce the joint with an iron plate. This should be the size of the pedestal circle, with three prongs or fingers extending over the bottoms of the legs. A countersunk hole in the center of the plate and one in each prong will permit attaching with wood screws.

DRAWER CONSTRUCTION

In a quality piece of furniture, good workmanship is essential in all structural details. Nowhere is this more true, or the evidence more easily seen, than in drawer construction. A well made drawer is strong, securely joined, and fitted in its place so that it slides easily without sticking or wobbling.

The most important structural detail of a free-sliding drawer is its rigidity. A drawer that can be pushed out of square from either end will bind, unless carefully closed with both hands in a straight line. Real, permanent rigidity can be assured only by well cut dovetail joints.

The front of a drawer matches the case, but the sides, back and bottom should be of well dried poplar. For most drawers these should be ½″ thick. For small drawers ⅜″ is sufficient.

After the drawer front, sides and back are cut to size, the only milling necessary is a groove for the bottom. This groove is ¼″ by ¼″, milled inside the full length of the sides and front. The groove should be placed ⅛″ higher than the thickness of the bottom, to provide clearance against dragging. The height of the drawer back is equal to that from the top of the sides to the top of the groove, leaving an opening through which the bottom may be slid in place after assembly. The bottom is held in place by three or four nails driven from the under side of the bottom into the back. With a ½″-thick bottom, a ¼″ by ¼″ tongue is milled on the front and side edges of the bottom panel to permit sliding into place. A ⅜″ bottom is chamfered at the edges to fit the groove. All four corners of a drawer are dovetailed, as instructed in the section "Dovetail Joints."

Drawers are supported on strips of wood attached to the frame of the piece. These strips are usually mortised into the frame at front and back, and screwed to the frame side. Drawer guide strips should be fitted on top of the drawer supports wherever these are necessary to keep the drawer straight.

Drawer handles and locks are of various types and are discussed in Chapter XI.

CORNER BLOCKS

The undersides of table or chair-seat corners should be reinforced with corner blocks. These are triangular blocks of wood, screwed to the rails, and usually notched to fit around the legs of the furniture. The grain of the wood in the block should run diagonally to that in the rails, providing greater bracing against strains. The blocks may be curved or scalloped along the open edge.

RUB BLOCKS

Occasionally an angle joint must be strengthened by the addition of some sort of brace. This is particularly true when the weight of a heavy piece of furniture is supported on a continuous foot, or when a thin decorative cresting stands on edge on a flat surface. In such cases the inside or back angle is strengthened with wooden blocks, glued to both angle surfaces, at frequent intervals. These are called rub blocks, because they are "rubbed" into position.

Clamping is seldom practical for this type of joint. For this reason it is necessary to use hot glue, which sets quickly. After cutting the block to fit the angle, apply the glue and place the block in its approximate position. Then, with short, gentle strokes, rub the block against the angle surfaces until it seems to "catch hold." Then let go.

Glue is often the only fastening agent required, but in some cases brads or screws are added for additional strength. These may be driven in after the glue has thoroughly dried.

HINGED TABLE-LEAF SUPPORTS

Figures A and *B* of *Plate 2* show the top and side views of a flat swing support, such as is used on small occasional tables where little strength is required. An opening is cut in the upper edge of the skirting under the table top, long enough and deep enough to accommodate the strip of wood which forms the leaf support. The strip is attached to the skirting by a single screw through its center. The screw, which is not turned too tightly in order to permit movement, acts as a pivot on which the strip swings out to support the leaf.

The best leaf support is the vertical hinge (*Figures C* and *D*). This consists of an extra skirting under the table top, made in two pieces which are joined at the center with an open finger or box joint. The "fingers" are meshed and held securely while a $\frac{3}{16}''$ hole is drilled vertically through the center. A $\frac{3}{16}''$ round iron pin is then driven completely through, and peened over on the top to keep it from working down. Although the joint should be firm, it must be loose enough to swing easily. The non-swinging section is screwed to the table skirting. The vertical hinge is stronger than the flat swing support, but it should terminate in an extra leg if the table leaf is large (*Figure E*).

FITTING THE TABLE HINGE

Plate 3 illustrates the fitting of a drop-leaf table hinge. This is an important and exacting operation. The rounded moldings, male and female, must be worked to the lines shown in the drawing. Before making the cutout for the hinge, the quarter-round should be $\frac{7}{16}''$ high and $\frac{3}{8}''$ wide. This slight variation keeps the leaf from binding when dropped. The cutout for the hinge is $\frac{1}{8}''$ deep, even though the hinge itself is only $\frac{1}{16}''$ thick.

The center line of the hinge pin must be carefully placed, as binding may

Plate 2

HINGED TABLE LEAF SUPPORTS

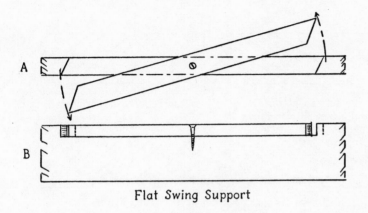

Flat Swing Support

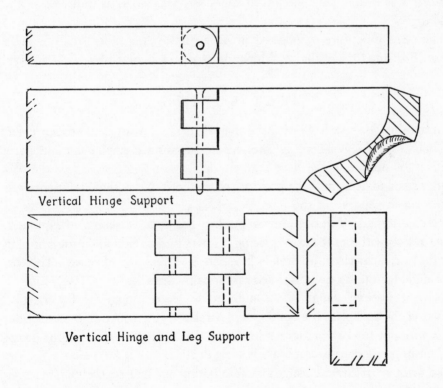

Vertical Hinge Support

Vertical Hinge and Leg Support

Plate 3

TABLE HINGE FITTING

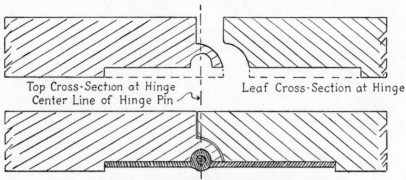

Top Cross-Section at Hinge   Leaf Cross-Section at Hinge
Center Line of Hinge Pin

Top and Leaf Cross-Section With Hinge Fitted

result if it is in line with the joined edges. Proper placing is indicated in the drawing.

The same procedure is followed in fitting hinges on either small or large tables. For small tables the 1⅛″ hinge is used; for large tables, the 1½″ size.

SEAT BORING

In making chair seats which have shaped surfaces, as in the Windsor chair, the holes for the legs should be bored before any surface shaping is done. After cutting the outline of the chair seat, check the seat-plan drawing of the particular chair to determine the positions of the holes. Mark these positions with pencil on the bottom of the seat.

Next, draw pencil lines from the marked positions, as shown in *Figure A, Plate 4.* You will find the exact placing of these lines indicated on the seat plan for the particular chair, by broken lines labeled "direction of brace." The correct angle for the leg holes is stated on the same drawing.

Now set a bevel gauge to the number of degrees suggested for the particular chair, and place the bevel gauge parallel to the pencil line on the seat. This will give the two angles for lining up the bit. *Figure B* shows the gauge and bit in position, at a sample angle of 63 degrees.

To assist in accurate boring, a simple boring jig will be useful. This may be made by boring a hole of the correct size at the correct angle through a solid block of wood. Use the bevel gauge to line up the bit for boring this hole. Then place the block of wood over the seat so that the bit, emerging from the

Plate 4

SEAT BORING AND COMMON MOLDINGS

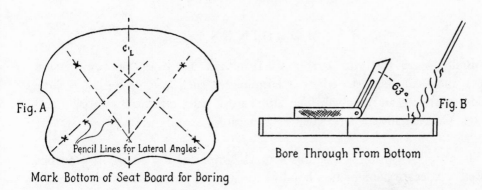

Fig. A

C L

Pencil Lines for Lateral Angles

Mark Bottom of Seat Board for Boring

Fig. B

63°

Bore Through From Bottom

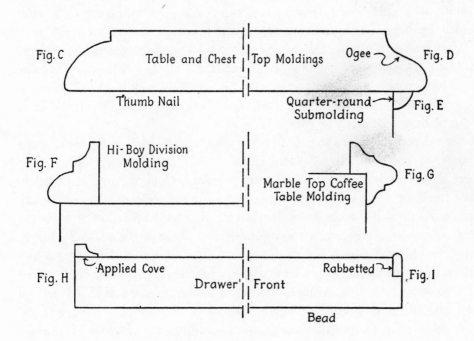

Fig. C

Table and Chest | Top Moldings   Ogee   Fig. D

Thumb Nail   Quarter-round   Fig. E
                          Submolding

Fig. F

Hi-Boy Division
Molding

Marble Top Coffee
Table Molding   Fig. G

Fig. H   Applied Cove   Drawer | Front   Rabbetted   Fig. I

Bead

bottom of the jig, will enter the seat at the correct position. Clamp the jig securely to the seat. The jig guides the bit and assures identical angle of splay for each leg.

MOLDINGS

Moldings are used on almost all furniture. They are of two general types: those cut along the edges of large pieces, such as table tops, and those made separately and applied. The latter are usually attached with glue and brads. Occasionally, where greater strength is required, wood screws are used.

The work of cutting a molding is much simplified if a shaper is available. Special blades for combination hand planes may be procured in various shapes for this purpose. Rough-shaping may also be accomplished by repeated trips across a circular saw, readjusted for the proper depth of each cut. The same effect may be achieved on short pieces with a band saw, using care to avoid cutting too deeply. The loosened stock is then removed with hand tools, after which the shape is thoroughly smoothed with sandpaper.

Most moldings are applied on the surface of the larger piece, but in some cases a bead, or half-round molding, is set into a recess or groove. When the bead projects beyond the adjacent surface, it is called "cock beading." When it is level with the surface, it is called "flush beading." A typical example of cock beading is shown in *Figure I, Plate 4.*

Several popular shapes of molding are illustrated in *Plate 4. Figure C* is the thumbnail, commonly found on the edges of tables and other large pieces. The ogee, *Figure D,* is a graceful shape most popular on Queen Anne or Chippendale furniture. *Figure E* is the convex quarter-round, or ovolo, used in inconspicuous angles. For more prominent angles, such as the division between top and bottom of a highboy, a more complicated shape is shown in *Figure F.* The molding in *Figure G* is well suited to its double purpose of decoration and support for the marble top of a table. *Figure H* is a concave quarter-circle, called cavetto or cove molding. A small half-round, such as *Figure I,* is called astragal or bead; a large half-round is called torus.

In addition to the profile shaping, some moldings are carved with conventional designs on the flat or convex surfaces. The egg-and-dart, dentil, acanthus, and water-leaf designs are traditionally popular. Tall pieces, such as secretary-bookcases, are occasionally trimmed with acorn molding. A series of arches is carved in relief on the molding. The acorns, made separately and applied, hang down from the arch divisions.

CONSTRUCTION OF BRACKET FEET

Bracket feet are made in various shapes to correspond with different furniture styles. These shapes are discussed historically in Chapter XI. Except for shaping, however, the construction principle is the same for all.

A bracket foot is made from two blocks of wood joined with a mitered corner. In *Plate 5* the progressive steps of construction are shown. *Figure 1* shows one of the two blocks, with sample measurements. Actual measurements, of course, will depend on the size of foot required. *Figure 2* shows the same block, mitered. The second block is identical except for the opposite direction of the miter. At this stage the two blocks should be placed together, and the miter joint checked for perfect fit.

The blocks are then sawed to the desired outline, as shown in *Figures 3* and *4*. *Figure 5* shows the method of assembling the blocks, with the miter corner glued and joined with corrugated fasteners at top and bottom. Screw holes are bored through the foot at each side, to prepare for vertical screws which will be driven up into the bottom frame of the case.

At this point a plain bracket foot is ready for sanding and finishing. A foot which requires profile shaping, such as an ogee foot, is completed by the steps shown in *Figures 6* and *7*. As in cutting moldings, the shape may be first roughed out by repeated trips across a circular saw, readjusting the depth gauge for each cut. Hand tools and sandpaper are then used to dress down the surface.

Furniture which is to stand against a wall does not require ornamental shaping at the back. In such cases it is customary to shape only the side of the back foot. This side is made like one-half of a front foot, except that it is not mitered. A plain wooden brace is firmly attached with glue and screws to provide the necessary support at the back. The inner edge of this brace is sawed on a diagonal line, so that it cannot be seen from the front of the piece.

Large pieces, such as chests and cupboards, frequently have a continuous foot instead of four separate feet. In such cases the feet are cut as part of the base molding. The long pieces are mitered and joined in the same way as other bracket feet. Between the front feet the lower edge is usually sawed in an ornamental shape. The sides are often left plain, to rest flat on the floor. The molded upper edge is fastened to the case with brads through the molding, and with rub blocks glued and screwed at frequent intervals in the angle formed by the case bottom and the back surface of the molding. (*Plate 5, Figures 8* and *9.*) Since the foot does not continue across the back, plain diagonal braces are used as described above.

Plate 5

BRACKET FOOT CONSTRUCTION

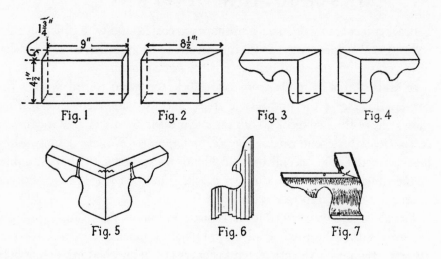

Fig. 1   Fig. 2   Fig. 3   Fig. 4

Fig. 5   Fig. 6   Fig. 7

CONTINUOUS FOOT MOLDING (SOLID OR CUT OUT)

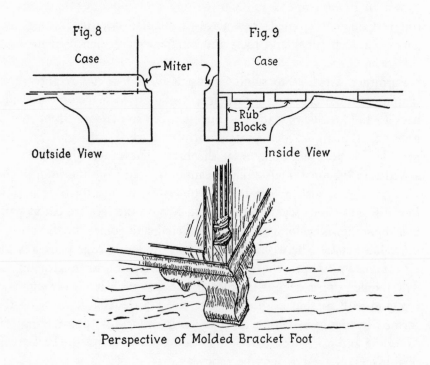

Fig. 8   Case   Miter   Fig. 9   Case

Rub Blocks

Outside View   Inside View

Perspective of Molded Bracket Foot

SHAPING A CABRIOLE LEG

The cabriole leg requires two sawing operations, since it curves outward as well as forward. The first step is to make a pattern, figuring from the drawings and leg cross sections given for the particular piece of furniture. This pattern should then be marked in pencil on two adjacent faces of the block to be cut. Study the drawing in *Plate 6, Figure A,* and note that the pattern is placed so that the knee on side No. 1 meets the knee on side No. 2 at the front corner.

After marking both faces, side No. 1 is sawed accurately along the marked lines, keeping the waste pieces intact for use in the next step. A band saw is most convenient for this operation, if available. *Figure B* shows the completed first cut, with the waste pieces *A, B, C,* and *D.*

Now fasten the waste pieces to the block with brads, in their original positions. Waste piece *A* is retained to provide a flat surface on which the block may rest during the second cut. Waste pieces *B, C,* and *D* are retained to keep the pattern markings complete on side No. 2. *Figure C* shows the block turned so as to rest on side No. 4, ready for the second cut. Note that the brads fastening the waste pieces are carefully placed in what will be waste wood, and as far as possible from the lines representing the second cut.

Now saw along the pattern lines on side No. 2. The waste pieces will drop away, leaving the leg with four definite sides, but with the cabriole curves as shown in *Figure D.* The final operation is to round the leg with hand tools. During this process, any required carving should also be done. Smooth the surface to finish condition with sandpaper.

UNUSUAL TURNINGS

Most lathe work on furniture is simple turning, and requires no special instruction. The following paragraphs, therefore, deal only with the procedures required for unusual turnings.

Off-center turning. Work in the lathe revolves about an axis represented by a straight line between the two lathe centers. For straight turning, therefore, the lathe centers are placed accurately in the end centers of the work piece, so that the turning axis is parallel with the outside line of the piece, before shaping. In order to turn a piece at an angle, the work must be placed in the lathe so that the turning axis is at the desired angle. This is accomplished by placing the lathe centers *off center* in the ends of the work piece.

Plate 6

BANDSAWING CABRIOLE LEGS AND FEET

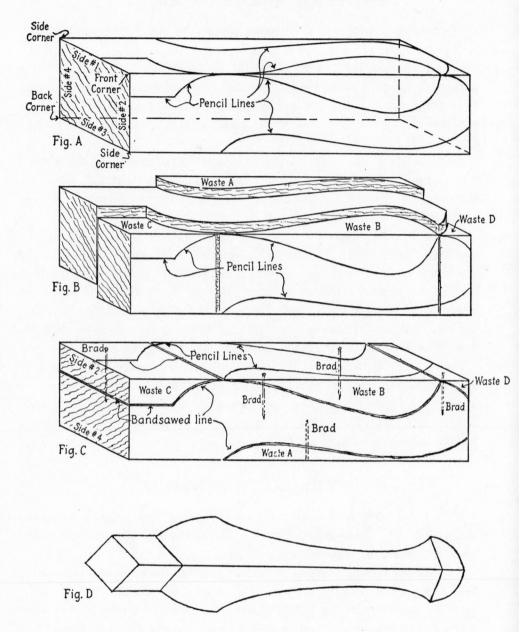

Fig. A

Side Corner
Side #1
Side #4
Side #2
Front Corner
Back Corner
Side #3
Side Corner
Pencil Lines

Fig. B

Waste A
Waste C
Waste B
Waste D
Pencil Lines

Fig. C

Brad
Side #2
Brad
Pencil Lines
Brad
Brad
Waste C
Waste B
Waste D
Brad
Side #4
Bandsawed line
Brad
Waste A

Fig. D

Plate 7

OFF-CENTER TURNING

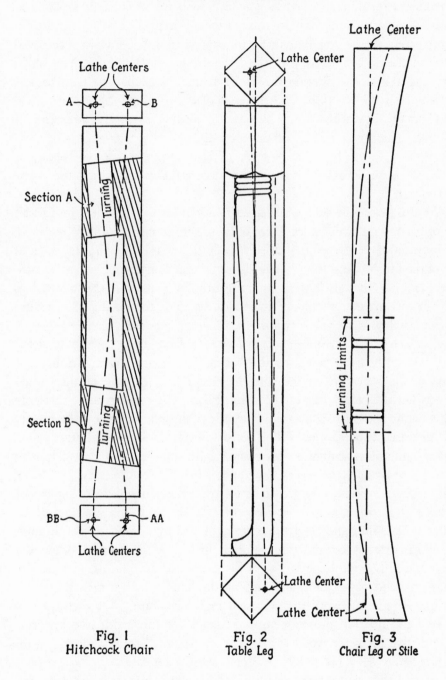

Fig. 1
Hitchcock Chair

Fig. 2
Table Leg

Fig. 3
Chair Leg or Stile

19

Plate 7, Figure 1, shows the top rail of a Hitchcock chair, which requires two off-center turnings. Section A is turned with the lathe centers placed at *A* and *AA*. The turning axis in this position is represented by the broken line connecting these two points. After turning Section A, the work is removed from the lathe and replaced with the lathe centers at *B* and *BB*. This shifts the turning axis so that Section B may be turned. Note that the lathe centers are placed in waste wood, beyond the ends of the turnings. This waste wood is later cut off or worked down by hand, according to the requirements of the design. The center section of the piece illustrated is not turned, since its oval contour requires hand shaping. A straight turning could, of course, be made between two angular turnings by centering the work in the lathe in the ordinary way.

Figure 2 in *Plate 7* shows a table leg such as was occasionally used on various types of early American tables. Here only one off-center turning is required. The distance off center of the lathe ends is determined by the diameter at ankle of the finished leg. It will be readily seen that this turning, when perpendicular, looks as though it were bent inward. To counteract this effect, legs turned in this manner should be joined to the table top at an angle, giving them some splay or spread outward.

The back-chair leg or stile shown in *Figure 3, Plate 7,* is turned only at the section where the seat rail joins the back. This is a straight turning, but because of the curvature of the stile the center line, or axis, of the turned section is not the center line of the whole piece. The turning must therefore be done before the convex surface of the stile is shaped, with the lathe centers placed in waste wood as shown. Further shaping is done by band saw.

Half- and quarter-columns   are turned as full columns, but the work piece is made up of two or four pieces, as required. For half-columns, two perfectly fitting pieces of wood are joined so as to form one square block. A piece of strong, tough paper is placed between the two halves, which are then glued together. The joining may be further strengthened by driving screws through stock which extends beyond the required turning at both ends. When the turning is completed, the two halves are separated by placing a wide flat chisel on the end paper joint, and tapping the handle with a mallet.

For quarter-column work the process is more elaborate. Since each quarter must be a full quarter, provision must be made for the width of a saw cut. Start with two pieces of wood the desired length, $1\frac{1}{4}''$ thick and $2\frac{5}{8}''$ wide (*Figure 6, Plate 8*). This allows $\frac{1}{8}''$ for a subsequent saw cut. Place strong, tough paper between the two pieces and glue them together. Allow time for the glue to set thoroughly, then saw at right angles to the original joining,

Plate 8

FLUTING, REEDING, AND QUARTER-COLUMN WORK

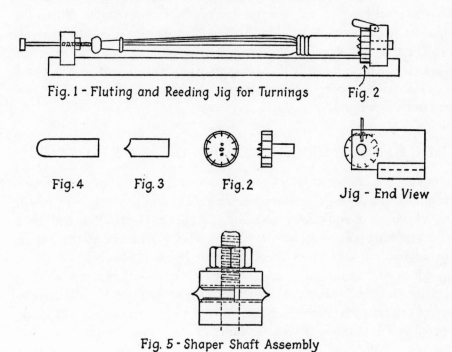

Fig. 1 - Fluting and Reeding Jig for Turnings   Fig. 2

Fig. 4   Fig. 3   Fig. 2   Jig - End View

Fig. 5 - Shaper Shaft Assembly

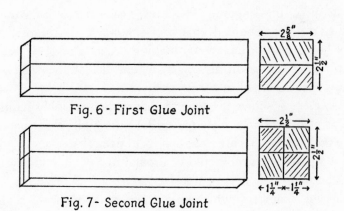

Fig. 6 - First Glue Joint

Fig. 7 - Second Glue Joint

leaving two pieces 1¼″ by 2½″. These pieces are then glued together with paper between (*Figure 7, Plate 8*). When the glue is thoroughly set, square the ends to exact length, and turn the desired shape on the lathe. When the columns are to be fluted, this is done before the quarters are separated (see section, "Fluting and Reeding of Turnings"). Four flutes to a quarter is the usual number. The column is then separated into halves with a chisel and mallet, as described above. In the same way, the halves are divided. This procedure results in four full quarters.

FLUTING AND REEDING OF TURNINGS

Fluting and reeding of turnings may be done on a shaper with the proper tool assembly. A simple jig should be made to hold and turn the piece on the shaper. This piece of equipment is shown in *Figure 1, Plate 8*. The end block with the centering bolt is movable, and the baseboard is slotted so that the jig can be adjusted to take turnings of different lengths. The bolt should be ⅜″ by 6″, ground to a taper point at the end. The other centering block is fitted with a turned wood division "wheel" (*Figure 2, Plate 8*). The circumference of this wheel is marked off into equal divisions, the number of markings equal to the number of reeds or flutes desired. Slots are then sawed at the marked positions. Wheels containing different numbers of slots may be made to fit the jig for different pieces of work. Three wood screws should be turned into the face of the wheel, one for a center, and one on each side to keep the piece from slipping. The screw heads are cut off with a hack saw and filed to a point. The end of a hack-saw blade can be used to keep the division wheel from turning while making a cut. The blade is mounted on the jig so that it can be firmly seated in one slot of the wheel, then raised while the wheel is turned to a new position.

Figure 5, Plate 8, shows the type of shaper tool assembly required for this work. Two of the collars are slotted to hold the high-speed shaper steel. The others are used for fill-in, either above or below the slotted set.

For reeding, the tool steel should be ground to a point as shown in *Figure 3, Plate 8*. The point cuts half of one reed and half of the next. This method avoids varying diameters, which might otherwise interfere with the equal division of reeds. With the turned piece fixed firmly in the jig, it is fed evenly past the cutter for the full length of the reed. The work is then turned in the jig until the next slot of the "wheel" is in place, and the process repeated.

For fluting, the cutter is shaped as in *Figure 4, Plate 8,* to cut one entire groove. The work is fed across the cutter in the same manner as for reeding, using the slots of the "wheel" to place the piece in position for each groove.

After shaping, the reeds or flutes are carefully smoothed with sandpaper. This may be done most easily by cutting blocks of wood with corresponding curves in reverse, to fit over the reeds or into the flutes. The blocks are then covered with sandpaper of the desired fineness.

FLUTING AND REEDING BY HAND

If a shaper is not available, reeding and fluting may be done by hand with a gouge. For this method a reeding box will be helpful. The box is made with two ends and two sides, but no top or bottom. The turned piece is held in the box by a screw at each end. The piece is then marked off for the desired number of reeds, and the vertical line of each reed is scratched with a marking gauge, adjusted so that it presses evenly against the side of the box while scratching a straight line down the center of the turned piece.

The piece is then firmly wedged in the box and each scratch mark is V-cut, after which the reed is rounded with a gouge or chisel. This method, of course, results in a much more uneven job than may be done on a shaper, and requires considerably more sanding. For fluting, a U-shaped gouge is used instead of the V-shaped tool, along the vertical scratch line. A router plane or machine router with a round-nosed cutter may also be used for fluting.

STOP FLUTING

Furniture legs and columns are sometimes decorated with a more elaborate form of fluting, known as stop fluting. In such cases a conventional flute extends from the top about three-fourths of the way down the leg or column. Below this point a bead is apparently embedded in the flute. This is accomplished by continuing the outside edge lines of the flute to the bottom terminal, without removing the center. This may be done with a small V gouge. Then round the top of the bead with a small chisel or, if the stop fluting is small, the rounding may be done with sandpaper. Brass flute-stops are formed by sliding brass rods into position in conventional flutes.

CARVING

Early American furniture frequently features carving, and in many cases the carving is an essential part of the over-all design. Fine carving is an art, and as such is not to be encompassed in the space available here. Fortunately, however, most common designs are relatively simple and within the abilities of the patient craftsman. In fact, it is a happy surprise to note how easily, after a little practice with the correct tools, simple but graceful patterns can be produced. It may, indeed, require some effort not to allow enthusiasm for the new skill to lead to excessive ornamentation. We have only to look at nineteenth century homes and furniture, with their gewgaws and gingerbread produced in the first flush of enthusiasm over the new woodworking machines, to realize how easy it is to be led astray.

A careful study of fine old pieces will show the wisdom of keeping patterns simple, and of placing them so as to form an integral part of the over-all pattern of the piece. When the lines and curves of the carving blend subtly into the lines and curves of the whole piece, a particularly happy result is achieved. The Hepplewhite chair shown in *Plate 16,* Chapter II, beautifully illustrates this point. *Figures 2* and *3* of *Plate 9* are details of the back slat of this chair, which combines fluting and carving to carry out the delicate grace of the design.

In *Figure 1, Plate 9,* are shown the most necessary tools for simple carving. Measurements refer to width across the bow of the gouge.

No. 3 is a slightly concave gouge. Two sizes, ¼″ and ¾″, will suffice for most work. No. 5, with slightly more curve, should be had in the same two sizes. No. 7, with still more curve, will be required in ½″ and ¾″ sizes, and No. 9, still deeper, in ¼″ and ½″ sizes. No. 11, a U-shaped tool, will be useful in three sizes: ¼″, ⅜″, and ½″.

No. 41 is a V-shaped tool used for parting, lining, and so forth. Two sizes are required, ⅛″ and ⅜″. In addition, a sharp flat chisel is desirable in two sizes, ⅛″ for cleaning and smoothing flat surfaces along edges and in corners, and a wider chisel for rough work on flat backgrounds. However, it will be found that, since the sharp edges of the chisel may cut into the surface, the No. 3 gouge will be better for all but the roughest background work. All woodcutting tools should be kept well sharpened. Best results will be obtained by making short cuts, working from each end toward the middle. If long cuts are made in one direction, the gouge is likely to dig into the wood more deeply than is desired.

A compass and dividers will be needed for laying out patterns. Garnet sandpaper in three degrees of fineness will be found essential for finishing of carved surfaces. No. 1/2 cabinet is used first, to remove uneven spots, marks, and bumps. No. 3/0 garnet finishing paper will remove the scratches left by the No. 1/2. Finally, No. 7/0 garnet finishing paper is used to obtain the smooth surface required for a satisfactory finish job.

Plate 9

CARVING

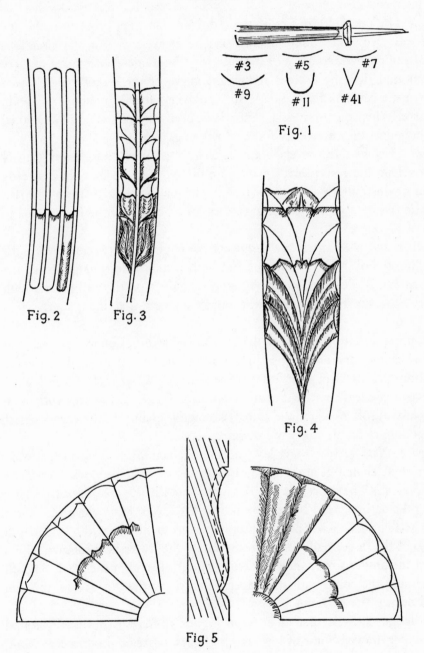

Fig. 1

Fig. 2   Fig. 3

Fig. 4

Fig. 5

Figure 2, Plate 9, shows a simple fluted piece (one detail of the Hepplewhite chair slat mentioned above). A No. 11 tool is used for this work, the size determined by the width of groove desired. Here the chief problem is to keep the grooves even. The pattern should first be marked with pencil along the edges of the grooves, to serve as a guide for the gouge. Note that the piece is curved, and that the grooves follow the curve of the piece. When this is the case, extra care must be taken in marking the pattern to obtain a smooth, even curve. When the grooves, or flutes, have been carefully cut and smoothed with the gouge, they are ready for sandpapering.

Figure 3 shows a more elaborate pattern, a shallow leaf design usually found on long, narrow pieces. In the case of the Hepplewhite chair already mentioned, this pattern is combined with that of *Figure 2* to form the slat. The various stages of the carving process are shown, reading from top to bottom of *Figure 3.*

The first step is to mark the center rib with pencil, then cut it with the No. 41 lining tool. Next, outline the leaf with pencil. Select gouges to fit the desired curves, and cut the outline by tapping lightly on the tool handle with a mallet. Cut the background away on a slope so that the pattern is in relief.

Next, using a shallow gouge of the appropriate width, hollow out each leaf along the center curve, leaving a slightly rounded swell at each edge. Finally cut a rib up the center of each leaf, using the small No. 41 tool, and following the curve of the leaf as shown at the bottom of *Figure 3.* Careful work with sandpaper will soften ridges and impart a flowing quality to the curves. After sandpapering, clean all edges thoroughly.

Figure 4, Plate 9, is a water-leaf carving such as is found principally on Duncan Phyfe chair legs and on the vase turning of some bedposts. (*See Plate 57,* Chapter V.) The process is similar to that used in *Figure 3, Plate 9.* After marking the outline, use a No. 41 tool to part the leaves. Mark the center curve of each leaf lightly. Selecting the proper gouge to fit the width and depth desired, cut the upper half of each leaf convex, the lower half concave. Use a gouge of the proper size to make a sloping cut at the end of each leaf. Smooth and highlight the curve with sandpaper. Finally, use the No. 41 tool to clean out and deepen the divisions.

Shell designs such as that pictured in *Figure 5, Plate 9,* are usually found on the center drawer fronts of lowboys, highboys, desks, and other case work, and on the center fronts, backs, and knees of Chippendale-style chairs. Using a compass, outline the outer circle, then the center radius. Cut the center curve deeply with the No. 41 tool.

The next step is to shape the surface roughly. A typical shape is shown in the cross section (*Figure 5*). Then use dividers to lay off the number of ribs desired, marking them first with pencil, then with the No. 41 parting tool. Cut the outer curves by tapping lightly with a mallet on the handle of the appropriate gouge, and cut away the background.

From this point the procedure may take various paths. For the conventional shell design shown at the left of *Figure 5*, alternate sections are hollowed out down the center, leaving a smooth ridge at each edge. This is done with gouges of the proper widths, working carefully so as to taper the width of the cut toward the narrow center. The remaining sections are convex. In the sunburst design shown at the right of *Figure 5*, every section is convex. There are also some shell designs made with every section concave, divided by ridges. For these designs the ribs are marked with pencil only, not with the parting tool.

The ball-and-claw foot was used frequently by early makers, who showed considerable individuality in its execution. The Philadelphia masters, for example, used a realistic carving which distinguishes their work from the more conventional designs of some others. The claws are thinner, with a suggestion of scales; the knuckles are more prominent, and the web is flattened or even concave toward the joining of the claws. The ankle is bent, and the whole effect is that of strained clutching of the ball. The ball-and-claw design may vary from this extreme realism to a purely conventional pattern.

The first step in making this foot is to band-saw the rough shape shown in *Figure 6, Plate 10*. The width and position of each claw is then indicated by pencil lines drawn down each side of the corner peaks. The large No. 41 tool is used to cut along the pencil lines, as shown in *Figure 7, Plate 10*. Cut away the sections between the claws in convex shape to form the ball and web (*Figure 8*).

At this point it is wise to examine the bottom of the piece to make sure that, except for the claws, the ball is nearly round. Next cut ¼″ from the bottom of each claw, as in *Figure 9*. Shape the claw as in *Figure 10*, leaving an apparent knuckle on each of the two high points, and cut the nail.

The ending of the web is next marked in pencil, as in *Figure 11*, then cut with the appropriate gouge, tapping lightly on the handle with a mallet. Cut the ball away to a depth of about ¹⁄₁₆″ to leave the web in relief. A very slight undercut at the edge of the web will enhance the effect. For additional realism, the carving may now be refined to the desired point. Finish with sandpaper, working carefully to round and highlight the knuckles, smooth the ball and web, and so forth. Lastly, clean out all crevices carefully, deepening the cuts

Plate 10

CARVING (*Continued*)

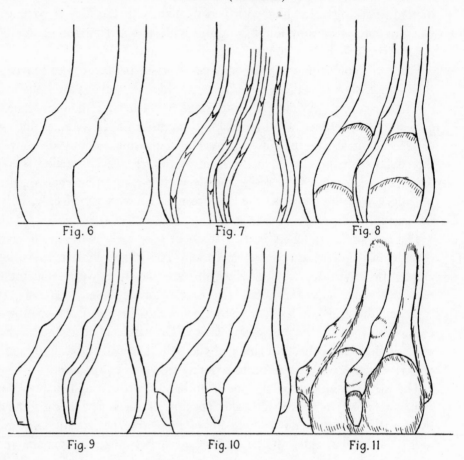

Fig. 6　　　　　Fig. 7　　　　　Fig. 8

Fig. 9　　　　　Fig. 10　　　　　Fig. 11

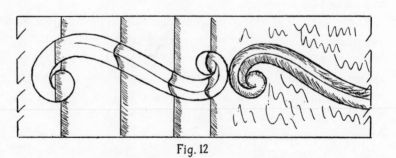

Fig. 12

along the sides of the claws, with the No. 41 tool held at a slant so as to make a slight undercut.

The procedure illustrated in *Figure 12, Plate 10,* applies to almost all flat surface carving. From left to right, the following stages are shown. First, outline the pattern in pencil, then cut away the background to the desired depth. The outline cut may be made with the No. 41 tool, after which the flat background is shaved away with a shallow gouge. Next, shape the pattern, using the appropriate gouges. Note that in the pattern illustrated, the curve of the upper half sweeps from convex to concave, that of the lower half from concave to convex. This gives a graceful effect when carefully executed.

It will be found that, in any type of carving, careful work in finishing will be well repaid. The appropriate tools should be used to sharpen outlines, clean out corners, and so forth. Thorough sandpapering is essential. Careful execution of a practice carving, on a piece of waste wood, will bring to light the most convenient techniques in handling the tools for the best results.

INLAYING

Many fine pieces of furniture owe much of their beauty to inlaying. Although this is one of the most effective means of decoration, the process is not difficult. It is only necessary to use great care in making the cutout section fit perfectly the design which it is to receive.

For simple line inlay, an excellent cutting guide may be made by clamping two straightedges in place on either side of the desired channel, after marking its position with pencil. Make sure that the strip of inlay fits snugly between the straightedges. Then, with a sharp knife, make several cuts along each edge of the channel. Use a chisel to remove stock between the cuts, to a depth exactly equaling the thickness of the inlay.

When the channel has been prepared, the edge guides are removed, and the strip of inlay is cut to the desired length. A thin coat of glue is applied to the strip, which is then tapped lightly into place with a mallet. Work carefully to avoid breaking the inlay.

When more elaborate patterns are used, a template may be made to serve as a cutting guide. When the inlay is glued in place, it should then be covered with a protecting layer and clamped securely until the glue is thoroughly dry.

Some inlay patterns, including rope or spiral inlay, may be purchased ready to apply. Line inlay may be obtained in various widths.

VENEERING

When a beautifully patterned surface is desired, veneer may be used over the solid wood. For matched veneering, care must be taken to cut the edges perfectly straight. A popular pattern is diamond-matched veneer, in which four pieces are joined so that the grain forms a diamond design. Veneers may also be used to form swirls and other pleasing patterns. The matched edges are joined by gluing veneering tape over the joint. Matched veneers may be bought joined and ready to apply.

Veneers are very thin (about $\frac{1}{32}''$). For this reason wrinkles may develop unless the veneer is carefully pressed smooth, from the center outward. Glue should not be applied to the veneer itself, but should be spread thinly and evenly on the surface to be veneered. The veneer is then carefully centered and laid with a rolling motion, making sure no air is trapped to form bubbles.

Most veneering should not be undertaken without a veneer press. Small pieces, however, may be veneered without elaborate equipment. After the veneer is applied, it may be covered by a hot zinc plate and then by a board, flat or curved to fit the surface. This is clamped with closely spaced C clamps, and allowed to dry for at least twenty-four hours.

FINISHING

The process of finishing furniture has always been so highly controversial that the authors hesitate to say "It must be done this way," or "It must be done that way."

If this discussion deals primarily with poor results under given conditions, it is in the hope that the reader will thus understand, and retain to a higher degree, the reasons for good finishing procedure.

The most important single factor is the condition of the wood surface to be finished. In almost every instance of poor finishing, the cause is the same: lack of adequate sanding with the proper grades of sandpaper. Even a slightly rough surface condition will persist and spoil the finish. This cannot be overcome after the first coat of finishing material has been applied, because the sanding necessary to get a smooth surface would cut through the stain and leave an uneven, undesirable color.

The next cause for disappointment in the finished product is insufficient drying time between coats. Humidity plays an important role at this point.

Contrary to popular belief, a hot summer day, for instance, is not ideal for drying finishing materials. There can be no set rule for drying time, but each coat must be thoroughly dry before the finishing process is continued.

The next and last cause for a disappointing finish is in the way materials are applied. Oil stain, even though it is wiped off with a cloth, should first be brushed well into the wood and applied evenly over the surface, always brushing *with* the grain of the wood. Other materials, such as shellac, are also applied by brushing with the grain.

FINISHING MATERIALS, AND HOW TO APPLY THEM

Sandpaper. Garnet cabinet paper No. 1/2 is most satisfactory for first or rough sanding. Coarser paper will scar the wood surface too deeply. The most convenient method of sanding is with quarter-sheets of sandpaper fastened over a block of wood or cork. Do not put too much pressure on the block while sanding, since this will hasten nothing except fatigue. Sand much longer with each number paper than you consider necessary. Always sand *with* the grain of the wood.

The next finer grit to be used is No. 3/0 garnet finishing paper. Thorough sanding with this will remove all the coarse scratches resulting from the previous operation. In like manner, and for the same reason, No. 7/0 garnet finishing paper should be used for the final sanding operation. Save the worn sandpaper to rub down the finish between coats.

To sum up: the chances for a satisfactory finish are excellent when the surface has been well sanded. The odds against a good finish increase as the quality of the sanded surface decreases.

Water and spirit stains are extremely hard to use, and while their deep penetration is desirable, it is offset by the difficulty of applying evenly; furthermore, these two stains will raise the grain of the wood considerably more than oil stain will, requiring extra sanding after the stain has dried.

Oil stain should be used as the first coat. Brush well with the grain. The longer it sets before wiping, the deeper will be the final color. Wipe with a cloth evenly, leaving no brush or cloth marks, especially in corners. Allow *at least* overnight drying.

Shellac, diluted with an equal quantity of denatured alcohol, forms the second coat. If applied with a soft, fine brush, coated quickly and without excessive brushing, the result will be satisfactory. Dry overnight, or longer if necessary. Using No. 7/0 finishing paper which has had the sharpness worn off, sand the shellac coat to a smooth, glassy surface. The finish is now ready for one of a choice of sealing materials.

Varnish   is full-bodied and easy to apply with a brush. Over a long period of time, however, it has a tendency to absorb enough dust to give it an uncared-for appearance. Another characteristic of varnish is that, with repeated expansion and contraction, fine lines or "crow's feet" may develop.

Lacquer   has a toughness and durability which make it one of the foremost finishing materials. It is not suited for brushing, but if a spray outfit is available, dull lacquer for the finish coats is highly recommended.

Shellac   may also be used for the final coats. Diluted half and half, two or three coats should leave a pleasing finish.

No matter which material is used for the final operations, sanding between coats with well worn No. 7/0 paper is necessary.

Fine steel wool   may be rubbed lightly over the surface after the last coat has thoroughly dried.

Wax,   preferably a good paste wax, should be applied last, wiped dry, and polished.

RUSH SEAT WEAVING

Rush seats are woven on the finished frame of the chair. The free end of a roll of fiber is tacked tightly to the inner side of one side rail, near the widest part of the seat. The roll is then passed over the front rail, back under it, and up over the top strand and the side rail, back under the side rail and across to the opposite side (*Figure 1, Plate 11*). There it is passed over the side rail, back under, over the strand and front rail, under and back against the inner side of the side rail, where it is tacked (*Figure 2*). This process is repeated with separate strands (*Figure 3*) until the wide corners have been filled and the remaining area is a perfect square (*Figure 4*). Regular weaving is then started by tacking the free end to the underside of the back rail, close to the post. The roll is then passed over the front rail, back under, over the strands and the side rail, back under and across to the other side rail, over and back under the strands, over and under the front rail, then the back rail, and so on, continuously (*Figure 5*) from corner to corner until the diagonal "seams" meet at the center (*Figure 6*). Care should be taken to keep the weaving flat, tight, and smooth. When splices are required, they should be made on the undersurface. The ends to be spliced should first be flattened and glued together, then bound tightly with stout thread.

Plate 11

RUSH SEAT WEAVING

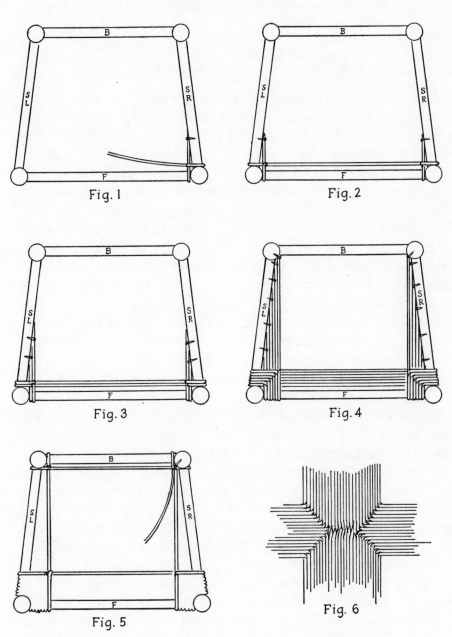

Fig. 1

Fig. 2

Fig. 3

Fig. 4

Fig. 5

Fig. 6

Rush seats should be protected by a coat of shellac or varnish. As the rush is porous, thin clear glue is often used as a sizing coat before the finish is applied.

BENDING HICKORY

Either green or seasoned hickory may be bent, but green is usually preferred when available. It may be procured easily in many areas of this country. Most farms, especially in the East, have wooded sections where small hickory trees can be found. The ideal tree for this purpose is four to eight inches in diameter, with a measurement of about five feet from the base to the first limb. This is the only part of the tree suitable for the purpose, and when green will split easily.

Using a wide wedge of steel, bisect directly through the center core. Then, depending upon the size of pieces needed, either quarter the two halves or split off wedge-shaped strips of desired thickness, always entering the wedge from the core outward. It will be found that on these wedge-shaped pieces a draw-knife will work with ease, for further shaping.

Work down the pieces needed (larger than finished size to allow for shrinkage: ⅛" to 1" oversize in thickness and width). Have prepared a wooden form with a slightly smaller radius than the desired curve. Clamp the hickory to this form, first in the center, then gradually outward toward each end, setting the clamps about six inches apart, and allowing fifteen to thirty minutes for each bend. Two days clamped on this form should be sufficient. After removal, the bent piece may be placed in a bar clamp and drawn inward to the proper radius. The length of time it should remain in this clamp depends to a great extent upon the humidity or drying condition of the atmosphere. It may vary from a few days to a few weeks. The piece should be kept in the bar clamp until there is no more pressure against the clamp jaws.

Seasoned hickory is much harder to work, but may be used when green wood is not available. Choose boards with the straightest grain, and cut oversize. Have ready a trough large enough to contain the pieces to be bent.

Mix a strong solution of water and ammonia, or of water and synthetic urea. Submerge the piece to be bent, and leave until saturated (about twenty-four hours), then remove from the solution and proceed as in bending green wood.

CHAPTER II

CHAIRS

THE DAWN of the eighteenth century was also the dawn of a new era in chair design. Up to this time English furniture had been massive, cumbersome, and uncomfortable. Chairs were scarce and were largely restricted to the heads of households, others being accommodated with stools. In 1688, however, William and Mary came from Holland to rule England, bringing with them ideas of domestic comfort and style hitherto unknown. Their reign was followed in 1702 by that of Queen Anne. Furniture designers eagerly copied and developed the Dutch style features and assimilated them into the distinctive Queen Anne style, the forerunner of the great designs of Chippendale and others in the later Georgian period. American designers closely followed the lead of the English, and the Dutch influence was further intensified here by the large Dutch settlement in New York. Later English designers, such as Hepplewhite and Sheraton, abandoned most features of the Queen Anne style, but retained the lightness and grace which distinguished it from previous designs.

An inflexible rule in chair making is that armchairs are always 1″ wider (back and seat) than side chairs. The one exception to this rule is a Hepplewhite shield-back chair, since a change in width without a corresponding change in height would destroy the pleasing proportions of the shield. Where side chairs and armchairs are used as a set, it is advisable to have all the same height. In most of the following illustrations, only the armchair of each set is shown. Measurements for side chairs to match are the same, except for the 1″ variation in width.

35

There is a long-standing controversy over which of two ways the top rail of a chair should be joined to the stile to give it the most strength. The oldest method is the mortise-and-tenon joint. An oblong tenon is cut on the top of the stile, while a matching mortise is cut into the top rail. The width of the stile will, of necessity, determine the width of the tenon. In any case the tenon will not be large, and the weakness of this method can be seen on any of the chair illustrations by studying the grain direction of the stile.

The other method, which the authors recommend, is to place two ³⁄₁₆″ dowels in each joint. Most chairs made today have only one ³⁄₈″ dowel in each joint.

———◆———

The chair shown in *Plate 12* is a typical Queen Anne design. The cabriole leg, the club or Dutch foot with a shoe, the fiddleback splat, the curved shaping of the front rail, and the carved knees are all features of this period. Despite its grace, the construction is sturdy. Both mortise-and-tenon and dowel joints are used, as indicated on the drawing. The rough-shaping of all parts of this chair, except the stretcher, is done by band saw. Those members that have a rounded or oval form are then worked to that shape with hand tools.

It should be noted that the front legs are doweled to the rails, because of the acute angle of side- and front-rail grain. The chair back is curved to a comfortable shape. The splat (about ⁷⁄₁₆″ thick) is sawed to follow the curve of the stiles. One turned stretcher reinforces the back legs. The cabriole leg is rough-shaped by band saw, then worked down by hand when the carving is done. Chairs of this period were usually made of walnut.

The stiles should be made first. Each stile includes the back leg and the side frame of the chair back, cut in one long piece. After cutting the rough shape by band saw, with a slight taper toward the top, round it with hand tools, except for the square section at the seat level. Cross sections at various points are shown in the drawings. Cut mortises in the stiles for the seat rails. Methods of cutting and fitting joints are described in Chapter I.

Next cut the back seat rail. Note that this rail is straight on the bottom edge, but has a shaped top edge rising above the seat level. This edge is grooved for the splat. Tenons are cut on the ends of the rail to fit the mortises in the stiles.

Turn the stretcher, cut to length, and bore matching holes in the stiles.

Plate 12

QUEEN ANNE CHAIR

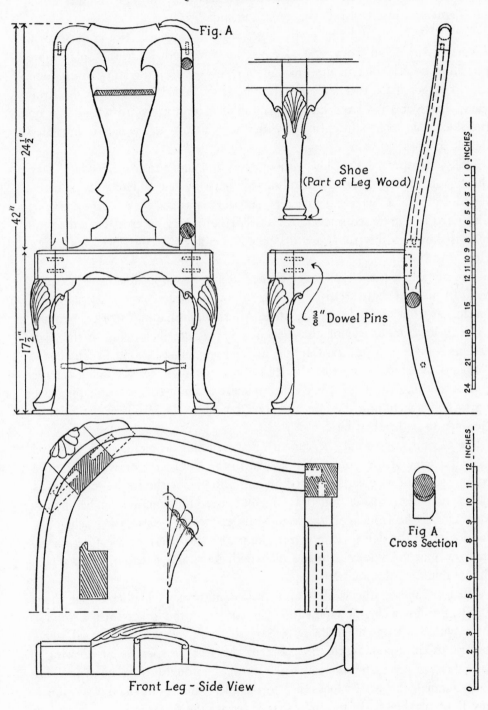

Fig. A

$24\frac{1}{2}''$

$42''$

$17\frac{1}{2}''$

Shoe
(Part of Leg Wood)

$\frac{3}{8}''$ Dowel Pins

INCHES

Fig A
Cross Section

Front Leg - Side View

INCHES

Assemble the stiles, back seat rail, and stretcher. Bore through the assembled rail joints and insert glued wooden tenon pins.

Cut the top rail, and round the edges with hand tools. (See cross section, *Figure A,* in detail drawing.) Groove the lower edge for the splat. Bore matching dowel holes in the rail ends and the tops of the stiles. Each joint should be bored for two ³⁄₁₆″ dowels. The front dowel is shown in the front view, the second is placed directly behind it. The dowels are not shown on the side view, to avoid confusion with the splat tongue, which is indicated by dotted lines.

Make a temporary assembly without glue, and measure for the splat. Make the splat, working down the band-sawed shape by hand. The splat is band-sawed from thick wood to give the necessary vertical curve. This curve is illustrated by the dotted lines on the side-view drawing. A cross section of the splat is shown in the front-view drawing. Assemble the complete back, using glue.

The cabriole legs are first rough-shaped by band saw, as described in Chapter I. In making the pattern for the leg, allow the necessary thickness for the carving at front and sides of the knee. After rough-shaping, work down the leg with hand tools, leaving the shell in relief. A detail drawing of the shell pattern is given in *Plate 12.* Carving instructions will be found in Chapter I.

Round the front corners of the legs, above the shell design, but leave the final smoothing until the chair is completely assembled. Finish shaping the leg by hand, including the foot and shoe, but leave the scrolls at the sides of the knee to be finished later.

Use a band saw to cut the curved front and side seat rails, and to shape the lower edge of the front rail as shown in the front-view drawing. Remove saw marks with a spokeshave or drawknife. Rout out the inside top edge as indicated in the cross-section drawing, but leave the molding to be shaped later. Dowel the front legs to the rails, using two ³⁄₈″ dowels in each joint. Positioning of the dowels is shown in the front-, side-, and top-view drawings, *Plate 12.* Join the side rails to the stiles with mortise and tenon, using tenon pins to reinforce the joints.

After assembling the complete chair and allowing the glue to set thoroughly, finish working down the top front corners of the legs to form a smooth curve with the front and side rails. Saw the wing blocks from wood thick enough to correspond with the bulge of the legs (corner detail drawing). Glue them in place and allow the glue to dry thoroughly. Use hand tools to finish shaping the wing blocks and to complete the scrolls on the adjoining legs. Rout out the tops of the front legs to receive the slip seat.

The shape of the molding at the top of the seat frame is shown on the rail cross section, *Plate 12*. Using a chisel and other hand tools, shape this molding all around the front and sides. Sand all surfaces, and apply the desired finish. This completes the side chair. The matching armchair, 1″ wider, is made as above, after which arms and arm supports may be made and assembled as described in the following text (*Plate 13*).

———◆———

Plate 13 shows a mahogany chair of Philadelphia design, with modifications of Queen Anne features. The cabriole leg is used, but the club foot is replaced by the drake foot. Shaping of the front seat rail is repeated in the side rails. The broad splat has a raised margin ending in scrolls, to match the characteristic scroll design of the Philadelphia arm. The top rail ends in a plain roll, and is ornamented with a carved fan at the center, a feature often found, with variations, in Philadelphia designs. An alternative ball-and-claw foot is also shown.

The chair is first completed without arms, after which the arms and arm supports are added. As in the case of the preceding chair, the first step is to cut the stiles, or back legs. Use a single piece of wood for each stile, rough-shape by band saw, and finish shaping by hand. Mortise the stiles for the seat rails.

Cut the back seat rail, mold the raised upper edge, and groove it for the splat. Cut tenons on the rail ends, and join to the stiles, using tenon pins for reinforcement.

Cut the top rail from wood sufficiently thick to allow for the horizontal curvature. The curve is shown in a detail drawing of the rail. Use hand tools for the final shaping, including the ears and the central fan design. A detail drawing of the fan is included in *Plate 13*. Carving instructions may be found in Chapter I.

Groove the straight section of the rail's lower edge for the splat, and bore matching dowel holes in the rail and the stiles. Two ³⁄₁₆″ dowels should be used for each joint. The front dowel is indicated by dotted lines on the front-view drawing. The second dowel should be placed directly behind the first.

Mount the rail on the stiles temporarily without glue, to determine exact measurements for the splat. Band-saw the splat outline, using thick enough wood to allow for the horizontal curvature. The curve may be determined

Plate 13

PHILADELPHIA DRAKE-FOOT CHAIR

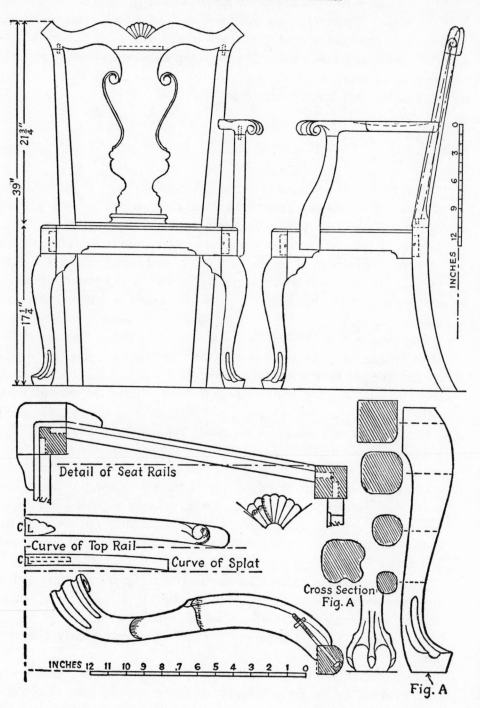

Detail of Seat Rails

C L
-Curve of Top Rail-
C
Curve of Splat

Cross Section
Fig. A

INCHES 12 11 10 9 8 7 6 5 4 3 2 1 0

Fig. A

from the detail drawing (Curve of Splat, *Plate 13*). Dress down the surface with hand tools, leaving the scrolls and raised edges in relief. Assemble the completed parts with glue.

Make a pattern for the front legs, conforming to detail drawings, including cross sections, in *Plate 13*. Extend the pattern at the top to include the square corner block. The cross section *Figure A* is to be used for the drake foot. If the ball-and-claw foot is preferred, the pattern at the base must be made to include this. Study the carving instructions in Chapter I for details of the ball and claw. The drake foot, after shaping, is grooved with a U-shaped gouge.

After shaping the legs, cut mortises for the seat rails in the square top sections, as indicated in the drawings.

The front and side rails are rabbeted inside the top edge to provide for the slip seat. (Refer to cross section of rail in *Plate 12*.) Cut the rails, tenon the ends, and band-saw the lower edges as shown in the front- and side-view drawings, *Plate 13*. Use a spokeshave or drawknife to remove saw marks. Join the rails to the legs (see detail drawing), using tenon pins through the joints for reinforcement. Join the side rails to the stiles in the same way. Then cut the wing blocks, glue them to the front legs, and allow time for all glue to set thoroughly. Final shaping with hand tools includes smoothing of joints between legs, rails, and wing blocks, rounding of upper-leg front corners, routing out of leg tops for the slip seat, and molding of the seat edge all around. Sand all outside surfaces to finish smoothness.

The arms and arm supports may be rough-shaped by band saw, then worked down by hand. The shape of the arm is shown in a detail drawing, *Plate 13*. The scroll ends are grooved with a U-shaped gouge. The shape of the arm support is shown in the front and side drawings.

After shaping the arm and arm support, bore dowel holes and dowel them together temporarily, without glue. Hold the assembly in place on the chair, and mark the position of the bolt (see detail drawing of arm). Bore a hole for the $\frac{1}{8}''$ by $3\frac{1}{2}''$ R.H. bolt, through the stile from the back, so that the point of the bit marks the position of the bolt hole in the arm. Then separate the arm and support, and bore the hole in the arm. Cut a slot in the underside of the arm, for inserting the nut. Counterbore the stile for the head of the bolt, as shown in cross section, detail drawing of arm and stile, *Plate 13*.

Join the arm and support permanently with glue, place in position, and insert the bolt and nut. Attach the arm support to the seat rail with three screws from inside the rail. Plug the holes in arm and stile with matching wood. After completing assembly of both arms, sand and apply finish as desired.

Side chairs to match are made 1″ narrower, with arms and arm supports omitted.

———◆———

The chair discussed above is typical of the early Chippendale period. In his later years the great designer "modernized" furniture styles, introducing the period now often called "Chinese Chippendale." The carved cabriole legs of early designs were replaced by square legs, often fluted. (Still later, Hepplewhite adapted the square leg to the delicate lines of his own designs, modifying it with a graceful taper.)

A popular chair design of the later Chippendale period was the ladder back. This style may have been inspired by an earlier type of chair which is also sometimes called a ladder back, but which most authorities call a slat back (*Plate 23*).

Ladder backs are popular in reproduction today, and are usually made of mahogany, like the best originals. The chair illustrated in *Plate 14* has gracefully curved ladders, with a cutout design. The square legs are molded along the outside corner. The inside corners are chamfered. Four stretchers give this chair a particularly sturdy construction.

The first step is to band-saw the stiles, then complete the shaping with hand tools. (Sand all parts after shaping, before assembly.) Then cut the back seat rail, rabbeting the top inside edge for the slip seat. Mortise the stiles, and tenon the rails to fit. Cut the back stretcher, using ⁷⁄₁₆″ wood. Because of the thinness of the wood, cut the ¼″-thick tenons on the extreme inside surface, to allow for greater strength of the outside wall of the matching mortise. Place the mortise so that the stretcher fits flush with the outside surface of the stile. This flush fitting is always used with rectangular stretchers entering square legs.

Before assembling the back, the three ladders must be made and tenoned, and the stiles must be mortised for the ladder joints. The curve of the ladders is indicated in the drawing labeled "secondary ladders." A detail of the ladder pattern is also shown. After sawing the rough shape, finishing is done by hand. The pierced design may be cut out with a jigsaw or coping saw, threaded through holes bored in the waste wood. The top rail is similarly made, but is longer and thicker and fits over the stile ends with dowel joints. Two ³⁄₁₆″

Plate 14

CHIPPENDALE FOUR-LADDER CHAIR

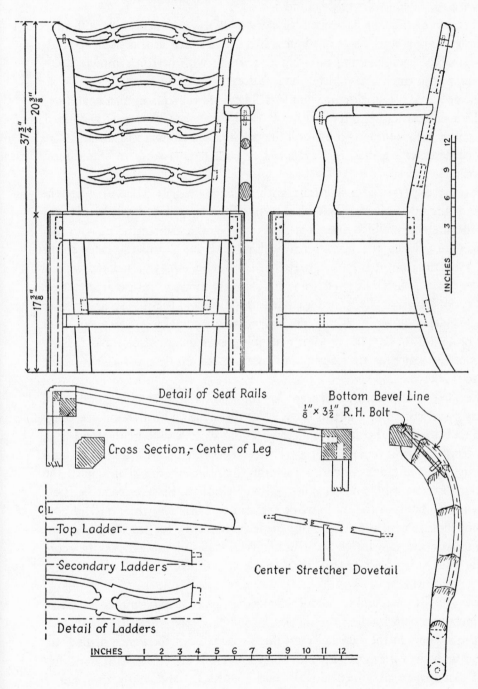

$37\frac{3}{4}''$ $20\frac{3}{8}''$ $17\frac{3}{8}''$

INCHES   3   6   9   12

Detail of Seat Rails

Cross Section, Center of Leg

Bottom Bevel Line

$\frac{1}{8}'' \times 3\frac{1}{2}''$ R.H. Bolt

C L

-Top Ladder-

-Secondary Ladders-

Detail of Ladders

Center Stretcher Dovetail

INCHES   1   2   3   4   5   6   7   8   9   10   11   12

43

dowels are used in each joint, the first placed as indicated in the front-view drawing, the second directly behind it.

After completing the back members, assemble the complete back with glue, using tenon pins in the seat rail joints. It is a good plan at this point to study the assembled back, making sure that all parts fit with perfect symmetry. Any necessary adjustments should be made before proceeding further.

The next step is to make the front legs. These are cut square, then chamfered on the inside corner up to the seat rail line. The front outside corner is molded. A detail of the molding is shown on the cross-section drawing of the leg. This may be done with a shaper, if available, or with hand tools (see "Moldings," Chapter I).

Next cut the front and side rails, with inside top edges rabbeted. Note the angle of the side rails in the detail drawing. The same angle will be used for the side stretchers, which are cut next. Prepare and assemble the mortise-and-tenon joints, fitting the side stretchers flush with the outside surfaces of the legs, as in the case of the back stretcher. Use tenon pins to reinforce the rail and leg joints. The front stretcher is cut after assembly, to insure a perfect fit. This is not joined to the front legs, but is dovetailed to the side stretchers (see center-stretcher dovetail, *Plate 14*). Instructions for making a dovetail joint may be found in Chapter I. After assembly, use hand tools to mold the top edges of the seat rails all around, and rout out the inside top surfaces of the legs to receive the slip seat.

The chair is now complete except for the arms. (The matching side chair, 1″ narrower, is complete at this stage.) Cut the arms and arm supports, using hand tools for final shaping (note cross sections of arm support in front view, also detail drawing of arm). Prepare the dowel joint, and assemble it temporarily without glue. Hold this assembly in place on the chair, mark the position of the bolt hole on the stile, and bore through the stile from the back, allowing the point of the bit to mark the arm end. Remove the arm and bore the bolt hole. Cut a slot in the underside of the arm, for inserting the nut. Counterbore the stile for the bolt head. Details of this process may be more clearly understood by a careful study of the arm drawing. The bolt used is a ⅛″ by 3½″ R.H. bolt.

Now glue the arm and arm support together, place in position on the chair, and insert the bolt, holding the nut in the slot to receive the bolt end. Attach the arm support to the side rail with three screws from the inside of the rail. Repeat with the other arm. Plug the bolt holes and arm slots with matching wood. Sandpaper all joints and all outside surfaces, and apply the desired finish.

Plate 15

THREE-LADDER CHAIR

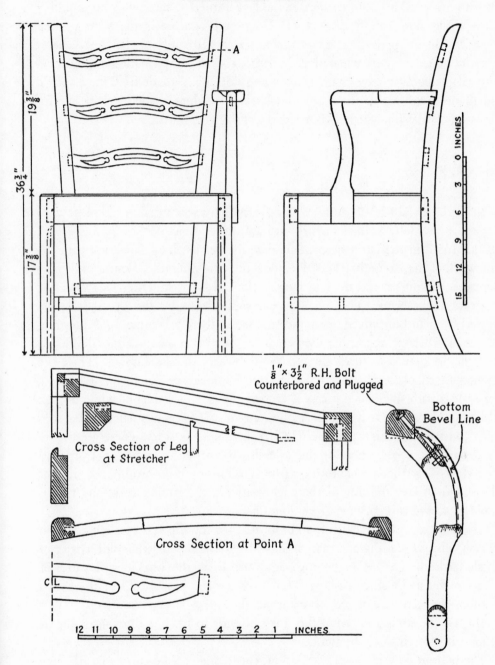

$\frac{1}{8}'' \times 3\frac{1}{2}''$ R.H. Bolt
Counterbored and Plugged

Bottom
Bevel Line

Cross Section of Leg
at Stretcher

Cross Section at Point A

12 11 10 9 8 7 6 5 4 3 2 1 INCHES

A modified version of the ladder back chair is shown in *Plate 15*. The top rail is omitted. The front corners of the legs are left square, with no molding. Except for these simplifications, construction procedure is the same as that described in the preceding text, *Plate 14*. A careful study of that text, and of the drawings in *Plate 15*, will provide all essential information for making this simple but attractive chair. If matching side chairs are desired, these should be 1″ narrower across the front and back. Procedure is identical except for omission of the final step: making and attaching the arms.

———◆———

In the latter half of the eighteenth century there was a definite trend toward lighter, more delicate lines in furniture and decoration. We see the beginning of this trend in the late Chippendale designs, but its finest flowering came in the work of the Adam brothers, Hepplewhite, and Sheraton. Veneer and inlay replaced carving as the chief ornamentation; slender, tapering legs took the place of the cabriole. The new fashion spread rapidly: the great designers copied from and improved upon one another, so there was much intermingling of detail. Each of them, however, had his particular genius, and developed certain distinctive features by which his work is best known. Thus the mahogany chair illustrated in *Plate 16*, with its shield back, and square-tapered, fluted legs with spade feet, is a perfect example of typical Hepplewhite design, although Hepplewhite by no means limited himself to these particular features.

In constructing this chair, the first step is to cut the stiles. These are square in cross section. The curve of the stiles is shown in the drawings, front and side view. The stiles are continuous from floor to top rail, forming the sides of the shield. Above the line of the back seat rail, the front face of the stile is molded. Leave this carving to be done later.

The back seat rail is next cut, and rabbeted for the slip seat (see cross section of seat rail). In cutting the rails, it should be remembered that side chairs of shield-back design are made the same width as the armchair, instead of 1″ narrower as in other designs. This preserves the proportions of the shield without the necessity of reducing the height.

Mortise the stiles and tenon the seat rail ends to fit. Use drawbore pins or tenon pins to reinforce the joints.

The bottom bow of the shield is now cut to shape. The curve of this piece is planned to join the curve of the stiles smoothly. When the face molding of the stiles and bow is completed after assembly, the result will be an appar-

Plate 16

HEPPLEWHITE SHIELD-BACK CHAIR

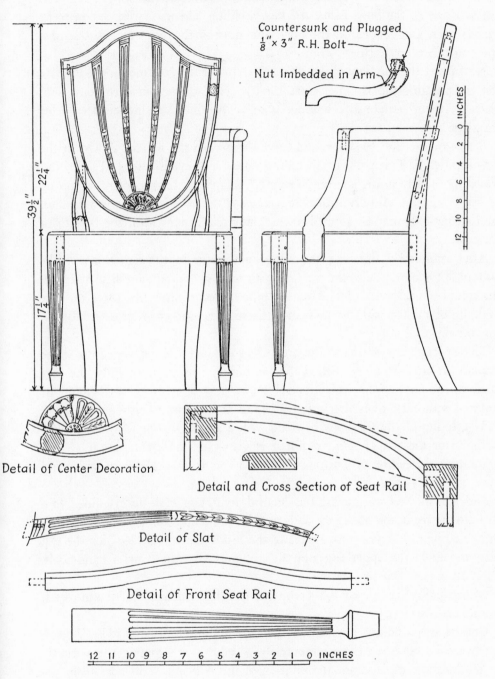

Countersunk and Plugged
$\frac{1}{8}'' \times 3''$ R.H. Bolt

Nut Imbedded in Arm

$39\frac{1}{2}''$

$22\frac{1}{4}''$

$17\frac{1}{4}''$

INCHES
0 2 4 6 8 10 12

Detail of Center Decoration

Detail and Cross Section of Seat Rail

Detail of Slat

Detail of Front Seat Rail

12 11 10 9 8 7 6 5 4 3 2 1 0 INCHES

47

ently uninterrupted curve. The ornamental semicircle at the bottom center is cut as a part of the bow. Leave the face molding and half-circle design to be carved later. Cut tenons on the bow, and mortise the stiles to fit. Assemble these members with glue.

Next make the top bow of the shield (except for the face molding). Prepare the ends of this rail and the stiles for two ⁵⁄₁₆" dowels in each joint, and assemble them temporarily without glue, to obtain exact measurements for the slats.

Band-saw the slats to shape, and carve them with the pattern shown in the detail drawing. This pattern (including fluted section) is discussed and illustrated more fully in the section "Carving," Chapter I. Instructions for carving a shell design are also given in that section. After studying these instructions, similar methods may be applied to the half-circle ornament at the bottom of the bow.

After completely finishing the slats, joint them to the half-circle at the bottom of the bow, and to the top rail, with mortise-and-tenon joints. Assemble the complete back with glue. After the glue has set thoroughly, carve the face molding of the top rail, the bow, and the stiles, as shown in cross section on the drawings.

The next step is to make the front legs. These may be sawed to shape (square in cross section). Below the bottom line of the seat rails, the legs taper to the ankle. The spade foot is cut as part of the leg, and should be finished with hand tools after rough shaping. It is square in cross section.

The fluting of the legs may be done with a shaper, if one is available. Description of the shaper setup required is given in Chapter I, in the section "Fluting and Reeding of Turnings." If no shaper is available, flute with hand tools.

Next cut the seat rails, using the detail drawings in *Plate 16* as guides. Join these to the front and back legs with mortise-and-tenon joints, reinforced with drawbore pins or tenon pins. Rout out the inside tops of the legs for the slip seat, and mold the upper edges of the seat rails all around, with hand tools. Sand all outside flat surfaces.

At this point the side chair is complete. For the armchair, make and attach arms as follows:

Cut the arms and arm supports, and finish shaping with hand tools. Prepare a dowel joint, and join them temporarily without glue. Holding the assembly in place on the chair, mark the position of the bolt hole, and bore from the back of the stile as indicated in the arm detail drawing. Allow the bit to penetrate far enough to mark the end of the arm. Remove the arm and bore the hole, then cut a slot in the underside of the arm for the nut. Counterbore the stile for the bolt head. A ⅛″ by 3″ R.H. bolt should be used.

After completing the bolt holes, assemble the arm and arm support permanently with glue, place in position, and insert the bolt and nut. Repeat with other arm. Then plug the bolt holes and nut slots with matching wood. Mold the lower edges of the arm supports to continue the seat-rail molding, as indicated in the side-view drawing. Sandpaper all surfaces, and apply the desired finish.

———◆———

As Hepplewhite favored the shield back and graceful curves, his contemporary, Sheraton, was partial to a lattice effect and delicate straight lines. The mahogany chair shown in *Plate 17* is an excellent example of the Sheraton influence. The central panel rising above the top rail line is also characteristic of this designer.

As usual in chair construction, the back legs, or stiles, are made first. These may be band-sawed to shape; they are square in cross section. Do not cut face molding at this time. Next, the back seat rail and the back stretcher are made. The seat rails are rabbeted along the top inside edge for the slip seat (see cross section). The stretchers are rectangular, of $\frac{7}{16}$″ wood. Dimensions shown are for the armchair. Side chairs are 1″ narrower; otherwise they are the same.

The seat rails and stretchers are joined to the legs with mortise-and-tenon joints. In preparing the stretcher joints, bear in mind that a rectangular stretcher entering a square leg is always fitted flush with the outside surface of the leg. Owing to the thinness of the wood, the ¼″-thick tenon is milled on the extreme inside surface of the stretcher, to allow the greatest possible thickness for the outside wall of the matching mortise.

The crosspiece at the bottom of the back lattice must also be prepared (except for the face molding), before assembly of the stiles and cross members. This piece is tenoned into the stiles, and is mortised in four places on its top surface to receive the vertical standards of the lattice. The stiles, back seat rail, stretcher, and lower back crosspiece may now be glued together. The rail joints should be reinforced by the drawbore method or by tenon pins (Chapter I, "Joinery").

The top rail should be made next. It is all one piece of wood, band-sawed to shape. Study the detail drawing before cutting. Leave the face molding to be cut after the chair back is completely assembled. Prepare dowel joints,

Plate 17

SHERATON LATTICE-BACK CHAIR

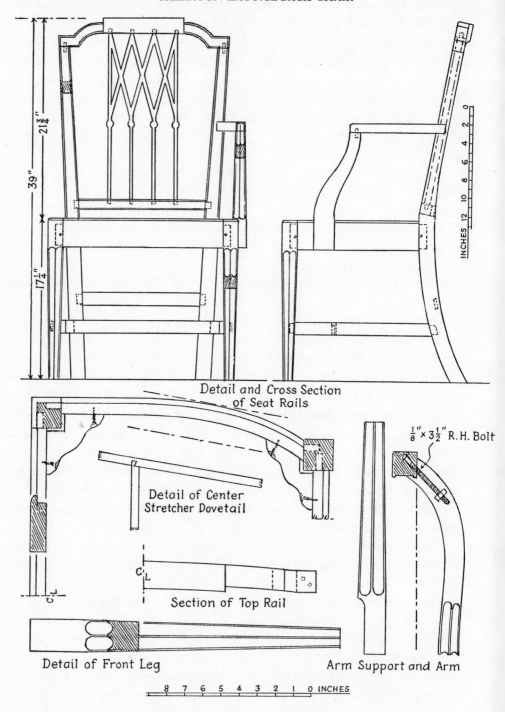

Detail and Cross Section
of Seat Rails

Detail of Center
Stretcher Dovetail

$\frac{1}{8}$" × $3\frac{1}{2}$" R.H. Bolt

Section of Top Rail

Detail of Front Leg

Arm Support and Arm

8 7 6 5 4 3 2 1 0 INCHES

using two ³⁄₁₆" dowels for each joint, and join the top rail to the stiles temporarily without glue, to determine the exact measurements for the lattice.

The lattice is cut from a single piece of wood. To make the cutouts, mark the diamond pattern on the wood, and bore a hole inside each section. A jigsaw or coping saw may be threaded through the hole to make the cut. Remove saw marks with a wood file and sandpaper. Cut tenons on the top and bottom projecting ends. Mortise the top rail for the lattice, measuring carefully for correct positions of the mortises. Make a trial assembly of the entire back, to insure perfect fit and symmetry, then assemble permanently with glue. After the glue has set, cut the face molding on the upper stiles, top rail, and bottom crosspiece, using hand tools. This molding is shown in cross section on the stile, front-view drawing.

The front legs are square-cut, with a slight taper commencing just below the bottom line of the seat rails and continuing to the floor, without a foot. After sawing the rough shape, groove the front and side surfaces with wide, shallow gouges. As the grooves taper with the narrowing of the leg, a succession of gouges of slightly different widths will be required. The groove pattern is shown in cross section on the leg detail drawing. Smooth the grooves with sandpaper.

Use the detail and cross-section drawing of the seat rails as a guide in cutting the front and side rails. Cut the side stretchers, prepare the mortise-and-tenon joints, and assemble. Reinforce the rail joints with tenon pins.

The front cross stretcher is cut last to insure a perfect fit. Use a dovetail joint, as indicated in the stretcher detail drawing. Instructions for cutting a dovetail joint are given in Chapter I, under "Joinery."

The corner blocks are cut and fitted after assembly, as shown in the seat detail drawing. Finally, use hand tools to rout out the inside of the leg tops for the slip seat, and to mold the top edge of the seat all around.

At this point the side chair is complete, except for sanding and applying the finish. (Dimensions of side chair are one inch narrower.) To complete the armchair, first make the arms and arm supports, using the detail drawings as guides. Carve the tapering grooves with gouges and sandpaper, as on the legs. Before grooving the arm, prepare the dowel joint and assemble temporarily, without glue, to insure perfect matching of the grooves.

Hold the arm and arm support in position on the chair, and mark the stile for the position of the bolt. Study the detail drawing of the arm before boring. Bore from the back of the stile, allowing the point of the bit to mark the arm end. The hole should be sized for a ⅛″ by 3½″ R.H. bolt. Remove the arm and bore the bolt hole, then cut a slot in the bottom of the arm for inserting the nut. Counterbore the stile to receive the bolt head.

Now glue the arm and arm support together, hold in position on the chair, and insert the bolt and nut. Fasten the arm support to the side seat rail with three screws from the inside of the rail. Repeat with the other arm.

Use matching wood to plug the bolt holes and nut slots. Sand all surfaces and apply the desired finish.

———◆———

As ideas of comfort grew in the eighteenth century, various types of upholstered chairs came into general use. An outstanding type was the wing chair, of which a fine example is shown in *Plate 18*. This chair was designed primarily for fireside use, its high wings protecting the neck of the occupant from drafts created by the fire.

The development of the wing chair took place chiefly in the Chippendale period, and the best surviving examples have the cabriole leg and serpentine curves of that era. The foot is usually some form of the Dutch foot, such as the drake foot shown, or the ball and claw.

Since the legs are the only exposed wooden parts, these are made of mahogany, while the other frame members may be of maple or birch. The back leg (shaded area on drawing) is 2″ thick; other parts are 1″ thick. This permits a 1″ shoulder to be cut in the outside surface of the leg from the bottom frame line upward, leaving 1″ of wood to fit against the inside surface of the seat frame. This is fastened to the inside of the frame by four screws. This method of construction requires considerably less mahogany than would be needed if the leg and stile were one piece.

The whole frame is doweled, and in most cases the dowel holes are bored from the outside, making measurements unnecessary. A ½″ opening must be left between the seat and arms, between seat and back, and between back and wings, to allow for tacking of upholstery material.

Cut the stiles, the back seat rail, and the top and bottom rails of the back. Shape the top rail as shown in the front-view and perspective drawings. Dowel these members together, leaving a ½″ gap between the seat rail and the bottom back rail. Cut the seat rails, allowing for the greater width at the front, as indicated in the seat plan. Shape the back legs with hand tools (including the shoulder) after rough-shaping with the band saw. Band-saw the cabriole front

Plate 18

WING CHAIR FRAME

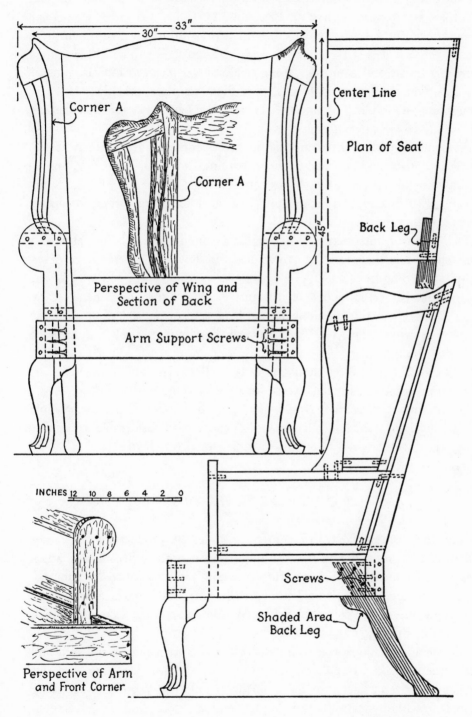

33"

30"

Corner A

Corner A

Center Line

Plan of Seat

45"

Back Leg

Perspective of Wing and
Section of Back

Arm Support Screws

INCHES 12 10 8 6 4 2 0

Screws

Shaded Area
Back Leg

Perspective of Arm
and Front Corner

53

legs, including the feet, as described in Chapter I. Complete the shaping with hand tools. Use gouges to carve the foot grooves.

Now dowel the side seat rails to the stiles, using three dowels in each joint. Attach the back legs with screws as described above. Complete the assembly of the seat frame and front legs, using triple dowel joints as indicated in the drawings. Cut the leg wing blocks, glue them in place, and drive a screw through each wing block up into the seat rail. Use hand tools for final shaping of the wing blocks after assembly.

All members of the arm frame (four pieces for each arm) are next cut, doweled together, and attached to the seat frame and stiles. Leave a ½″ opening between the arm and seat frame, and between the arm and stile. Study the side-view drawing, and the perspective of arm and front corner, for details of the arm assembly.

Cut the wing frame pieces, and assemble them completely before attaching to the chair. The shaping of the wing pieces is shown in a perspective drawing, *Plate 18*. The front and top edges of the wings, and the top edge of the back, should be well rounded on the inside. Dowel the wing members together, then dowel this assembly to the back and arms as indicated in the side-view drawing. Leave a ½″ gap between the wing and back, and between wing and arm.

The exposed leg surfaces should now be well sanded, and finished as desired. This completes the chair except for upholstering.

Upholstering is a separate craft which has no place in this book. Simple upholstering is not difficult, but unless the reader has considerable experience he would be well advised to employ a professional for this chair.

COTTAGE CHAIRS

While the fashionable world enjoyed the elegant productions of master cabinetmakers, humbler homes were by no means unfurnished. There was a parallel development in the class of furniture now variously called "provincial," "rustic," "cottage," or "colonial," though the latter, at least, is a misnomer. Why apply the term "colonial" to the Windsor chair, for example, which originated in England?

Early cottage furniture was well or poorly made according to the skill and patience of its maker. In either case it was usually of simple design, and this simplicity is a large factor in its enduring popularity. While the surviving originals are highly prized by collectors, reproductions find a welcome in modern homes, even where more elaborate antique styles would be rejected as "old-fashioned."

An outstanding example of this timeless quality is found in the Windsor chair, still modern despite its ancient beginnings. Structurally, this is a stool with a back added, having no stile. The earliest known Windsor dates from about 1680, but exact dating of cottage furniture styles is, of course, impossible.

Many variations of the Windsor chair were made in England during the eighteenth century. Travel and communication were difficult, and each small region developed its own styles. However, certain general characteristics of each period may be found: some early Windsors had cabriole front legs, Chippendale scrolls in the top rails or combs, a plain or pierced splat in the center of the back. More delicate, tapering lines may be noted in later examples, such as the "Sheraton Windsors" (*Plate 19*).

In America, Windsors were apparently first made in Philadelphia, about 1725. Although inspired by the English style, American makers introduced some differences: the central splat of the back was omitted, and the legs were more sharply raked, with the top ends placed farther in from the seat corners.

The woods used were those at hand and best suited to the purpose. English seats were usually of elm, American of pine or poplar, and green wood was often used to insure tighter fit around the legs and spindles. Yew, oak, or hickory commonly formed the bows. Legs were of ash, birch, maple, cherry, or other woods. Many American Windsors were painted, dark green being a common color. Present-day reproductions are often natural maple.

The seat is nearly always hollowed out in a clearly defined saddle shape. Where the design of the back is such as to require added strength, the seat has a projecting "bobtail" at the back center, and two extra spindles are placed at an angle from this to the top rail (*Plate 20*).

The legs are nearly always turned, and are set in holes bored at an angle through the seat. They are reinforced with turned stretchers.

The back is completely independent of the legs, being formed of spindles set into holes bored in the upper surface of the seat. Other features of the back vary, and the different types of Windsor chairs are named from these features. A few of the best known American types are described below.

Low-Back Windsor. This was the earliest type of American Windsor, and was not made in England. Never popular, it is important only as the forerunner of other American Windsors. The top rail was semicircular, its ends serving as arms.

Comb-Back Windsors. This is structurally a low-back Windsor with the back spindles extending up through the semicircular rail to a top rail or comb.

The lower rail, or bow, is made of a single piece of bent wood. In some cases a secondary comb was added above the first. A fine example of this type is shown in *Plate 21*.

Hoop-Back Windsors.   In this type a vertical semicircular hoop of bent wood forms the upper rail. It is mortised into the lower bow at each side. The spindles are graduated in length, projecting up through the lower rail and mortised into the hoop. This is the most common type of Windsor reproduced today.

New England armchairs.   In this form the lower bow is omitted, and the arms are formed by bending forward the ends of the vertical hoop. Occasionally such backs are strengthened by use of the bobtail seat and bracing spindles. A small comb is sometimes added above the hoop.

Fan-Back Windsors.   These are side chairs, lacking the bow. The upper rail resembles the comb of the armchairs. Backs are sometimes braced. *Plate 20* is an example of this type. The back was often less tapered, with thicker side spindles turned to match the legs. Tenoned arms were sometimes added.

Loop-Back Windsors.   These were usually side chairs, resembling a hoop-back with the horizontal bow omitted and the hoop extended to the seat at each side. Some loop-backs have tenoned arms.

Sheraton Windsors.   In some of the later Windsor chairs, the Sheraton influence is seen in straight-line backs and slender, tapered legs. Some of these had wide top rails with stencil decorations, others had a cross rail below the top rail, as shown in *Plate 19*.

The above are basic types of American Windsors. Many variations of each type are found.

———◆———

Plate 19 shows a graceful Windsor side chair with both top and secondary rails. The shaping of these rails may be seen in the front view and in the curve plan. The upper is a graceful serpentine. Three of the spindles pass through the secondary rail, then through the top rail, where they are wedged. The heavier side turnings have a $\frac{5}{16}''$ round tenon turned on the top end, which also passes through the top rail and is wedged. The alternate spindles end at the secondary rail. The lower ends of all spindles rest in holes bored in the top surface of the seat. The holes for the side turnings are bored completely through the seat, as are the leg holes. These joints are also wedged.

Plate 19

SHERATON WINDSOR SIDE CHAIR

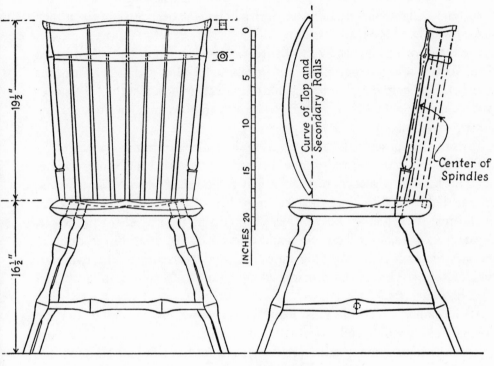

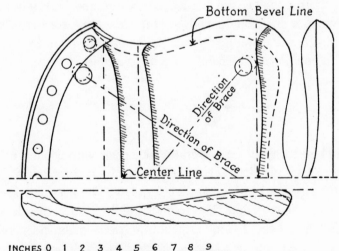

Angle for Leg Holes in Seat, 68°

The detail drawings of the seat show the positions of the holes and the plan for the saddle shape. After cutting the outline of the seat with a band saw, holes should be bored before any shaping is done. Exact instructions for seat boring are given in Chapter I. The angle for the leg holes is 68 degrees. The seat is then shaped with hand tools, and sanded.

Use the drawings in *Plate 19* to figure the turning plans. Turn the legs, fit them to the seat without glue, and measure for the stretchers. Turn the stretchers, and bore holes in the legs for the stretcher ends. Slot the leg tops for wedges, assemble the legs, stretchers, and seat with glue, and drive wedges into the leg tops. Smooth with sandpaper.

Turn the side posts of the back, figuring the pattern from the drawings.

The top and secondary rails should be made of hickory, bent before shaping. Since the bending is a slow process, this may be done beforehand if desired. Use a form slightly smaller than the piece to be bent. Clamp the hickory piece to the form at the center of the arc, then place clamps at each side of the center, about six inches apart. Clamping should proceed slowly, using fifteen to thirty minutes for each bend, working outward from the center to the two ends simultaneously. This process is described more fully in Chapter I, in the section "Bending Hickory."

After bending, work the rails down with a drawknife, and sand. Cut the pieces for the spindles, and shape with a drawknife and sandpaper. Then bore holes in the seat for the spindles (1″ deep), and for the side rails (through the seat). Bore the side posts for the ends of the secondary rail, and bore spindle holes in the two rails. Slot the bottom ends of the side posts for wedges. Assemble all parts with glue, and wedge the side posts under the seat. Smooth down the wedges. This completes the chair, ready for the finish.

———◆———

Plate 20 is a graceful but sturdy fan-back Windsor side chair with bobtail seat. The shovel shape of the seat is unusual. Legs are turned with no taper, but with vase turnings above the stretchers, which are set very low. The back is a fine example of skillful two-purpose design. The second spindle from each side is drawn back and set into the bobtail. This provides the required bracing and also permits a sharply tapered outline, as the outer spindles are drawn inward to "close ranks." Structural details are shown in the drawings. In general, procedure is the same as that for *Plate 19,* and a study of the preceding text will supply all necessary information. The angle for the leg holes in this seat is 70 degrees.

Plate 20

FAN-BACK WINDSOR CHAIR

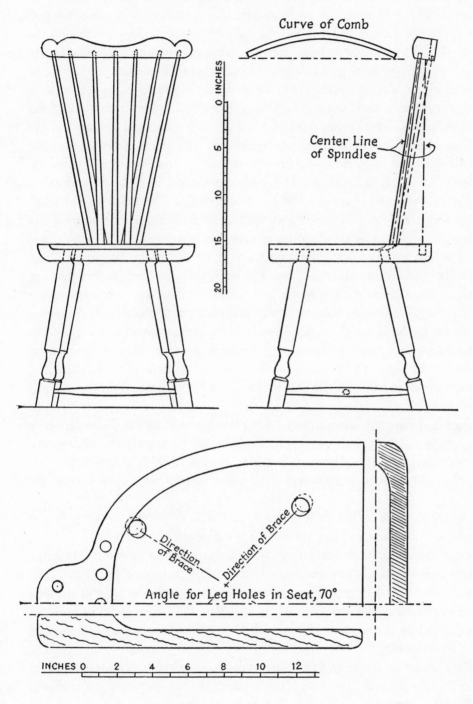

Curve of Comb

Center Line
of Spindles

0 INCHES

5

10

15

20

Direction
of Brace

Direction of Brace

Angle for Leg Holes in Seat, 70°

INCHES 0   2   4   6   8   10   12

An unusually impressive armchair with a double comb back is shown in *Plates 21* and 22. The seat is saddle-shaped. The spindles curve gracefully outward, the five central spindles passing through the secondary comb into the high comb. The arms extend well forward, with sharply raked turned supports. Arm and comb ends are scrolled. Legs are vase-turned above the stretchers, and tapered below. Turning plans are given in the detail drawings, as are working plans for the seat, bow, and comb. Arm ends are built up with well glued and doweled pieces, before being worked into the scroll with hand tools.

Procedure for making and assembling the seat, legs, and stretchers is the same as that described in connection with *Plate 19*, except that the angle for the leg holes in the seat is 64 degrees. Turning plans are given in *Plates 21* and 22.

The next step is to bore the seat for nine spindles. The holes should be 1" deep. Shape the spindles with a drawknife and sandpaper, tapering them upward as indicated by the diameter measurements on the spindle detail drawing, *Plate 21*. Spindles should be cut extra long at the top, to allow for bending.

The bow and combs are of hickory. The wood should be bent before shaping, by the method described in Chapter I, in the section "Bending Hickory." After bending and shaping the bow, attach the end pieces with glue and $\frac{3}{16}$" dowels, as shown in the detail drawing, *Plate 22*. Shape the scrolls with hand tools, using a carving gouge for the grooves. Sand the bow, bore it for the nine back spindles, and place it in position on the spindles, without glue. Measure and mark the bow and seat for the position of the arm spindles and the turned arm supports.

Turn and sand the arm supports, using the turning plan in *Plate 22*. Make the arm spindles. Bore the seat holes at the required angles, and glue in the supports and spindles. The arm supports extend through the seat and are wedged. The bow may be removed to avoid interference while boring the seat.

Replace the bow on the back spindles, and hold in position while boring it for the arm supports and arm spindles. Then glue the bow in place.

Shape the combs with hand tools and sandpaper, after bending. Mark the lower comb for the position and angle of the spindle holes, and bore these. The five central holes should be bored completely through the comb. Cut the side spindles to length (two on each side), then glue the lower comb in position. The position of the holes should be such as to bend the spindles outward (see front-view drawing).

Mark the position and angle of the spindle holes in the top comb. Bore these holes 1" deep. Glue the comb in place, bending the spindles outward as shown in *Plate 21*. The chair is now complete, ready for the finish.

Plate 21

DOUBLE COMB-BACK WINDSOR CHAIR

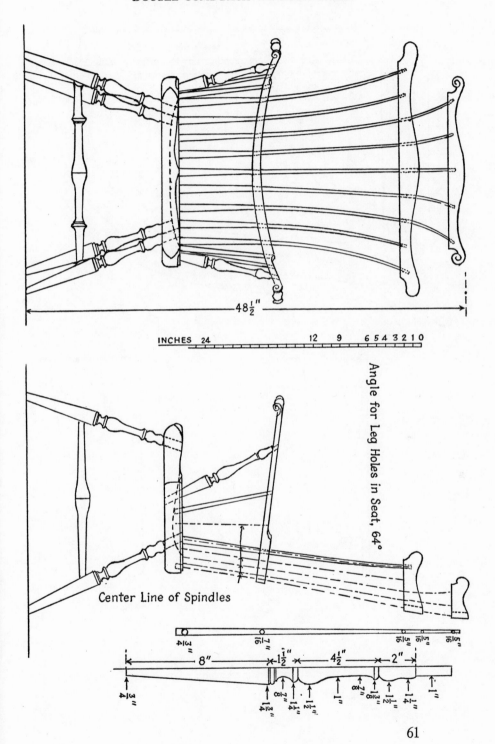

48½″

INCHES 24   12   9   6 5 4 3 2 1 0

Angle for Leg Holes in Seat, 64°

Center Line of Spindles

8″   1½″   4½″   2″

Plate 22

DOUBLE COMB-BACK WINDSOR CHAIR

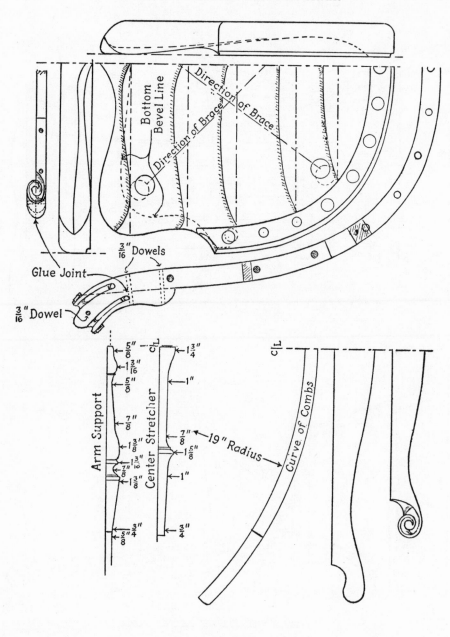

Another early chair which has retained its popularity to the present day is the type which antiquarians call the slat back, but which is also sometimes called a ladder back. This type originated about three centuries ago, and may have been the inspiration for the fine ladder backs of the Chippendale period.

American slat backs were usually of maple, with woven rush seats. They were made as straight chairs and rockers, as side chairs and armchairs. The backs were high, with the number of slats varying. Those made in New England generally had four slats, while Pennsylvania chairs often had five or even six. The vertical side posts were turned, usually plain in Pennsylvania, ornamented with rings or other designs in New England. Slats varied from simple arches to elaborate scroll shapes. The number of stretchers varied, five being common, but as many as seven were occasionally used. The front stretchers and legs were sometimes elaborately turned.

The chair in *Plate* 23 may be made either as a straight chair or as a rocker. The slats have a shallow tapering arch which is shown in cross section (front view). The curve is shown in a detail drawing.

The wood for the slats should be bent before shaping, and in the best old chairs these were of hickory or oak. Use a form of slightly smaller radius than that of the piece to be bent, clamping the ⅜″ wood to the form at the center of the arc. Then place clamps at both sides, about 6″ from the central clamp. Allow fifteen to thirty minutes for each bend, gradually adding clamps 6″ apart, working from the center toward both ends simultaneously. Since the bending process requires considerable time, it should be started beforehand, and continued while other work is in progress. (See Chapter I, section on "Bending Hickory.")

Turn the stiles, which are plain except for a slight V cut at the center line of each cross member (see side view drawing). Turn the acorn finial on the top end of the stile, and round the bottom end as shown in the drawing.

Shape the seat frame pieces as shown in cross section on the seat plan. Edges should be well rounded and sanded, to avoid fraying the strands of the rush seat. Turn the back stretcher, then cut the back seat rail to length, working round tenons on the ends with hand tools. Bore matching holes in the stiles. Before assembling these members, shape the slats from the bent wood, using hand tools to work them down. Cut mortises for the slats in the stiles, then assemble the complete back with glue. Bore and insert tenon pins through the back of the stiles to reinforce the slat joints.

While the glue is drying, prepare the front assembly. Turn the front legs with a ring near the bottom, and a slight V cut at the center line of each stretcher and seat rail, as shown in the drawings. Round both ends, and sand.

Plate 23

SLAT-BACK CHAIR

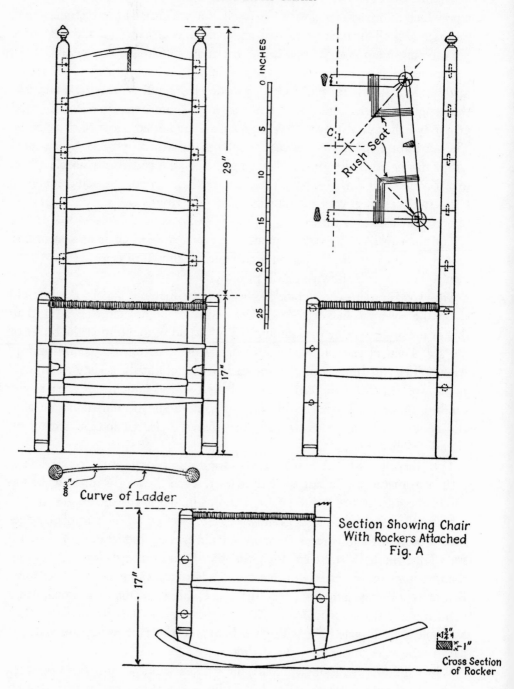

INCHES

29"

17"

C L

Rush Seat

Curve of Ladder

3/8"

17"

Section Showing Chair
With Rockers Attached
Fig. A

1 3/4"

x—1"

Cross Section
of Rocker

Turn and sand the two front stretchers, cut the front seat rail to length, and work a round tenon on each end. Note that the front is wider than the back (see plan, *Plate 23*). If the chair is to be fitted with rockers, use the rocker plan, *Figure A,* to determine the length and end shaping of legs.

The side stretchers and side seat rails are made and fitted last. This completes assembly of the straight chair. If rockers are desired, these are band-sawed to shape, smoothed with hand tools and sandpaper, and bored for the lower ends of the legs. Before assembling, slot the leg ends for wedges. Glue the rockers to the legs, wedge, and sand smooth.

There is a legend that rockers made of walnut will not "walk," whereas rockers made of any other wood will do so. The reader is invited to test the old tale if he desires.

The chair is now ready to apply the desired finish. The rush seat is woven on the finished chair. Instructions for seat weaving will be found in Chapter I.

HITCHCOCK CHAIRS

During the "American Empire" period (about 1815 to 1840), small painted and stenciled chairs enjoyed great popularity. Of these, the best known today are the chairs made by Lambert Hitchcock of Connecticut, from 1826 to 1843. Recently the old Hitchcock factory has been restored to manufacture faithful replicas of the original chairs.

Green as well as seasoned wood was used in these chairs, which were consequently very sturdy. Rock maple was the favored wood. The seats were slightly dished, and the earliest were rush. Cane and solid seats were also used.

The chairs were usually painted black over an undercoat of red. Gold and colors were used to decorate the fancy turnings, and to make the stencil designs on the back rails.

The turned members varied in design. The chair in *Plate 24* has a bolster top rail. This is rough-shaped before turning, as shown in the left half of the detail drawing, *Figure E*. Owing to the curve, two off-center turnings are required for the end sections. The center section is oval, and is shaped by hand. Detailed instructions for the off-center turning are given in Chapter I. Note that a ⅝" round tenon is worked with hand tools on each end of the top rail. This is done after turning is completed, when the waste wood (required for lathe centers) is removed.

The stile is turned only at the section marked *A* on the side-view drawing. The turning must be done before the waste wood is cut away above and below it, as the lathe centers *A* and *AA* are in this waste wood (Chapter I, "Off-Center

Plate 24

HITCHCOCK CHAIR

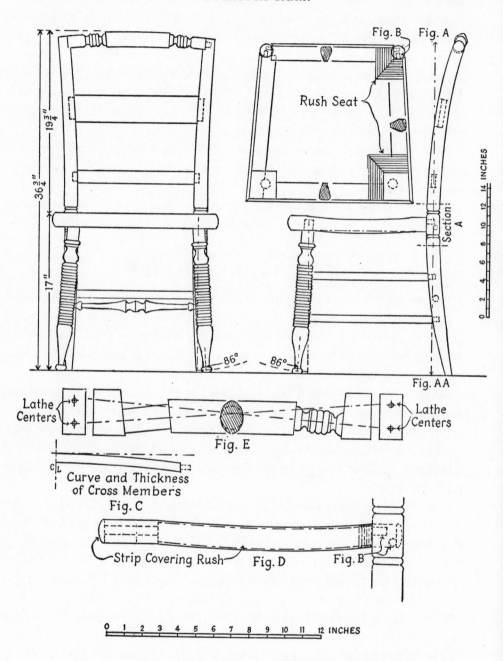

Fig. B   Fig. A

Rush Seat

Section: A

$36\frac{3}{4}$"

$19\frac{3}{4}$"

17"

86°   86°

Fig. AA

INCHES
0 2 4 6 8 10 12 14

Lathe
Centers

Lathe
Centers

Fig. E

C L
Curve and Thickness
of Cross Members
Fig. C

Strip Covering Rush   Fig. D   Fig. B

0 1 2 3 4 5 6 7 8 9 10 11 12 INCHES

Turning"). The stile above the turned section is rectangular in cross section, and may be shaped by band saw. The lower end of the stile is rounded by hand, after sawing. It is tapered at the bottom, as shown in the side-view drawing. After shaping, the stile is mortised for the cross members, and sanded.

The back stretcher is a plain turning, with ⅝" round ends. The back seat rail is worked down with hand tools to the shape shown in cross section on the seat plan. This rail has a round tenon of ½" diameter worked on each end below center (*Figure B* in detail drawings). Edges of seat rails must be well rounded to avoid fraying the strands of the rush seat.

The two back slats or ladders are band-sawed to a slight curve, as shown in the curve plan, *Figure C*. They are then sanded, cut to length, and tenoned to fit matching mortises in the stiles. When all back members are completed, the entire back is assembled with glue.

Study the seat plan in *Plate 24* before cutting the side and front rails. The two front corner squares are included in the cutting of both front and side rails. The squares are then milled so as to fit together sandwich-like: the side-rail squares, with top and bottom cut away, form the "filling"; the front-rail squares are correspondingly grooved. Except for the squares, the rails are shaped as shown in cross section on the seat plan. The opposite end of each side rail, joining the stile, is worked into a round tenon above center (*Figure B*). After shaping and sanding the front and side rails, glue the square tongues into the grooves, clamp, and allow to dry.

Turn and sand the front legs, front stretchers, and side stretchers. The legs are heavily ringed, with vase forms above and below, and small bun feet. The front stretcher has trumpet turnings, side stretchers are plain. Turning patterns may be easily figured from the drawings. Bore stretcher holes in the legs at an angle, to compensate for the forward and outward rake of the legs. Glue the legs and stretchers together.

The leg holes in the underside of the seat frame should be bored at an angle of 86 degrees (see front and side views). A boring jig will be helpful in insuring the identical angle for both legs. Instructions for making the jig will be found under "Seat Boring," Chapter I. However, note that in this case the holes do not go completely through the seat frame. Use a bit gauge to insure identical depth for both holes. Glue the legs to the seat frame.

The stiles should now be bored to receive the round ends of the side seat rails and stretchers. After gluing these joints, the chair is ready to apply the finish. The strips which are to cover the rush at the seat edges (*Figure D*) may be made and finished at the same time as the chair, but are not attached until the seat weaving is completed (see Chapter I, "Rush Seat Weaving").

Rush-seat weaving is explained in Chapter I. In the case of this chair, the preliminary corner-weaving process is reversed from front to back, because of the front corner squares, which are left uncovered. The back corners are first filled in until the unwoven section of the back rail equals the measurement of the front rail between squares. The seat is then woven in the usual way. After the seat is finished, the edge strips are attached with brads.

CHAPTER III

STOOLS

In EARLY England chairs were rare and were reserved for the head of the household and important guests. The rest of the family sat on stools. As the chair gradually came into general use in the eighteenth century, the stool lost some of its importance. It has, however, survived as a convenience to the present day, and while used chiefly as a footrest, its lightness and easy movability make it popular for occasional seating use.

In America the earliest stool of importance was the "joint" stool, so named because it was made by a "joiner," as a certain type of skilled woodworker was called. The joint was the mortise and tenon, which was used almost exclusively in fine old furniture, and is recommended today as best for most joints. Procedure for making this joint is described in Chapter I.

Joint stools were made in this country until about 1700, and were frequently of maple, though other native woods were used. They varied greatly in shape, style of turning, quality of finish, and other features. *Plate 25* presents a stool of a type popular between 1660 and 1700. The legs are vase-turned with rings above and below. On this stool the legs rake one way only. Some joint stools had vertical legs all around, some had legs raking all ways. The mortise-and-tenon joints are reinforced with drawbore pins.

The legs are first turned, then cut to length with the tops slanted to provide the proper rake. Mortises for the skirt pieces and the stretchers are cut in the legs, which are then sanded on the inside flat surfaces.

Next, cut the skirt pieces and stretchers, with tenons to fit the leg mortises.

69

Plate 25

JOINT STOOL

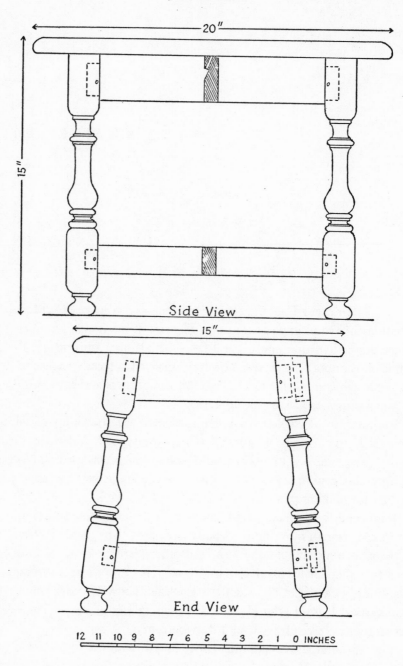

20″

15″

Side View

15″

End View

12 11 10 9 8 7 6 5 4 3 2 1 0 INCHES

Bore and counterbore the inside surface of the skirt as shown in cross section, *Plate 25,* for the screws which will attach the top. Sand the inside and top surfaces of the stretchers.

Measure and drill drawbore holes in the tenons and mortises, then assemble the joints with a good casein or hot glue. The drawbore pins should be driven into place before the glue has set. With this method, clamping is unnecessary. Sand all outside surfaces.

The top may be made of two or more boards. Glue these together, then cut the top to size, mold the edges, and sand the upper surface. Attach the top with sloping screws through the counterbored skirting. The stool may then be finished with wax, stain, or any desired finish.

———◆———

During the Queen Anne and Georgian periods, chairs were supplanting stools for seating purposes, and for this reason stools in these styles are very rare. Their graceful lines make them well worth reproducing. *Plates 26* and *27* show stools of the Queen Anne style, the first probably made about 1730, the second somewhat later, possibly 1760. Both have the typical cabriole leg, with slightly different forms of the Dutch foot.

The shell carving on the knees of the second stool, though used occasionally in the early Queen Anne period, was more popular in the time of Chippendale. Both these stools were of walnut, and both were upholstered, probably in rich brocade or tapestry.

For the stool in *Plate 26,* first make a leg pattern from the scale drawings and cross-section plan. The pattern includes the square leg tops as well as the shaped portion. Mark the pattern on the leg blocks, and band-saw ("Shaping a Cabriole Leg," Chapter I). After shaping, mortise the legs for the rails.

Next cut the rails, shaping the skirt with a band saw. Rabbet the top of the rails to receive the slip seat. A similar rabbet is shown in cross section, *Plate 27.* Tenon the rail ends to fit the leg mortises. Assemble the joints, using the drawbore method described in "Joinery," Chapter I.

Cut the wing blocks roughly to shape, and glue them to the rails and legs (see corner detail drawing). After the glue has set, finish the shaping with hand tools. Use hand tools also to round the front corners of the legs, rout out the leg tops to receive the slip seat, and mold the top edge all around. Sand all outside surfaces, and apply the desired finish.

Plate 26

EARLY QUEEN ANNE STOOL

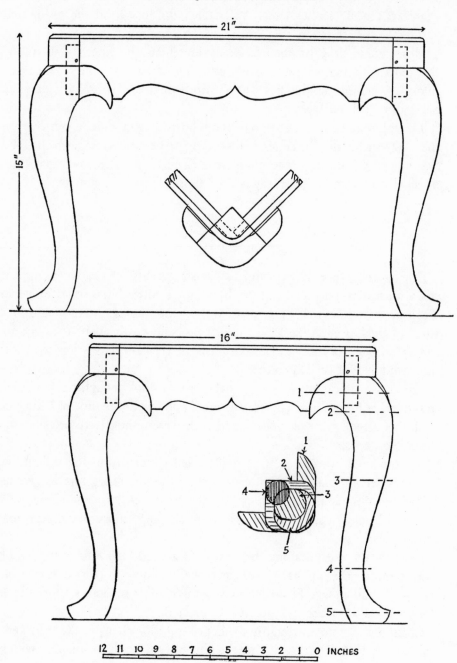

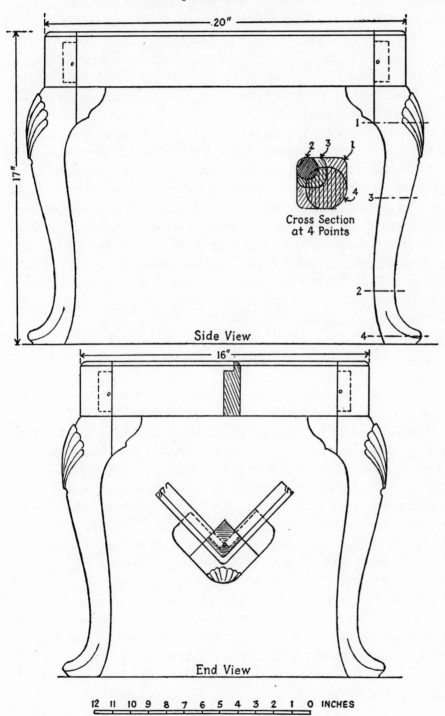

Plate 27

LATE QUEEN ANNE STOOL

20"

17"

Cross Section
at 4 Points

Side View

16"

End View

12 11 10 9 8 7 6 5 4 3 2 1 0 INCHES

73

The cabriole legs of the stool in *Plate 27* are ornamented with shell carving on the knees. This must be allowed for on the leg pattern. Use the scale drawings and the cross-section plan as guides in making the pattern. Mark the pattern on the leg blocks, and saw the rough shape as instructed in "Shaping a Cabriole Leg," Chapter I. Cut mortises for the rails in the square tops of the legs. Use hand tools for the final shaping, including the shell design on the knees ("Carving," Chapter I).

Cut and rabbet the rails (cross section in *Plate 27*), and tenon the ends to fit the leg mortises. Assemble the joints, using the drawbore method ("Joinery," Chapter I). Then saw the wing blocks. Unlike those in *Plate 26,* these wing blocks do not cover the rails, but are fitted below them (corner detail drawing). Glue to the leg only, not to the rail. This allows for shrinkage of the wood without weakening the joint. Final shaping of the wings with hand tools is done after assembly. Round the front corners of the legs, rout out the leg tops to receive the slip seat, and mold the top edge all around.

Corner support blocks may be made and attached, if desired, for greater strength ("Corner Blocks," Chapter I). All outside surfaces are then sanded, and the desired finish applied.

———◆———

Early eighteenth century stools, such as those described in the preceding pages, were designed for use as seats. Their height is usually about fifteen inches. Low footstools were rare; the chairs of that era were not adapted to comfortable sprawling. The well worn stretchers of many antique chairs and tables bear witness to man's early method of keeping his feet off drafty floors.

The advent of the wing chair and other comfortably upholstered chairs made the use of a footstool practicable. *Plate 28* illustrates a true footstool, eight inches in height. The Chippendale influence is seen in the ogee bracket feet and the ogee shaping of the stool frame. The wood is mahogany. This stool is an appropriate companion piece for the wing chair in *Plate 18.*

Construction of this stool is extremely simple. The four side rails are bandsawed to the shape shown in cross section on the end-view drawing. They are then sanded smooth and cut to length, with mitered corners ("Miter Joints," Chapter I). The corners are joined one at a time with glue and corrugated fasteners. The ogee feet are then made and attached with screws as described in Chapter I, "Construction of Bracket Feet." Finish as desired.

Plate 28

CHIPPENDALE FOOTSTOOL

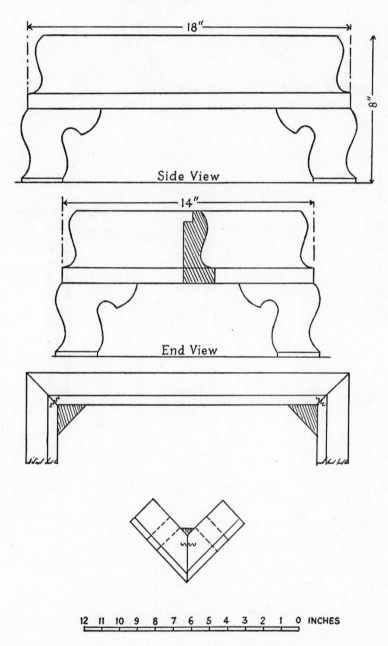

18″

8″

Side View

14″

End View

12 11 10 9 8 7 6 5 4 3 2 1 0 INCHES

Plate 29

EARLY AMERICAN FIRESIDE BENCH

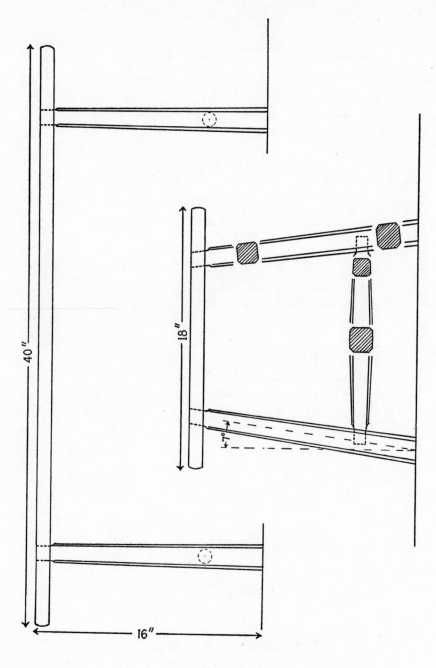

1 2 3 4 5 6 7 8 9 10 11 12 INCHES

Plate 29 shows an early American fireside bench. The legs are slightly raked, or splayed. They are square-cut, with chamfered corners, and taper slightly from base to top. An interesting feature is the shaping of the two end stretchers, which are also square-cut, chamfered, and taper gradually toward the ends. This bench may be appropriately made in any good solid wood, depending on the degree of elegance or rusticity desired.

The first step is to glue up the top (if more than one board is used), and cut to size. Round the edges, and smooth the surfaces by sanding. (If the bench is made of pine, smoothing is done with a hand plane.)

The leg holes are bored at an angle of 70 degrees, to give the legs an outward rake. The method of lining up the bit is similar to that for a Windsor chair seat, described in Chapter I.

Saw the legs, taper, and chamfer the corners, as indicated in the cross sections. Turn the top ends to fit the holes, and insert these temporarily, without glue, in order to determine the exact measurements for the stretchers. Make the stretchers, shaping them as shown in the cross sections, with chamfered corners. Bore stretcher holes in the legs at the same angle as that of the leg holes in the top. Turn the ends of the stretchers to fit. Make a saw cut in the top of each leg, for wedges. Assemble the parts, using a good casein or hot glue. Insert wedges in the leg tops, and drive them in to tighten the joints. Sand the top and other outside surfaces, and apply the desired finish.

CHAPTER IV

TABLES

NUMEROUS TYPES of tables were made by early American craftsmen. These varied not only with the use for which they were intended, but also with the period and style preference of the maker. The great designers developed certain distinctive styles which, though widely copied, came to be known by the names of their creators. American craftsmen imitated the styles of the English Chippendale, Adams, Hepplewhite, and Sheraton, but added variations of their own. Later some Americans, notably Duncan Phyfe, originated designs which still bear their names. The distinctive style features of the great designers will be pointed out as they occur in our illustrations.

We present a group of tables which range from the simplest to the most complex; among them the reader will find represented the major techniques required in making any type of table.

With the reign of William and Mary in England, the massive, awkward furniture of the Elizabethan and Jacobean periods gave way to the lighter, more graceful designs of the Dutch. The transition was gradual, but by the time of Queen Anne, who followed William and Mary in 1702, these characteristics were firmly entrenched in English design.

Coffee Tables. The coffee table shown in *Plate 30* is an adaptation of the Queen Anne style with its graceful lines, the typical cabriole leg, and the Dutch or spoon foot. Although at this early period the low coffee table was unknown, the side table of the time lends itself well to such adaptation. The marble top,

78

Plate 30

QUEEN ANNE MARBLE TOP COFFEE TABLE

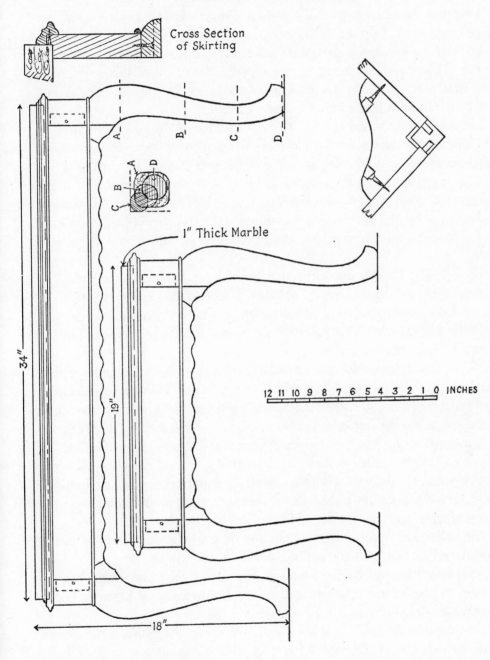

Cross Section
of Skirting

1" Thick Marble

12 11 10 9 8 7 6 5 4 3 2 1 0 INCHES

34"

19"

18"

79

then much in vogue, has recently regained some popularity. This is due partly to its beauty, but perhaps even more to its practicality.

A marble-topped serving table is a delight to any hostess in the present era of informal serving, since neither hot dishes nor spilled liquids will damage it.

The skirting is joined with mortise and tenon, reinforced by corner blocks as shown. This provides a sturdy base to support the weight of the marble slab. The effect is lightened by the gracefully scalloped lower edge of the skirting, and by the molded frame which encloses the top.

The legs should be made first. The cross section *A, B, C, D,* will assist in determining measurements for the cabriole leg pattern. Detailed instructions for band-sawing a cabriole leg are given in Chapter I. After the sawing operation the shape is worked down by hand. Mortises for the skirting should be cut before final shaping. Chapter I contains instructions for making the mortise-and-tenon joint, and other required processes. The legs should be sandpapered to finish smoothness, except the square top section, which will be sanded later.

The next step is to cut the skirt frame pieces to size, and tenon the ends. The top inside edge of the skirting is rabbeted to receive the marble top. Join the legs and skirt, using drawbore pins or tenon pins to reinforce the joints.

Corner blocks should now be cut to shape, and attached as indicated in the corner detail drawing, *Plate 30.*

The scalloped lower skirting pieces and the leg wing blocks may be first rough-shaped by band saw, then worked down by hand. Thicker wood must be used for these pieces, to allow for the bulging shape which matches the bulge at the side of the leg (see cross section of skirting, *Plate 30*). Use a spokeshave or drawknife to remove saw marks. After rough-shaping, fit these pieces in place, with mitered joints as shown at the meeting of skirt and wing. Glue the wing block to the leg only: shrinkage would pull it away if glued to the skirt. After assembly, dress down the bulging skirts and wing blocks with hand tools and sandpaper, and sand the flat surfaces of skirting and leg.

The half-round bead molding at the top of the bulge may now be made, sanded, and applied with brads. The corners are mitered.

Now make the top molding, sand it, and fit it to the table with mitered corners. Fasten the molding with screws from inside the skirt, as shown in the cross-section drawing.

The table is now ready to apply the desired finish. Furniture of the Queen Anne period was usually made of walnut; mahogany came into general use slightly later, but would also be appropriate for this style. Much of the beauty of this table will depend on the selection of a fine piece of marble for the top.

Plate 31 shows a coffee table in the Chinese Chippendale style. The square, fluted leg and the pierced bracket are authentic Chippendale features, while the smoothly rounded edge of the wood top subtly blends the style with that of the most modern furniture. Note on the leg cross-section drawing that the inside corner of each leg is chamfered. This is invariably done with square legs, to give them a desirable effect of lightness.

Instructions for fluting the legs may be found in Chapter I. After fluting, chamfer the inside corner, and cut mortises for the skirt pieces.·

Next cut the skirt frame pieces and tenon the ends. Assemble the legs and skirts with drawbore pins or tenon pins through each joint. Cut and attach corner blocks as shown in the corner detail drawing, then sand all surfaces before proceeding further.

Make a pattern for the corner brackets, using the bracket detail drawing as a guide. The pierced design may be cut out with a jigsaw or coping saw, threaded through holes bored in the waste wood. Remove saw marks with a sharp chisel or file, and sand smooth. Attach the brackets to legs and skirts with long thin brads.

Next cut strips to fit inside the top of the skirting, and screw these to the skirting as shown in the cross-section drawing.

Select the boards for the top, glue them together, and cut to size. Using hand tools, round the top outside edges of the skirting, then the edge of the top, as indicated in the cross-section drawing. Sand the top to finish smoothness, and attach it to the frame with vertical screws driven through the inside strips. Finish as desired.

Bedside Tables. In *Plates 32, 33,* and *34* are shown three bedside tables in styles prevailing around 1800. *Plates 32* and *33* are Sheraton designs with turned legs; *Plate 34* is a Hepplewhite design with square-tapered legs and concave front. The drawers of all three tables are of dovetail construction, with sides and bottoms of ⅜" wood.

Plate 32 has slender turned legs with a graceful taper above a "false foot." This foot rests on a tapered stilt, which is turned in one piece with the leg. Above the ring turnings the legs are square, forming corner posts for the table frame.

After turning and sanding·the legs, mortise them for the skirting. Note that the mortises for the side and back skirt pieces are long grooves (see side and back view). The front frame strips are marked *A* and *B* on the drawings. The upper strip, *A,* requires a dovetail mortise. Instructions for making these joints will be found in Chapter I.

The skirt pieces and the front frame strips should next be cut to size and

Plate 31

CHINESE CHIPPENDALE COFFEE TABLE

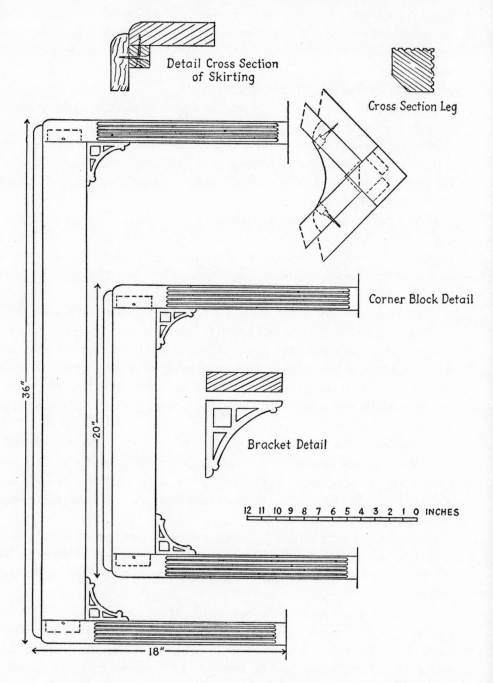

Detail Cross Section
of Skirting

Cross Section Leg

Corner Block Detail

Bracket Detail

12 11 10 9 8 7 6 5 4 3 2 1 0 INCHES

36"

20"

18"

Plate 32

SHERATON BEDSIDE TABLE

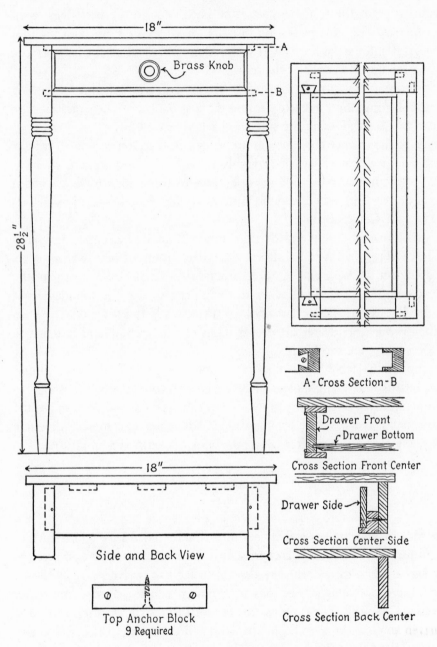

18"

Brass Knob

A

B

28½"

Side and Back View

18"

Top Anchor Block
9 Required

A · Cross Section · B

Drawer Front
Drawer Bottom

Cross Section Front Center

Drawer Side

Cross Section Center Side

Cross Section Back Center

12 11 10 9 8 7 6 5 4 3 2 1 0   INCHES

83

tenoned, including the dovetail tenons on the upper frame strip. Fit and glue the front strips to the front legs, and the back skirt to the back legs; then glue in the two side skirt pieces. Be sure the top edges are flush with the tops of the legs. Reinforce the skirt joints with tenon pins. Sand all the flat surfaces, including the upper sections of the legs.

Next, cut nine short strips (top anchor blocks) and screw them to the inside top of the skirting, three at each side and three at the back. Their positions are indicated by dotted lines on the side and back view.

Details of the drawer construction are shown in the cross-section drawings. At each side is a drawer support, roughly L-shaped in cross section, which is screwed to the inside of the side skirting, flush with the bottom edge. Careful fitting of drawer and drawer support is necessary for smooth operation (Chapter I, "Drawer Construction").

The decorative beading is added to the drawer front after assembly and sanding. The beading strip is $\frac{1}{8}''$ wide and $\frac{5}{16}''$ deep, rounded on the front edge. Make a saw cut $\frac{1}{8}''$ wide and $\frac{1}{4}''$ deep around the extreme outside edge of the drawer front. The bead should fit into this rabbet so that the rounded front protrudes $\frac{1}{16}''$ from the surface of the drawer, while the outer edge is flush with the drawer edge. Miter the corner joints of the beading, and fasten it to the drawer with glue and brads.

The top of the table overhangs the frame $\frac{1}{2}''$ all around. After gluing selected boards into a single piece of sufficient size, cut the top and sand it to finish smoothness. Fasten it in place with vertical screws driven up through the nine top anchor blocks at the back and sides. Construction complete, the table is now ready for finishing, after which the brass drawer-pull is installed.

———◆———

The table in *Plate 33* has elaborately turned and reeded legs, and is further distinguished by the outthrust corners which were often featured by Sheraton.

The legs are first turned, then reeded. Each leg has twelve reeds, as shown on the leg cross section. Instructions for reeding with a shaper, or by hand, are given in Chapter I. The leg tops are not mortised for the skirting; instead, a right-angle notch is cut as indicated in the detail drawing of the leg top. The skirt pieces (including the front, with the drawer opening cut out) are fitted together inside the notch with rabbet joints. After the skirt joints are glued, long triangular corner blocks are glued inside the joints. Two screws are then driven through each block, through the rabbet joint, and into the leg

Plate 33

SHERATON BEDSIDE TABLE

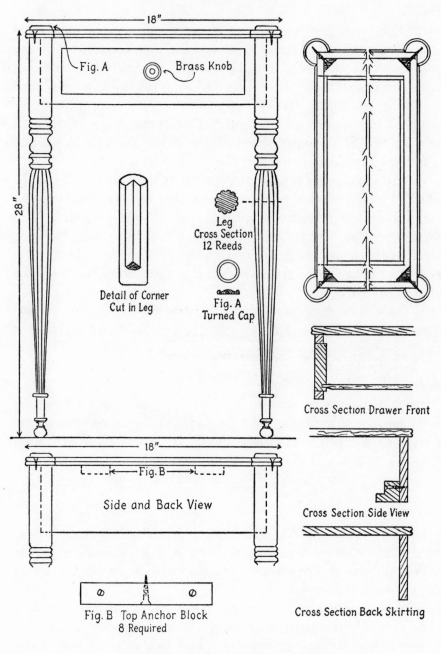

18"

Fig. A   Brass Knob

28"

Detail of Corner
Cut in Leg

Leg
Cross Section
12 Reeds

Fig. A
Turned Cap

18"

Fig. B

Side and Back View

Fig. B   Top Anchor Block
8 Required

Cross Section Drawer Front

Cross Section Side View

Cross Section Back Skirting

12 11 10 9 8 7 6 5 4 3 2 1 0 INCHES

(see top-view detail drawing). The flat surfaces should be sanded before assembly.

Next cut eight short strips (top anchor blocks, *Figure B*), and screw them inside the skirting, two on each side, front, and back, flush with the top edge.

Cut two drawer support strips, roughly L-shaped in cross section, as shown in the cross-section side view. Screw them flush with the inside lower edge of the side skirting, one on each side.

Make the drawer as instructed in Chapter I. Careful measurements are necessary for a perfectly fitting drawer. Sand all drawer surfaces. The drawer pull will be installed after the finishing operation.

The table top slightly overhangs the vertical line of the frame, including the legs. Glue the boards together to form a single piece, then cut it to size and shape, with a two-bead edge molding. Use the outline of the top-view detail drawing as a guide for your pattern. Sand the top, then fasten it in place with vertical screws driven up through the eight top anchor blocks. In addition, drive a screw down through each corner into the leg. These screw heads will be covered by the turned caps.

The two detail drawings marked *"Figure A"* show the surface and cross section of the turned cap. This ornament simulates the top of the leg, and is sized accordingly, slightly smaller than the corner circle of the table top. The four caps may be shaped on the lathe, and are attached to the table top with glue. The table is now ready for the finish.

The drawer pull should be installed last. The large brass knob illustrated is suitable for the style of this table. The leg ends below the reeded sections may also be brass, but normally in reproductions they are turned as part of the leg.

———◆———

The Hepplewhite table in *Plate 34,* with its simple lines, is adaptable to any decorative scheme. Made of mahogany, with oval brass drawer pulls as shown, it is traditionally correct. For the modern taste, it will be attractive in blond mahogany or other light wood.

The entire front surface is concave, which means that all front members (including drawer fronts) must be cut from thicker wood.

Use a jointer, if available, to taper the legs. Lacking this, a band saw or ripsaw may be used with a jig to guide the leg. Two jigs are required for this method. The first is made with the correct taper for each side of the leg, and is used for cutting the first two right-angle sides. Jig No. 2 is cut with double the

Plate 34

HEPPLEWHITE BEDSIDE TABLE

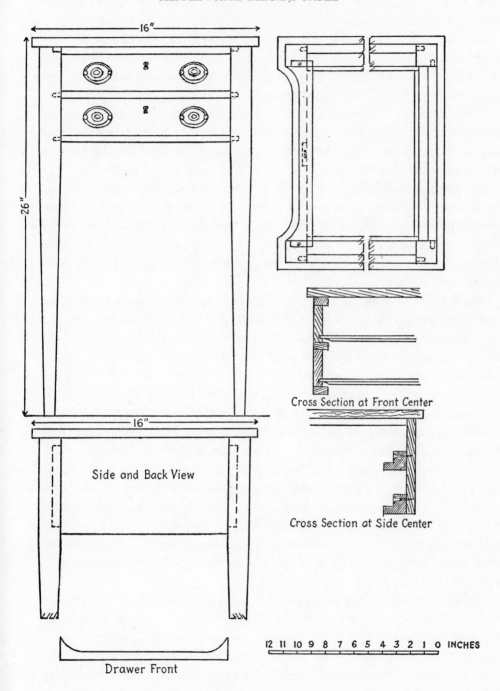

26"

16"

16"

Side and Back View

Drawer Front

Cross Section at Front Center

Cross Section at Side Center

12 11 10 9 8 7 6 5 4 3 2 1 0 INCHES

87

taper, so that when the tapered sides of the leg are placed against the jig, the next trip over the saw will cut the original correct taper on the last two sides.

After shaping the leg, sand the tapered section to finish smoothness, then cut long mortises in the square upper section for the side and back skirting (see side and back view). Instructions for making mortise-and-tenon joints, and other processes, will be found in Chapter I.

Mortises for the two lower front frame strips are also cut in the front legs (front-view and top-view drawings). Note that the tenon on the upper front strip is cut on the top edge of the strip. The leg top is cut down, making an open mortise, to allow the upper strip to rest flush with the top of the leg.

The side and back skirt pieces should next be cut, with long tenons to fit the leg mortises. Use wider wood to make the front frame strips, cutting the concave shape with a band saw or scroll saw, if available. The top-view drawing contains the outline of one of these pieces, which may be used as a guide. After shaping the strips, tenon the ends, placing the tenons on the top piece flush with the top surface.

Glue the back skirting into the back legs, and the front frame strips into the front legs. After gluing, reinforce the joints of the upper front strip with a screw through each tenon into the leg (top-view drawing). Then glue the side skirt pieces into the front and back assemblies. Sand all flat surfaces.

Drawer construction is discussed in detail in Chapter I. Cut and attach the drawer support strips as shown in the cross section at side center, *Plate 34*. Careful fitting is necessary for a smooth-running drawer. Make the drawer fronts from thick wood, cut to follow the same concave line as that of the front frame strips. A detail drawing of the drawer front is given in *Plate 34*.

The top overhangs the vertical line of the frame one-half inch, as shown in the drawings. Make a pattern, using the outline of the top-view drawing as a guide. After gluing together the boards of the top, cut it to shape and sand it before attaching to the table. Fastening the top is accomplished by sloping screws through the side and back skirting, and vertical screws through the top front frame strip. Apply finish as desired. Drawer pulls are attached after finishing.

Butterfly Tables. The butterfly table is an American development, not found in England. During the latter half of the seventeenth century, the gate-leg table was popular here as in England, but between 1700 and 1725 many butterfly tables were made in our New England states. The name refers to the shape of the leaf supports, which resemble the wings of butterflies. Sizes of these tables varied considerably, some being quite large. The tops were usually oval, but occasionally rectangular.

A characteristic feature of the butterfly table is the splay of the legs and skirting, the top being narrower than the lower part. Without this angle the leaf supports, or "wings," would not be workable.

———◆———

Plates 35 and *36* show two butterfly tables, similar in construction but of different sizes, 24″ and 30″ respectively. The legs are turned, and are reinforced by plain stretchers. The wing swings on a ½″ pivot, which is worked round on the end of the wing unit and set into the side stretcher. It is hinged at the top with a 1½″ butt hinge. A fill-in wedge is used between the wing top and the skirting, as shown in the cross-section detail drawing, *Plate 35*. Each leaf is hinged to the top with two 1⅛″ table hinges. Note the well fitted curve of the top and leaf edges.

It should also be noted that on splayed-leg butterfly tables, the tops of the legs and of the sloped skirting must be cut at an angle to compensate for the splay. This provides a straight flat surface for attaching the top.

The legs should first be turned and sanded to finish smoothness on the lathe. The sections which are to be mortised for skirting and stretcher joints are left square, with rounded corners. After removing from the lathe, cut the top ends of the legs at an 8-degree angle to provide the splay. The flat bottom of the ball foot must be cut at the same angle.

Determine the lengths of the end skirt pieces and the longer end stretchers, and cut these pieces with the proper angle at the ends (see end-view drawing). Then cut the side stretchers and side skirt pieces. These are identical in length. The top edge of the side skirting must be beveled to match the angle of the leg top.

Cut tenons on all skirtings and stretchers, and cut mortises for these pieces in the legs (see "Mortise and Tenon," Chapter I). Place the mortises so that the outside surfaces of skirting and stretchers will be flush with the outside flat surfaces of the legs. The distance from the leg top to the top of the mortise is approximately ⅛″ greater for the side skirting than for the end skirting, owing to the angle of the leg top. Measure carefully for position before cutting the mortises.

Before assembling, sand the inside flat surfaces of the legs, and the inside surfaces of the stretchers. Round and sand the top edges of the stretchers (see cross sections of stretchers in drawings.)

Plate 35

TWENTY-FOUR-INCH BUTTERFLY TABLE

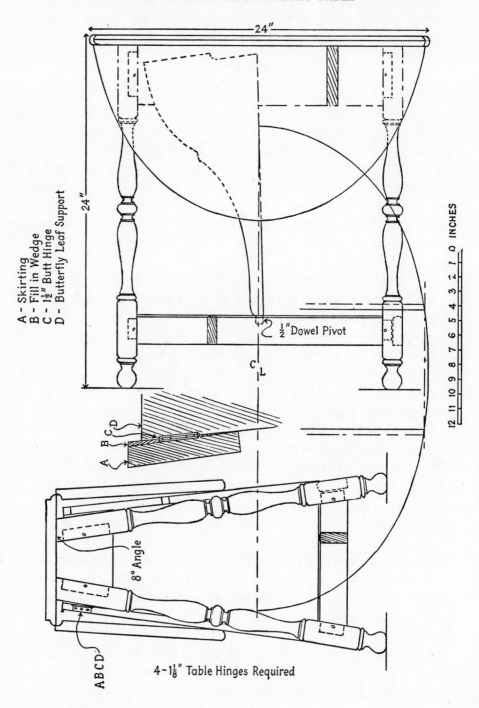

24"

24"

A - Skirting
B - Fill in Wedge
C - 1½" Butt Hinge
D - Butterfly Leaf Support

½"Dowel Pivot

C L

A B C D

12 11 10 9 8 7 6 5 4 3 2 1 0 INCHES

8° Angle

A B C D

4-1⅛" Table Hinges Required

Plate 36

THIRTY-INCH BUTTERFLY TABLE

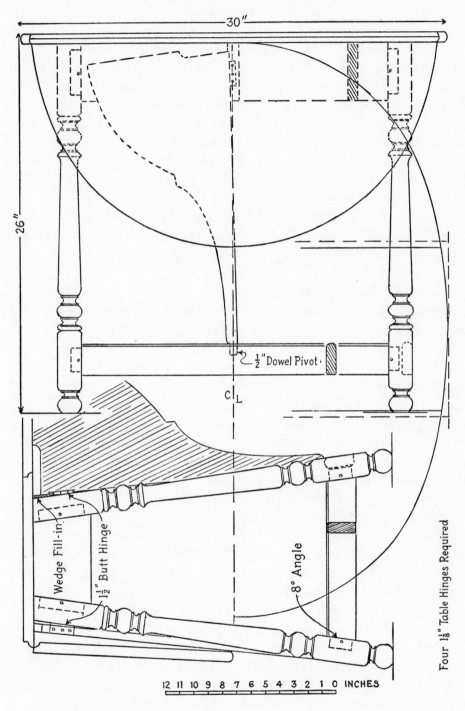

30"

26"

½" Dowel Pivot

C L

Wedge Fill-in

1½" Butt Hinge

8° Angle

Four 1⅛" Table Hinges Required

12 11 10 9 8 7 6 5 4 3 2 1 0 INCHES

Assemble the legs, skirting, and stretchers with glue, and reinforce the joints with tenon pins. Then sand all outside flat surfaces.

The butterfly leaf supports should next be cut, except for the top edge. Work the ½″ pivot at the lower end to a perfect round with hand tools and sandpaper, and sand all surfaces. Bore the pivot holes at the top centers of the side stretchers, and place the supports in open position, just touching the lower edge of the sloped skirting. Measure the gaps to determine the size and angle of the fill-in wedges required between the skirts and the leaf supports. Cut and fit these wedges, and glue and brad them to the skirting.

Cut the required indentations for the 1½″ butt hinges, placing them as indicated in the detail drawing, *Plate 35*. Attach the hinges to join the leaf supports to the table.

Now open both supports wide and lay a straightedge across the top edge of the side skirt, extending it alongside the leaf supports. Mark the supports with pencil for the level top edge. Saw the tops of the supports, and smooth the edges.

Next, select the boards for the top and the leaves, and glue them together to form pieces slightly larger than required. Mold the adjoining edges as shown in the end-view drawing. Directions for cutting moldings are given in Chapter I. Join the leaves to the top with 1⅛″ table hinges, two for each leaf. Fitting of table hinges is an exacting task. The method is described in Chapter I. After joining the top and leaves, cut the complete oval outline of the extended top. Round and smooth the outside edge, and sand the entire top surface. Sand both top and bottom surfaces of the leaves.

To attach the top, bore and counterbore at intervals in the inside surface of the skirting near the top edge, for screws to be inserted and driven up at an angle into the top. The desired finish may now be applied.

Drop-Leaf Tables.   In the middle of the seventeenth century, the gate-leg table evolved and was popular on both sides of the Atlantic. In the early eighteenth century, when all furniture design was undergoing the refining influence of the Queen Anne period, drop-leaf tables were made without the gate-like features. The leaves were supported by legs which swung out on a vertical wooden hinge. In some cases these were two of the regular table legs; in other cases two extra legs were provided to swing out under the leaves.

Small drop-leaf tables, with swinging bracket supports for the leaves, were a slightly later development. Designed as individual breakfast tables, they were popular during the Chippendale, Hepplewhite, and Sheraton periods. These "Pembroke tables," as they were called, were made in a variety of shapes, and were frequently used in America as tea tables. Most of them had one drawer.

Plate 37

SMALL QUEEN ANNE DROP-LEAF TABLE

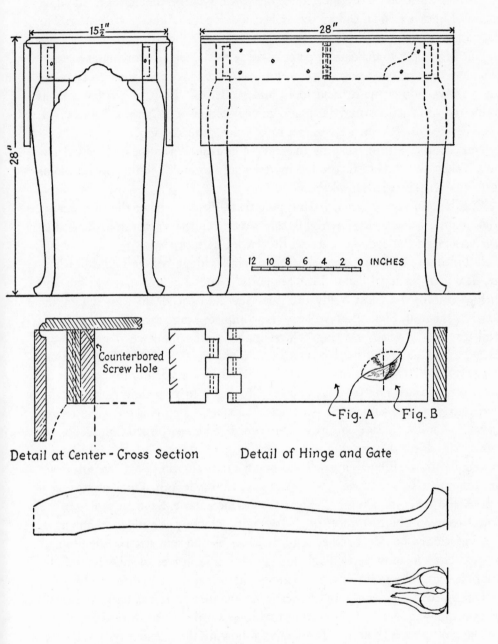

15½"

28"

28"

12 10 8 6 4 2 0 INCHES

Counterbored
Screw Hole

Fig. A   Fig. B

Detail at Center - Cross Section   Detail of Hinge and Gate

12 11 10 9 8 7 6 5 4 3 2 1 0 INCHES

Plate 37 illustrates a drop-leaf table of typical Queen Anne design. Its light, graceful lines are enhanced by the arched lower edge of the end skirting. The legs are cabriole, with either the plain Dutch foot or the ball and claw.

The first step is to make a leg pattern, using the leg detail drawing as a guide. The legs may be band-sawed according to instructions in Chapter I. They are then worked down with hand tools, and sanded. If the ball-and-claw foot is preferred, instructions may be found in the section on "Carving," Chapter I. The leg tops are left square, and are mortised for the skirting.

Next cut the skirting, shaping the end pieces as shown in the end-view drawing. Tenon the ends to fit the leg mortises, and assemble with drawbore pins or tenon pins, in addition to the glue.

Cut the four leg wing blocks and glue them in place. After the glue has set thoroughly, work them down with sandpaper to blend with the leg and skirt surfaces. Sand the end skirting and the flat leg surfaces.

Detailed instructions for constructing a vertical hinge will be found in Chapter I, under "Hinged Table Leaf Supports." After reading that section, and before cutting the parts, study the side view and the detail drawing of the vertical hinge in Plate 37. Note that the complete hinge assembly extends the full length of the side skirting. The swinging section (*Figure A* in *Plate 37*) is to be band-sawed at the free end in a decorative ogee curve. The piece cut off (*Figure B*) is not discarded, but is attached to the skirting, to continue an unbroken surface line between the legs. In order to provide an opening for the fingers to grasp and swing out the leaf support, a section about 3″ in length is beveled on the outside ogee edge of *Figure B,* and a corresponding section on the inside edge of *Figure A*.

Cut and fit the hinge "fingers" and make a trial assembly to determine exact measurement, before cutting the swinging section to length. Then saw the ogee curve, and bevel the adjoining edges as described above. Sand these edges, the lower edge and both surfaces of the swinging section; assemble as shown.

Glue selected boards together to form pieces of sufficient size for the top and leaves. The top must be wide enough to allow the leaves to fall clear of the cabriole legs. The grain of the wood should be carefully matched. Mold the adjoining edges of the top and leaves to fit together, as indicated in the cross-section drawing. Methods of cutting moldings are described in Chapter I.

The table hinges should be fitted next, following the detailed instructions in Chapter I. Two 1⅛″ hinges are required for each leaf. Then, with leaves extended, mark the straight edges and saw. Smooth the edges and sand the entire top, including the undersides of the leaves. Attach with sloping screws driven up through counterbored holes in the inside surface of the skirt, as shown in the cross-section drawing. Apply the desired finish.

The clear-cut differences between "typical" examples of various periods tend to obscure the fact that style transitions were actually gradual. The cabinetmaker, with customers of varying tastes, often kept one lingering eye on the past while the other peered into the future. The results were not always happy, but occasionally a transition piece blends the best features of two periods in perfect harmony. The attractive table in *Plate 38* is such a blend. The carved and pierced corner brackets and the leg molding are Chinese Chippendale in inspiration; the line inlay on the drawer front, the slender taper of the legs, and above all the general effect of pert grace are pure Hepplewhite.

The legs may be tapered on a jointer, if available, or with saw and jig. A detailed discussion of the latter process may be found in the text for *Plate 34*. After tapering, mold the outside surfaces of the legs as shown in the cross sections *A* and *B, Plate 38*. Sand to finish smoothness.

Next, cut the skirting, including the flat swing supports. Instructions for these may be found in Chapter I. Mortise the legs and shape the long skirt tenons to match, as indicated in the side-view drawing. Before assembling these members, cut the two front frame strips from wider wood, with convex front surfaces, as shown in the detail drawings *A* and *B*. Mortise the front legs and cut corresponding tenons on the lower strip, *Figure B*. The upper strip, *Figure A*, should be dovetailed into the leg top. Glue the back skirt to the back legs, and the front strips to the front legs; then join with the side skirt pieces. Sand the outside flat surfaces.

The bracket detail drawing may be used as a guide in making a pattern for the four brackets. Cut out the open section with a jigsaw or coping saw threaded through a hole bored in the waste wood. Use a V gouge to carve the rosette. Sand and attach to the table with brads.

Drawer construction is discussed in Chapter I. For the sides, back, and bottom of the drawer, ⅜″ wood may be used. The front is cut from thicker wood to the shape shown in the drawer detail drawing, *Plate 38*. Trim the drawer front with line inlay ("Inlaying," Chapter I). Install drawer support strips at the inside lower edge of the side skirting (see cross section at center).

Glue selected boards together to form pieces slightly larger than required for the top and leaves. Mold the adjoining edges to fit smoothly, as indicated in the cross-section drawing. Refer to Chapter I for methods of cutting moldings, and for fitting table hinges. Fit and attach the 1⅛″ table hinges, then lay out the complete top with leaves extended. Mark the outline as shown in the top detail drawing. Saw and mold the edges, then sand the entire upper surface and the undersides of the leaves. Bore and counterbore the inside surface of the skirting for sloping screws to attach the top (cross section at center). The table is now ready for finish.

Plate 38

SMALL TRANSITION DROP-LEAF TABLE

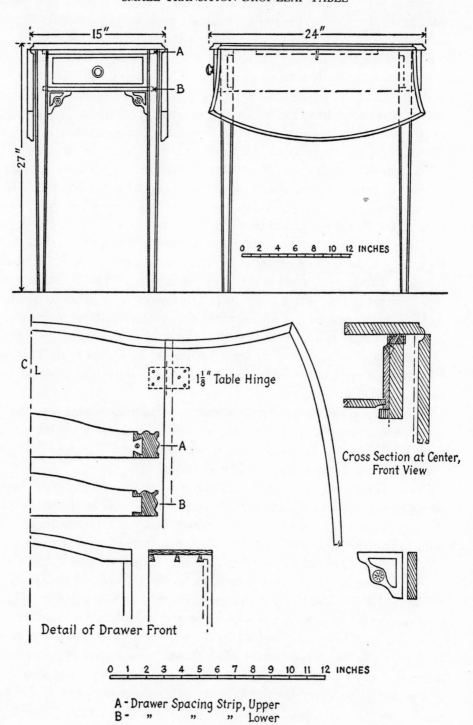

0 2 4 6 8 10 12 INCHES

C L

1⅛" Table Hinge

A

B

Cross Section at Center,
Front View

Detail of Drawer Front

0 1 2 3 4 5 6 7 8 9 10 11 12 INCHES

A - Drawer Spacing Strip, Upper
B - "   "   "   Lower

Plate 39

SMALL HEPPLEWHITE DROP-LEAF TABLE

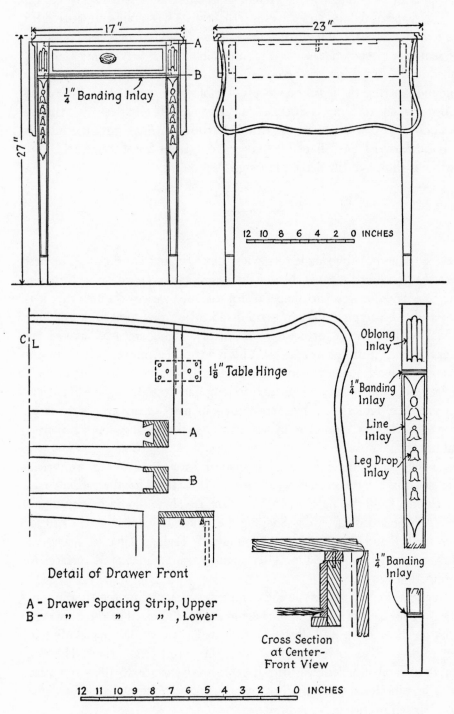

17"

A

B

¼" Banding Inlay

27"

23"

12 10 8 6 4 2 0 INCHES

C L

1⅛" Table Hinge

A

B

Oblong Inlay

¼" Banding Inlay

Line Inlay

Leg Drop Inlay

¼" Banding Inlay

Detail of Drawer Front

A - Drawer Spacing Strip, Upper
B - " " " , Lower

Cross Section at Center-Front View

12 11 10 9 8 7 6 5 4 3 2 1 0 INCHES

Plate 39 is an exceptionally fine Hepplewhite table with elaborate bellflower inlay. The shape of the top and leaves is serpentine. The square-cut, tapered leg has no foot, but a foot is suggested by the ¼″ banding inlay near the bottom.

The sequence of operations in making this table is so nearly identical to that described in the preceding text, *Plate 38,* that no repetition is necessary. After cutting and tapering the legs, the process of molding is omitted, and the inlay is applied instead. Inlaying is discussed in Chapter I. The patterns for cutting the designs may be made from the detail drawings in *Plate 39.* Line inlay is used on the drawer front. Shape the drawer front, front frame strips, table top, and leaves as shown in the detail drawings.

In *Plates 40* and *41,* two six-leg drop-leaf dining tables are shown. The first has turned legs with ball feet. Tables of this description were common throughout the East. Sizes of tops and shapes of leg turnings varied so much that it is hard to find two originals alike in every detail. The wood used for turned-leg tables was walnut, cherry, or occasionally maple. Mahogany was favored for tables of the type illustrated in *Plate 41.* This is a Queen Anne or early Chippendale design, with cabriole legs and either the Dutch foot or the ball and claw.

The leaves of both tables are large and rectangular. Straightedged leaves were popular, as these tables were frequently used in pairs to accommodate large families. Each leaf is supported by an extra leg that swings outward on a vertical hinge.

The six legs should be made first. The pattern measurements for the turned legs are given in a special drawing, *Plate 40.* The pattern for the cabriole legs may be figured from the leg cross section, *Plate 41.* These should be sawed and worked to shape as instructed in "Shaping a Cabriole Leg," Chapter I. Instructions for the ball-and-claw foot may be found in "Carving," Chapter I. Legs of both tables are square at the top. After shaping, sand the shaped surfaces to finish smoothness.

Next, cut the skirting, tenon the ends, and cut corresponding mortises in four of the legs. The size and positions of these joints are indicated in the drawings. Note that in *Plate 40* the end skirting is indented ⅛″ from the outside line of the leg, while in *Plate 41* it is set flush with the outside leg surface. The side skirting of both tables is set flush with the *inside* leg surface, to allow room for the extra legs in closed position. The end skirting in *Plate 41* is cut in cyma curves, as shown in the end-view drawing.

Plate 40

SIX-LEG DROP-LEAF TABLE

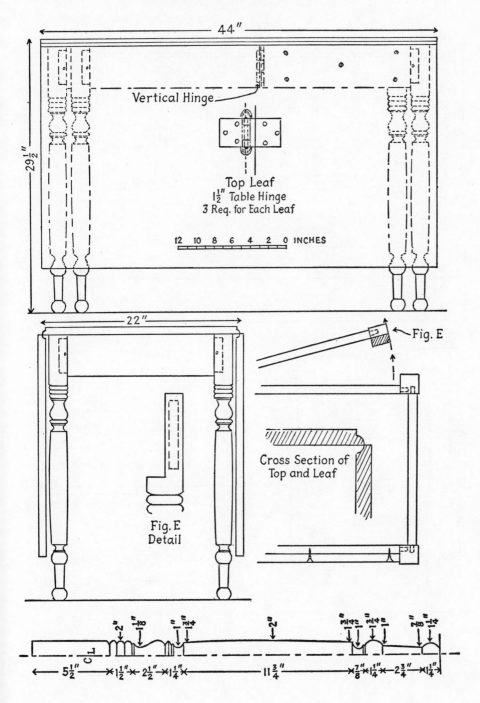

44"

29½"

Vertical Hinge

Top Leaf
1½" Table Hinge
3 Req. for Each Leaf

12 10 8 6 4 2 0 INCHES

22"

Fig. E

Fig. E
Detail

Cross Section of
Top and Leaf

2" 1⅛" 1" 1¾" 1¼" 2" ¾⅓½" ¾½1¼" ⅞" 1¼"

5½" C L 1½" 2½" 1¼" 11¾" ⅞" 1¼" 2¾" 1¼"

Plate 41

SIX-LEG CABRIOLE DROP-LEAF TABLE

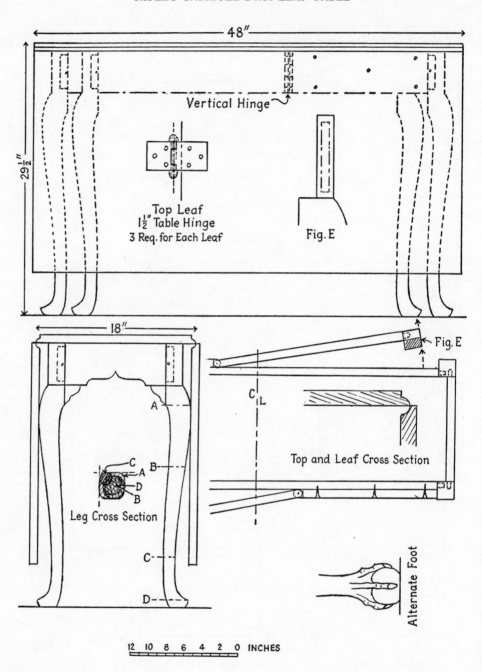

48"

29½"

Vertical Hinge

Top Leaf
1½" Table Hinge
3 Req. for Each Leaf

Fig. E

18"

A

B

C
A
D
B

Leg Cross Section

C

D

C L

Fig. E

Top and Leaf Cross Section

Alternate Foot

12 10 8 6 4 2 0 INCHES

Glue together the four legs and the skirt pieces, using drawbore pins or tenon pins to reinforce the joints. Then sand the end skirt and upper leg surfaces.

The procedure for constructing the two vertical hinges is described in Chapter I, under "Hinged Table-Leaf Supports." After assembling the hinge, mortise the free end of the swinging section into the extra leg. The detail drawing, *Figure E*, shows the position of this mortise and the shape of the leg top, which is cut away to allow the leg to pass under the skirting. (See also *Figure E* in top-view drawing.)

The fixed section of the vertical hinge support is fastened to the side skirting with screws, as shown in the side-view and top-view drawings.

The boards for the top and leaves should now be glued together, matching the grain for greatest beauty. For No. 41, make the top wide enough so that the leaves will clear the cabriole legs when dropped. Mold the adjoining edges as shown in the cross section of top and leaf. Then fit the 1½" table hinges, three for each leaf, as instructed in Chapter I, under "Fitting the Table Hinge."

With leaves extended, mark the straight edges, and saw. Smooth the edges, sand the entire top surface and the undersides of the leaves. Bore and counter-bore the inside surface of the skirting at intervals, and attach the top with screws driven upward at an angle through the bored holes. Finish as desired.

———◆———

Plate 42 illustrates a Chinese Chippendale serving table with one drop leaf. Construction of this table differs from the foregoing chiefly in the fact that, instead of an extra leg, one of the four regular legs swings out to support the leaf. This type of support, while not rigid enough for a large dining table, is well suited to a medium-sized table where an extra leg would appear cumbersome.

The square, fluted legs and pierced brackets are typical of Chippendale's later years. The style has a simplicity of line that makes it particularly adaptable to modern—even modernistic—home decoration.

The legs should first be cut to size, then mortised for the long tenons of the skirting. Omit the end-skirt mortise on the leg which is to be attached to the vertical hinge (see drawing). The leg sections marked *A* and *B* on the front view are then fluted and stop fluted, respectively, as shown in the cross sections *A* and *B*. Both processes are explained in Chapter I. Next chamfer the inside corner up to the bottom of the skirting, and sand the leg to finish condition.

Cut the four skirt pieces, and cut the opening for the drawer in one end piece. Study the drawing before proceeding. Note that front and end skirts are set

Plate 42

CHINESE CHIPPENDALE SERVING TABLE

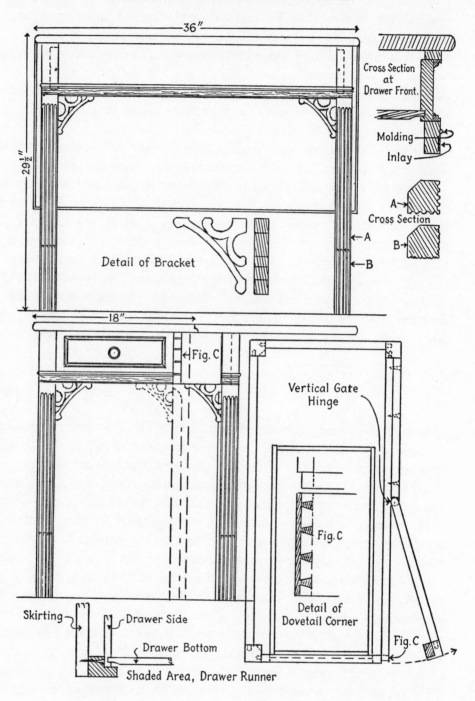

36″

Cross Section
at
Drawer Front.

Molding

Inlay

$29\frac{1}{2}$″

Detail of Bracket

← A

← B

A

Cross Section

B

18″

←Fig. C

Vertical Gate
Hinge

Fig. C

Detail of
Dovetail Corner

Fig. C

Skirting

Drawer Side

Drawer Bottom

Shaded Area, Drawer Runner

flush with the outside leg surfaces, while the back skirt is set flush with the inside leg surface to allow room for the vertical hinge assembly. At three corners the skirting is tenoned into the legs; at the fourth corner the skirt pieces (including the end with the drawer) are joined together with a series of dovetails (*Figure C*). Instructions for making these joints are included in Chapter I.

Prepare the joints as required, and assemble the four skirt pieces and three legs with glue. Reinforce the tenoned joints with drawbore pins or tenon pins.

After assembly, cut a dado groove 1″ wide and $\frac{1}{16}$″ deep around the front and ends of the table, including the legs, $\frac{1}{16}$″ above the lower edge of the skirt. Cut a matching groove on the end surface of the remaining leg. Set in your choice of inlay (see "Inlaying," Chapter I). Allow the glue to dry thoroughly, then sand all outside flat surfaces to finish smoothness.

Make a strip molding $\frac{3}{8}$″ by $\frac{3}{16}$″, and cut it to length with mitered corners. Apply it to the surface with glue and brads just above the inlay, as indicated in the cross-section drawing. Methods of cutting moldings are discussed in Chapter I.

Cut the two pieces for the vertical hinge, and construct the hinge as directed in Chapter I. Cut a recess in the top of the swinging leg as shown in the top-view detail drawing. The leg top should fit perfectly around the dovetailed skirt joint, while the leg below the recess fits under the skirting. Tenon the free end of the swinging hinge section to fit the leg mortise, and glue in place with a drawbore pin or tenon pin to strengthen the joint. Screw the nonmoving section of the hinge to the back skirting, as shown in the drawing.

Make and attach drawer runners of the type illustrated in the detail drawing. Drawer construction is discussed in Chapter I. Study the cross section at drawer front, *Plate 42,* and note that the front of the drawer is set in from the front line of the table, the angle being filled by a mitered molding. This molding is applied to the drawer front after the drawer is assembled and sanded.

The corner brackets may be easily cut with a jigsaw or coping saw. Six are required. After cutting, remove saw marks with a sharp chisel, and sand smooth. Fasten the brackets to the legs and skirts with thin brads. On the swinging leg corner, fasten to the leg only.

Select the boards for the top and leaf, and glue them together to form pieces of sufficient size. Mold the joining edges as shown in the end-view drawing. Install three $1\frac{1}{2}$″ table hinges, as instructed in Chapter I, under "Fitting the Table Hinge." Then, with the leaf extended, mark and saw the complete outline. Round the edges as shown in the cross-section drawing. Sand the entire upper surface and the underside of the leaf. Attach with sloping screws, driven up into the top from counterbored holes in the inside surface of the skirting. Apply finish as desired.

———◆———

Plates 43 and *44* illustrate two Hepplewhite serving tables of different patterns. As in the case of the preceding table (*Plate 42*), the leaf is supported by one of the back legs which swings out on a vertical hinge support. In this case, however, the leaf is not a drop leaf, but folds over on top of the table when not in use, as in a card table.

It is of interest here to note the reason for using this type of support design on some folding-leaf tables. The simplest form of leaf support is that provided by the table framework itself, when the top swivels in a quarter-turn. An example of this type is shown in *Plate 45*. In many cases, however, as in *Plates 43* and *44,* the shape of the top is such that it would not completely cover the framework when swiveled. The hinged-leg support is therefore necessary.

The legs may be tapered on a jointer, if available, or with a saw and jig. The method has been described in connection with *Plate 34.* After shaping, the leg mortises should be cut. Study the drawings to determine the positions and sizes of the joints. Note that the end skirting and the two front frame strips (above and below the drawers) are to be set flush with the outside surfaces of the legs. The back skirting is set in to allow room for the vertical hinge assembly. The swinging leg has only one mortise, for the free end of the hinge. The top of this leg will later be cut out so as to fit around the dovetailed corner of the skirting. Mortises for the wide skirting pieces should be long (nearly the width of the skirt).

The legs of No. 43 are trimmed with simple line and banding inlay. The crossband which separates the tapered section from the square top post should not be inlaid until after assembly. With this exception, inlay the legs (see "Inlaying," Chapter I); then sand the tapered section to finish smoothness.

Cut and tenon the front horizontal strips and glue them into the front legs; then measure and cut the vertical strips which separate the drawer openings, and glue them in place.

Cut the side and back skirting, and make a dovetail joint at the corner marked *Figure A* on the drawings. Tenon the remaining ends and glue them into the leg mortises, with drawbore pins or tenon pins to reinforce the joints.

After assembly, cut the groove for the ¼″ banding inlay across the front and

Plate 43

HEPPLEWHITE SERVING TABLE

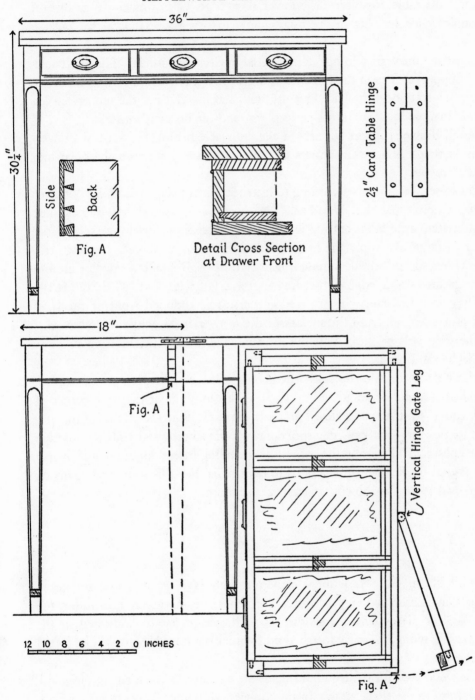

Fig. A

Detail Cross Section
at Drawer Front

$2\frac{1}{2}''$ Card Table Hinge

Vertical Hinge Gate Leg

Fig. A

12 10 8 6 4 2 0 INCHES

Shaded Areas are Cross Sections
of Drawer Supports or Runners

sides of the table, just above the lower skirt edge. Cut a matching groove on the unattached leg. Set in the inlay, allow to dry, then sand all flat outside surfaces.

Construct the vertical hinge as instructed in Chapter I, under "Hinged Table-Leaf Supports." Tenon the free end and glue it to the swinging leg. Fasten the stationary section to the back skirting with screws. Cut out the top of the leg so that in closed position it fits perfectly around the dovetail corner.

Install drawer support runners at the ends and behind the vertical drawer-division strips. Shape the runners as shown in cross section on the open top-view drawing.

Construct the drawers according to instructions in Chapter I, under "Drawer Construction." For the sides, back, and bottom, $\frac{3}{8}''$ wood will suffice. The front matches the other outside wood. After assembling the drawers, sand the front surfaces and apply the bead molding as follows: Make a beading strip $\frac{1}{8}''$ wide and $\frac{5}{16}''$ deep, rounded on the front edge. Make a saw cut around the extreme outside edge of the drawer front, $\frac{1}{8}''$ wide and $\frac{1}{4}''$ deep. Set the beading into this cut, with mitered corners. The rounded front of the bead will protrude $\frac{1}{16}''$ from the surface of the drawer front, while the outer edge of the strip will be flush with the drawer edge. Fasten the beading in place with glue and brads.

The boards for the top and leaf should next be glued together, sanded, matched, and cut to length. Fit a $2\frac{1}{2}''$ card-table hinge at the back corner of each end. With the leaf in closed position, mark and saw the outline of top and leaf. Remove saw marks with a spokeshave or drawknife, and sand the edges in closed position. Then sand the entire top, including both sides of the leaf. Apply the desired finish, then install brass drawer pulls. For this style, brass bails on large oval plates, as shown, are most appropriate.

———◆———

The table in *Plate 44* is more elaborate than *Plate 43* in shape and ornamentation. Construction procedures are the same, however, except for the curved skirt pieces which are doweled to the front legs as indicated in the top-view drawing, *Plate 44*. Instructions for making dowel joints will be found in Chapter I.

The wood used for the front and side skirting must be thick enough to allow for cutting to the shape shown in the top-view drawing. Drawers are omitted, the front being a full skirt instead of a framework. An enlarged detail draw-

Plate 44

HEPPLEWHITE SERVING TABLE

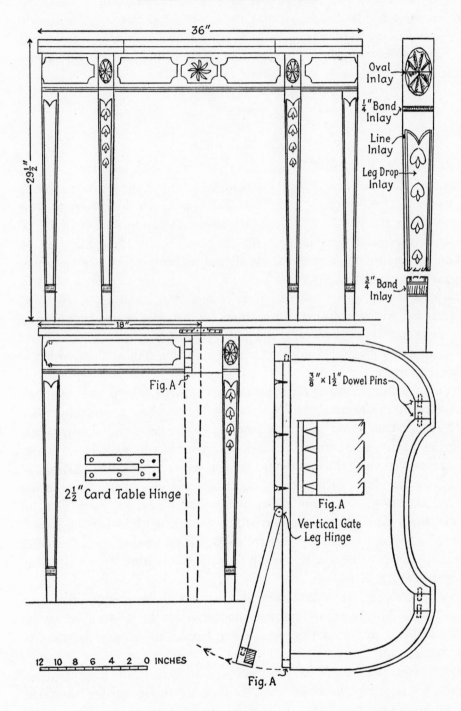

36"

29½"

18"

Oval
Inlay

¼" Band
Inlay

Line
Inlay

Leg Drop
Inlay

¾" Band
Inlay

Fig. A

2½" Card Table Hinge

⅜" × 1½" Dowel Pins

Fig. A

Vertical Gate
Leg Hinge

Fig. A

12 10 8 6 4 2 0 INCHES

ing of the leg shows the inlay pattern to be used. The skirting is decorated with line inlay and with a floral inlay pattern at the center front, as shown. Inlay patterns may be purchased ready to use, or may be made up from contrasting pieces of veneer. The continuous band across the skirt and legs should be inlaid after assembly.

———◆———

Plate 45 shows a beautiful Hepplewhite card table with inlaid legs. As on the serving tables just preceding, the leaf folds over upon the top when not in use. Extended, the leaf rests upon the table frame, which is brought into position under the leaf by a quarter-turn of the table top. This method of supporting the leaf is simpler than the hinge-leg construction, but may be used only where the top and leaf are so shaped that they will cover the frame completely in the pivoted position.

The legs may be tapered with a jointer or with a saw and jig, as discussed in connection with *Plate 34.* Long mortises for the skirt tenons should then be cut in all four legs ("Joinery," Chapter I). As shown in the top-view drawing, the mortises should be so placed that the skirting will fit flush with the outside leg surface.

The inlay pattern is shown on the leg detail drawing. The process of inlaying is described in Chapter I. All leg inlay should be set before assembly except the ¼″ band at the lower skirt line. Since this band runs continuously across the legs and skirting, it should be inlaid after assembly, in a single operation. The tapered sections of the legs should be sanded before and after inlaying.

Next cut the back skirting, tenon the ends, and glue them into the leg mortises. Use drawbore pins or tenon pins to strengthen the joints. Cut the side and front skirt pieces from wood thick enough to allow for the curved shape. The patterns for these pieces are shown in the second and third lines of the top-view drawing, the first being the table-top outline. Tenon the skirt ends to fit the leg mortises.

Before assembling, set in the rectangular patterns of line inlay on the front and side skirts. After assembly, cut the dado groove for the ¼″ band across the skirting and legs, and inlay this band. Then sand all the outside flat surfaces to finish smoothness.

Glue together the boards for the top and leaf, and cut to length in rectangular pieces. Sand the upper surfaces and lay them together in closed position. Sand the back corners of the ends, cut the required indentations, and

Plate 45

HEPPLEWHITE CARD TABLE

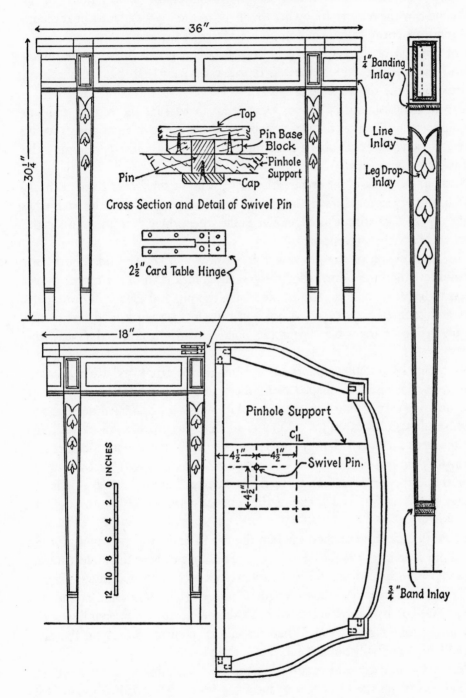

36"

30¼"

Top

Pin Base Block

Pinhole Support

Pin

Cap

Cross Section and Detail of Swivel Pin

2½" Card Table Hinge

¼" Banding Inlay

Line Inlay

Leg Drop Inlay

18"

Pinhole Support

C_{1L}

4½"   4½"

Swivel Pin

4½"

INCHES

0 2 4 6 8 10 12

¾" Band Inlay

109

fit a 2½″ card-table hinge at each end. With the leaf in closed position, mark and band-saw the outline, following the shape in the top-view drawing. Smooth and sand the entire top, including both surfaces of the leaf.

The position of the swivel pin is worked out in pencil lines on the underside of the top (see dotted lines on top-view drawing). In placing the lines, proceed as if the top were rectangular.

The first line should be drawn from front to back at the center, dividing the top in half. Then on the right-hand side draw a line at right angles to the other, dividing this half of the table top into two equal areas (presuming the top to be rectangular).

Next, in the back right rectangular area, draw a line from front to back, 4½″ from the original halving line; then draw a line parallel to the back edge of the top, 4½″ in from this edge. The point where these two lines cross is the exact center of the swivel pin.

The construction of the pin assembly is shown in cross section. First turn or band-saw the round disc called the pin base block, and in the center of this bore a tight-fitting hole for the 1″ pin. Turn the pin and glue it into the hole. Bore and counterbore two screw holes in the pin base block, and fasten it to the underside of the table top at the point already determined (swivel-pin center).

Next, cut the pinhole support to fit between the front and back skirting. The front edge must be shaped to fit the inside curve of the skirt (see top-view drawing). It is joined to the front skirt with two concealed dowels, at a height and position carefully calculated so that the pin base block will rest on the upper surface of the support when the top is in position. Measure and mark the positions of the corresponding dowel holes in the front edge of the support and the inside surface of the front skirting. Bore the holes, glue in the dowels, then fasten the back end of the support with two screws through the back skirting.

Repeat the marking method used on the top to find the center point for the swivel-pin hole in the pinhole support. Use a 1″ bit to bore this hole, sanding the bored edge so that the pin will turn freely but without too much play.

The swivel pin is then cut to length (flush with the underside of the support). Turn or band-saw a cap with 2″ diameter, and countersink a screw hole in the center of the cap. When the cap is screwed to the pin, the table top will turn but will not lift off.

Detach the pin cap and remove the top for finishing. It is advisable also to sand and finish the top edges of the table frame. This will eliminate deep scratches underneath the top, which otherwise would result from swiveling.

Plates 46, 47, and *48* illustrate a three-part set of tables in a beautiful Hepplewhite design. Mahogany tables of this type were used, in Colonial days, in large urban homes and southern mansions. They are particularly desirable today because of their compactness when closed.

The center table of this set, *Plate 46,* is constructed like other six-leg dropleaf tables, except that the long outside edges of the leaves are molded to the same shape as the long edges of the top. The straight edges of the end-table tops are molded with the same shape in reverse. Thus the tables fit together with the leaves either up or down, as indicated in the two detail drawings, *Figures C* and *D,* in *Plate 47.* The dotted lines at each joint represent centering tenons, which keep the tables in line and also give greater rigidity to the extended leaves.

One of the two identical end tables is illustrated in *Plate 47.* The only unusual construction feature involved is the laminated skirting. Each half-round table has three curved skirt pieces, each of which is composed of five layers of wood. This method of construction permits the skirt pieces to be tenoned into the legs. Because of the sharpness of the curve, the angle of the grain in a single-piece skirt would be too great for any but a dowel joint, lacking the required strength for a dining table.

The laminations may be prepared beforehand, to allow ample time for drying while other work is in progress. After determining the correct radius for each curved piece, screw form blocks to the floor or to a worktable in the required position (see *Figure F, Plate 48*). Cut the five layers of wood slightly larger than the finished dimensions, to allow for trimming. Spread a slow-setting casein or resin glue on all surfaces, except those which will form the outside surfaces of the finished piece. Place the five laminations in position over the form blocks, and clamp them securely at the center of the curve. Add clamps gradually, working outward from the center to each end. For best results in the clamping process, place a block of scrap wood under each clamp on the convex surface. This will increase the pressure area, and eliminate the bruise marks ordinarily left by the clamp jaws. When all clamps are in place, allow time for the glue to set thoroughly before removing the piece from the form blocks.

All three tables should be made at the same time to insure uniformity. The legs should first be cut to size and tapered, as described in connection with *Plate 34.* They should then be inlaid completely. The pattern is shown on the leg detail drawing, *Plate 46.* Inlay patterns may be purchased ready to use, or made up from pieces of veneer. Inlaying procedure is described in Chapter I. Sand the tapered sections of the legs thoroughly before assembly.

Next, cut the skirt pieces to size, including the curved laminated skirts of the end tables. Inlay the end skirts of the center table and the curved skirts of the end tables with ¼" banding inlay, measuring carefully to insure perfect continuity with the band on the legs.

Study the assembly details thoroughly before marking the positions of mortises and tenons on the legs and skirt ends. The curved skirts of the end tables and the end skirts of the center table are set back ⅟₁₆" from the leg front surface. The long skirts of the center table are set flush with the *inside* leg surfaces, to allow room for the vertical hinge assembly. Other skirt pieces are set flush with the outside leg surfaces. The swinging legs of the center table are cut back at the top to fit around the skirting. Similar hinge and leg-top details are illustrated in *Plates 40* and *41*.

After marking for position, cut the mortises and tenons as instructed in the section "Joinery," Chapter I. Glue the joints, using drawbore pins or tenon pins for extra strength. Sand all outside flat surfaces.

Study the drawings and text of *Plates 40* and *41,* and the discussion of vertical hinge construction in Chapter I, under "Hinged Table-Leaf Supports." Make, assemble, and attach the swinging leg supports of the center table.

Select the boards for the tops and leaves for all the tables. Glue them together to form pieces of sufficient size, cut to shape, and rough-sand. Cut the molded edges as shown in the detail drawings *C* and *D, Plate 47.* Molding procedures are described in Chapter I. The center table top should fit either the adjoining leaves or the straight edges of the end tables. The outside long edges of the leaves should also fit the end tables.

Hinge together the top and leaves of the center table as instructed in Chapter I, under "Fitting the Table Hinge." Then plane and sand the ends of tops and leaves to uniform length when the tables are placed together. Attach the tops to the table frames with sloping screws, driven upward through counterbored holes in the inside surface of the skirting.

The centering tenons are glued to the end tables. Detail drawings of this feature are given in *Plate 48.* First cut the mortises in the straight edges of the end-table molding, one near each end of the table. Then make the tenons and glue them in place.

Now set the end tables in position against the center table, with the leaves down. Mark and cut mortises in the center table top to fit the centering tenons, then place the tables in position with the leaves extended. Mark and cut mortises in the leaf edges.

Fit the tables together with leaves down, and plane any unevenness of the

Plate 46

HEPPLEWHITE THREE-PART SET OF TABLES

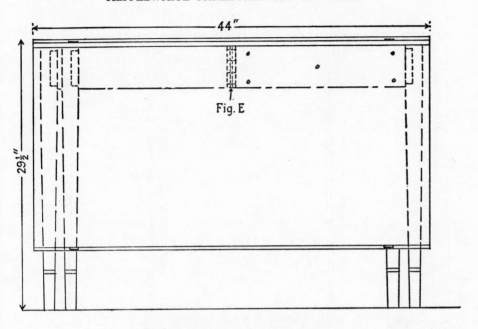

44"

29½"

Fig. E

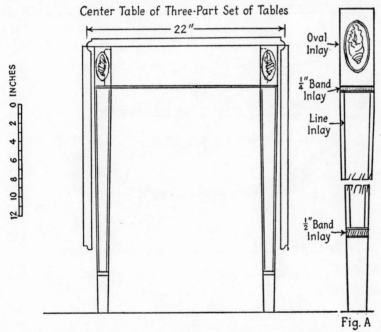

Center Table of Three-Part Set of Tables

22"

INCHES 0 2 4 6 8 10 12

Oval
Inlay

¼" Band
Inlay

Line
Inlay

½" Band
Inlay

Fig. A

Plate 47

HEPPLEWHITE THREE-PART SET OF TABLES (*Cont'd*)

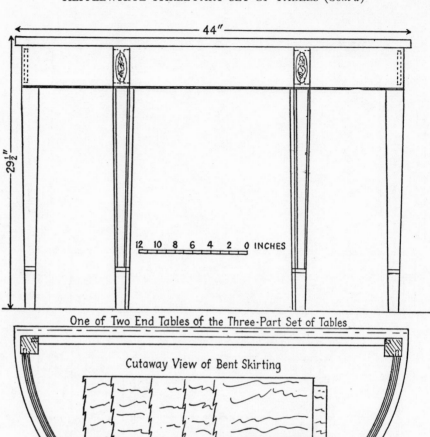

One of Two End Tables of the Three-Part Set of Tables

Cutaway View of Bent Skirting

Fig. B

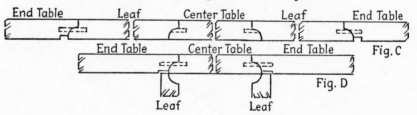

Side View of Table Tops: Fig.C, Extended; Fig.D, Closed

| End Table | Leaf | Center Table | Leaf | End Table |

Fig. C

| End Table | Center Table | End Table |

Fig. D

Leaf   Leaf

Plate 48

DETAIL OF PARTS AND EQUIPMENT FOR THREE-PART TABLE

Fig. F

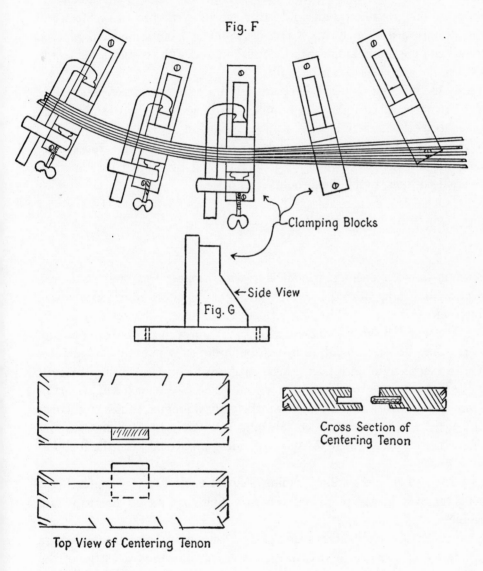

Clamping Blocks

←Side View

Fig. G

Cross Section of
Centering Tenon

Top View of Centering Tenon

meeting edges. Repeat with leaves extended. Sand completely, then apply the desired finish to all three tables.

Tripod Tables.   In the latter half of the eighteenth century, tripod tables became popular both in England and in America. They were usually of mahogany, but cherry, walnut, and other woods were also used. Sizes and shapes of tops varied widely. Most were of plain wood, but some were inlaid in patterns ranging from simple bands to elaborate designs covering the entire top. The tops were usually made to tilt.

Tables of this type required comparatively little time to make. They were therefore inexpensive, and great numbers of them were in use. They are popular today, both as antiques and in reproduction.

A characteristic feature of the revolving tilt-top table is the "crow's nest" which supports the top and allows it to turn and tilt. When the top is in horizontal position, a table catch holds it in place.

———◆———

Plate 49 shows a dish-top tripod table with cabriole legs and snake feet, typical of the Chippendale period. The top may be either tilted or revolved, or both. Study the section "Joining Tripod Table Legs," Chapter I. Turn the post to the shape shown in *Plate 49,* with a 1¼" pin turned on the upper end. This pin must be long enough to pass through the crow's nest, but should not be cut to exact length until later. Make a pattern for the legs, using the cross sections shown on the leg drawing as a guide. The shoe is included as part of the foot. Hip dimensions must allow for the vertical tongue. Band-saw the legs as instructed in Chapter I, under "Shaping a Cabriole Leg." Finish shaping by hand, then use a V gouge to cut the dividing groove between the foot and shoe.

As instructed in the section "Joining Tripod Table Legs," Chapter I, cut dovetail grooves in the post, and corresponding tongues on the legs, and assemble.

Next, cut the top and bottom plates of the crow's nest. These are two square pieces of wood, identical in size and shape except that the back edge of the top piece is extended to form a protrusion at each end. This piece is shown in the detail drawing, "Top View Crow's Nest," *Plate 49.* The protrusions are to be worked to ⅝" rounds with hand tools, to form the pivots on which the table top will tilt.

Sand the squares and clamp them together, to bore the postholes indicated by dotted lines on the detail drawing. These should be bored completely

Plate 49

QUEEN ANNE TILT-AND-TURN TABLE

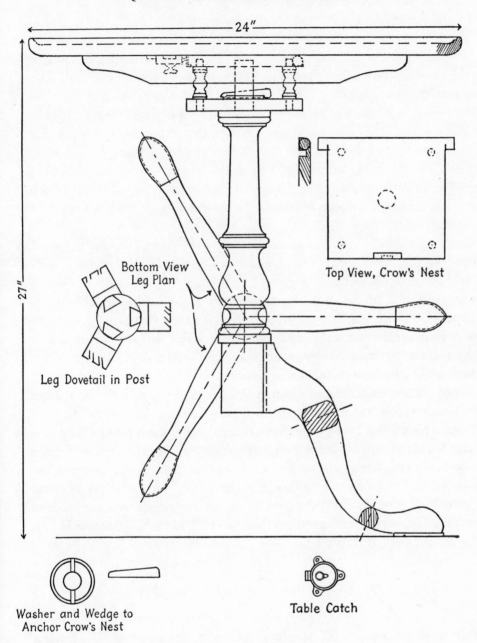

24"

27"

Bottom View
Leg Plan

Top View, Crow's Nest

Leg Dovetail in Post

Washer and Wedge to
Anchor Crow's Nest

Table Catch

12 11 10 9 8 7 6 5 4 3 2 1 0 INCHES

through the bottom plate but not quite through the top (⅜″ deep). Use a ½″ bit for the corner holes, a 1¼″ bit for the center hole.

Turn the four corner posts with ½″ pins at the ends. The top pins should be ⅜″ long to fit the holes in the top plate. The length of the bottom pins is the thickness of the bottom plate. The distance between shoulders of all four posts should be identical.

Make a trial assembly and measure the exact length required for the 1¼″ pin on the base post. This pin should pass through the bottom of the crow's nest and into the top to a depth of ⅜″. Cut the pin to length. Make a plain wood washer about ¼″ thick, with a 1¼″ hole in the center. Slip the washer on the base post pin between the top and bottom of the crow's nest. With the crow's nest seated firmly, mark the height of the washer top in pencil on the base post pin.

Remove the crow's nest, and cut a slot in the pin slightly below the pencil mark. The slot should be ¼″ wide, and tapered; that is, the bottom is horizontal but the top is about ¾″ high on one side and ⅝″ on the other. Make a tapered wedge to fit the slot. The top surface of the washer should have a shallow groove cut into it, to seat the wedge firmly. This will prevent the washer from turning with the crow's nest. The wedge and washer are shown in detail drawings. This will make a firm but freely revolving joint.

Next make the battens by which the table top will be mounted on the crow's nest. The shape of the battens may be more clearly seen in *Figure B, Plate 50*, where a similar top mounting is used. Bore holes in the battens to fit the ⅝″ round protruding ends of the crow's-nest top. Sand the insides of the holes.

Glue boards together to form a single piece for the top, and turn it to shape on the face plate of the lathe. The shape of the molded edge is shown in the drawing. Attach the battens to the underside of the top in proper position, with the battens mounted on the crow's nest. Fit and attach the table catch so it will hold the top in horizontal position. Sand all surfaces. The table is now ready for the desired finish.

———◆———

Plate 50 is a tripod table of simpler design than the preceding. The top is a plain oval which tilts but does not revolve. The legs are serpentine vertically, but are not cabriole. The base post is turned so as to show a graceful vase shape below the edge of the tilted top.

Turn the post with a pin 1″ in diameter at the top. Band-saw the legs to

Plate 50

OVAL TILT-TOP TABLE

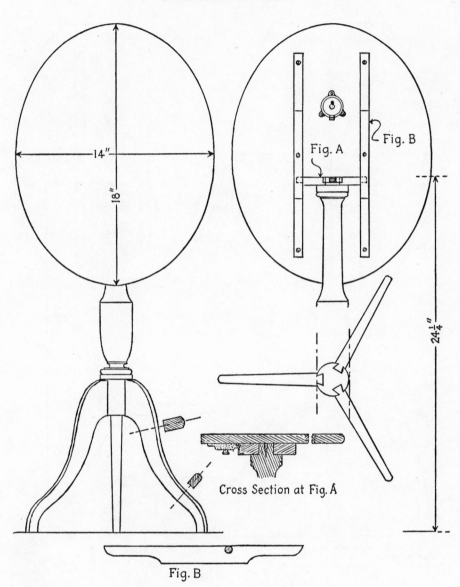

14"

18"

Fig. A

Fig. B

24¼"

Cross Section at Fig. A

Fig. B

12 11 10 9 8 7 6 5 4 3 2 1 0 INCHES

Plate 51

OCTAGONAL TILT-TOP TABLE

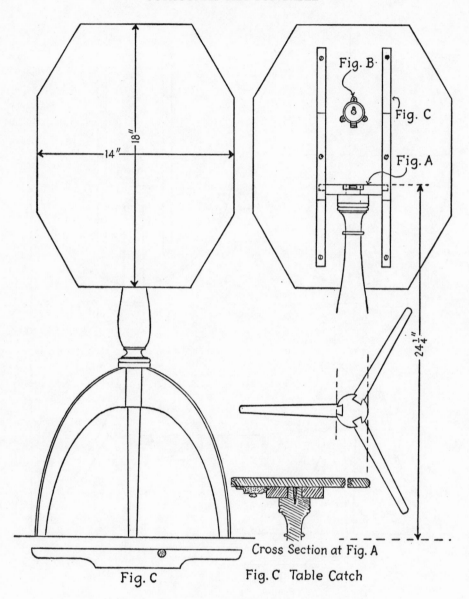

18"

14"

Fig. B

Fig. C

Fig. A

24¼"

Fig. C

Cross Section at Fig. A

Fig. C Table Catch

12 11 10 9 8 7 6 5 4 3 2 1 0 INCHES

shape, sand them, and cut dovetail tongues on the legs, with corresponding grooves in the post, as instructed in the section "Joining Tripod Table Legs," Chapter I. Glue the legs to the post.

The square top support block should be made like the top of the crow's nest in *Plate 49,* with a ⅝" pivot worked on each end of the back edge. Bore a 1" hole in the center of the block to fit over the base post pin. Slot the top of the pin, glue the block in position, and drive a wedge into the pin (see cross section at *Figure A*).

Cut the battens (*Figure B* on the drawings), and bore them for the ⅝" pivot pins on the top block. Glue, cut and sand the top, and attach it to the battens. Fit and attach the table catch. Sand completely, and finish as desired.

The table in *Plate 51* is identical with that in *Plate 50* in all respects except that the top is octagonal and the legs are simple convex curves. All construction details are the same.

Tavern Table. A tavern table with two drawers is shown in *Plates 52* and *53.* The legs are vase turned and reinforced by low plain stretchers. A scalloped edge below the skirting adds a graceful touch. Early tavern tables were often made of oak, but they are effective in any wood, depending on the degree of elegance or rusticity desired.

A distinguishing characteristic of tavern tables is the method of fastening the tops with removable wooden pins. In early England tables of this type were more or less standard in the inns and taverns, where the tops received hard wear. The wooden pins were designed to meet the need for frequent replacement of tops.

There was a good reason, also, for the low stretchers which we find somewhat inconvenient today. Floors were drafty in early times, and these stretchers enabled the tavern's patrons to sip their ale in comfort, with their feet off the floor. The practical value of these features is less important today, but they are valued for their decorative effect.

The legs should first be turned, using the turning plan in *Plate 53.* The upper and lower sections are left square, with slightly rounded corners. The ball foot is turned as part of the leg. Sand the turnings before removing them from the lathe.

Mortises for the stretchers and the side and back skirting should be cut in the square sections of the legs, as indicated in the front and end views, *Plate 52.*

Plate 52

TAVERN TABLE

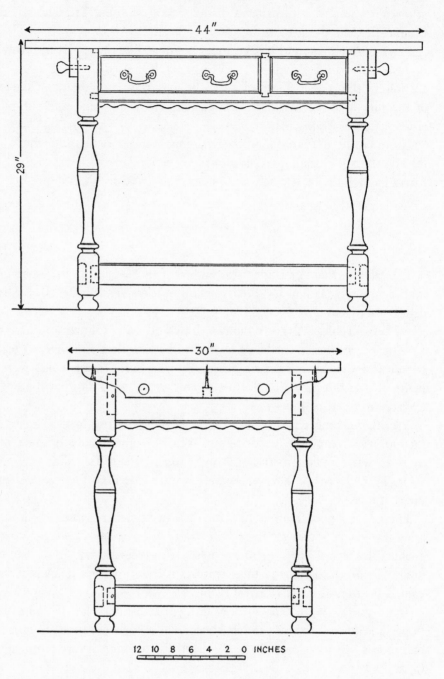

44"

29"

30"

12 10 8 6 4 2 0 INCHES

Plate 53

TAVERN TABLE (*Continued*)

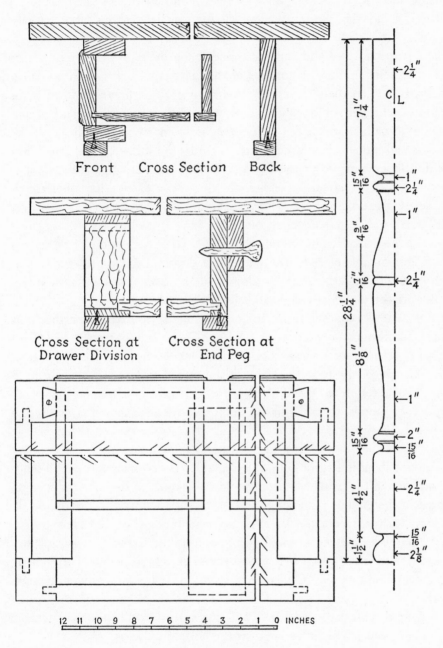

Front   Cross Section   Back

Cross Section at
Drawer Division

Cross Section at
End Peg

12 11 10 9 8 7 6 5 4 3 2 1 0 INCHES

These pieces are fitted flush with the outside leg surface. Instructions for fitting mortise-and-tenon joints may be found in the section "Joinery," Chapter I. Sand the inside surfaces of the square sections after mortising.

Next, cut the skirting and stretchers, and tenon the ends. The front of the table has no skirting, but is composed of two horizontal strips, with a vertical piece fitted between them to separate the drawers. The depth of these strips is equal to that of the leg tops (see top view detail drawing, *Plate 53*). Cut and tenon the horizontal strips: the lower strip to be mortised into the legs; the upper strip, with dovetail tenon cut flush with the top surface, fitted into a corresponding open mortise in the leg top. (See detail drawing, *Plate 53*, also "Dovetail Joints," Chapter I.) Assemble the entire front (legs, horizontal strips, and stretchers), then the entire back. Use drawbore pins or tenon pins to reinforce the skirt and stretcher joints.

Measure the exact length required for the vertical division between the drawers, and cut this piece to size with vertical grain. Make a dovetail tenon at each end, with corresponding mortises in the horizontal frame strips. When the joints are fitted perfectly, glue and slide in place.

Place the side skirts in position without glue, and measure between the front and back framework at the drawer division. Cut a drawer runner to fit this space, and prepare mortise-and-tenon joints. Then assemble the entire framework with glue, inserting the side skirts, stretchers, and drawer runner simultaneously. Reinforce the skirt and stretcher joints with tenon pins.

Cut drawer support strips, L-shaped in cross section, for each end, and screw them inside the end skirting. Attach a guide strip to the runner at the drawer division. Make the drawers as instructed in Chapter I, and sand.

Next, select boards for the top, glue together, cut to size, and rough-sand. Make and attach the battens. These should be as thick as the top, and shaped as shown in the end-view drawing. They should be screwed to the underside of the top with just enough clearance to avoid binding on the table frame. Place the top, with battens attached, in position on the frame. Using a ½" bit, bore two holes through each batten and the skirt behind it. The positions of the holes are indicated by the large wooden pins shown in the drawings, *Plate 52*.

Turn the pins with large heads and ½" shanks as shown in the cross section at end peg, *Plate 53*. The pins should fit the holes snugly.

Make the scalloped skirt edging with a band saw or scroll saw, the length carefully measured to fit between the legs. Remove saw marks with a drawknife or sharp chisel, and sand. Attach the edging to the skirt with screws, placing them in the narrowest part of the scallop. Sand the entire table, and finish as desired.

Candlestand. In the days when candles were a chief source of light, the tall, easily portable candlestand was an obvious convenience. Today it is often used to hold a plant, a choice piece of bric-a-brac, or a bedside lamp. It is a graceful and decorative piece, and may be made of mahogany, walnut, cherry, or maple to harmonize with other furnishings.

Plate 54 illustrates a fine stand with dished top, gracefully turned pedestal, and tripod serpentine legs. The foot is the elongated version of the Queen Anne, usually called a snake foot, with a shoe.

The post should be turned first. The shape is clearly shown in the drawing. A round shank is turned at the lower end, for attaching the tripod legs. The upper end has a short pin, 1″ in diameter, to support the top (see cross-section drawing).

A leg pattern may be made with the aid of the leg cross sections in *Plate 54*. The legs may be shaped by the method described in Chapter I, under "Shaping a Cabriole Leg." Instructions for cutting and fitting the sliding dovetail joints are given in the section "Joining Tripod Table Legs," Chapter I.

After assembling the pedestal, turn the round block which supports the top, and bore it to fit over the 1″ pin (see cross section of top). The block may be glued in place if desired.

Next turn the top to a round dished shape with molded edge, as indicated in the cross section. Attach it with screws driven straight up from the lower surface of the support block. Sand the entire assembly, and finish as desired.

Butler Tray. *Plate 55* shows a tray table, or butler tray. Its design is wholly functional, belonging to no particular period or style. It may be made of mahogany, maple, or any desired wood to harmonize with other furnishings. It may also be lacquered and stenciled.

This is a particularly convenient piece for the recreation room, porch, or indeed any room where informal refreshments are served. With its short legs, it performs the functions of a coffee table, with the added feature of easy portability.

The top should be made first. This is composed of a rectangular frame with a central crosspiece, enclosing two panels set flush with the top surface of the frame. Joints are tongue and groove ("Joinery," Chapter I).

After assembling the top, cut a reversed drop-leaf molding on all four sides (see cross section, *Plate 55*, also "Moldings," Chapter I).

Cut four rectangular pieces to length for the leaves. Mold the inside edges to fit the molded edges of the top. Fit and attach BT hinges. These are special

Plate 54

CANDLESTAND

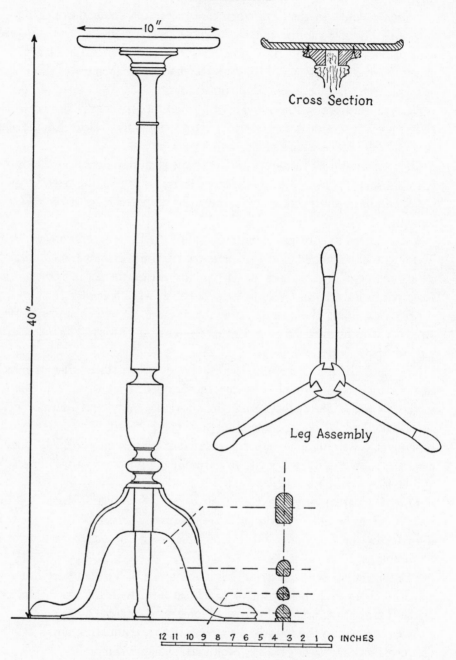

10"

40"

Cross Section

Leg Assembly

12 11 10 9 8 7 6 5 4 3 2 1 0 INCHES

126

Plate 55

BUTLER TRAY

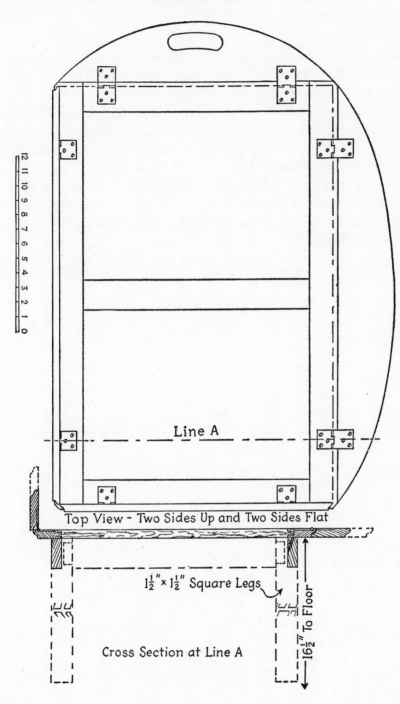

Line A

Top View - Two Sides Up and Two Sides Flat

$1\frac{1}{2}'' \times 1\frac{1}{2}''$ Square Legs

$16\frac{1}{2}''$ To Floor

Cross Section at Line A

127

hinges, made with a spring which holds the leaves in vertical position when desired, forming a guard rail around the tray.

After attaching the leaves, lay them out flat and mark the oval outline in pencil. Band-saw and mold the edges (see cross section).

Now remove the end leaves and cut out handholds, as shown in the drawing. Reattach the leaves and sand both sides of the top assembly.

Cut the legs and mortise them for the skirting. Sand the inside leg surfaces. Cut and tenon the skirting, assemble, and sand all outside surfaces. Attach the base to the top with sloping screws, driven upward from counterbored holes in the inside surface of the skirting (see cross-section drawing).

Style variations may easily be introduced into this basic design, if desired. The legs may be tapered or turned; the leaves may be cut to any ornamental shape. For outdoor use the tray may be made of cheap wood and painted to match other garden furniture.

CHAPTER V

BEDS

THE EARLIEST beds were crude affairs. Built into an alcove or into a corner of the room, the walls themselves formed the supports for one end and one side of the frame. A single post supported the remaining corner. A corded or laced canvas foundation formed the "spring," upon which was usually placed a husk mattress topped by a feather bed. The evolution of the "four-poster" freed the bed from the walls and permitted it to stand alone.

In the early eighteenth century, in England, the master bedroom became one of the important rooms in the house, in which the lady held formal morning receptions. Bedroom furniture during this period was designed with great elegance, and the bed itself was elaborate and draped with rich fabrics. The draperies were designed for semiprivacy as well as for decoration. These draped four-posters remained in fashion until nearly 1800. Later bedsteads lacked the draperies, and the posts were greatly modified.

Even during the period when elaborate high-posted, draped bedsteads were used by the master and mistress of a pretentious house, the beds for others of the household remained relatively simple. The children had trundle beds; servants and poor people generally used plain frames supported by low corner posts.

The earliest bedsteads were seldom carved, since the draperies usually hid the wooden parts. As the quantity of drapery was gradually reduced, and finally omitted, the amount of ornamentation on the bedstead itself was increased. The posts were usually fluted or reeded, and carved. If a canopy was used,

129

it was attached just below the finial, which in this case had an iron dowel instead of a wooden one, for greater strength. The bases of the posts were square until the Sheraton period, when they were often turned. In the Hepplewhite style the square base was tapered and usually ended in a spade foot. The long tapered upper section of the post was frequently separated from the base by some variant of the urn shape, with turned rings above and below it. The urn was often richly carved.

The canopy and drapery at the head of the bed remained in fashion long after the foot had emerged from its shroudings. For this reason bedsteads throughout the Chippendale period had simple headposts and headboards, however elaborate the footposts might be. On many later beds, however, all four posts were carved, and some decoration given to the headboard as well. Footboards were not used on early beds.

The elaborate bedsteads of England were not common in America. Colonial beds were usually plain, and were made of the abundant native woods, rarely of mahogany. The pineapple post bed became popular in the early nineteenth century, but, while ornate, it lacked the grace and fine proportions of the earlier English styles.

Twin beds are a modern innovation. The old-style beds were full-sized, with the exception of an occasional single bed which was slightly smaller. However, as twin beds are now in great demand, reproductions may be made in this size. It should be remembered that, in thus altering the over-all proportions, an awkward effect may result unless the design is carefully chosen with this in mind. A heavy or ornate style is never appropriate for a small bed.

In order to use as large a scale as possible, we have used the twin size in our drawings. Full-sized beds may be made from these drawings by lengthening the headboard and the headrails and footrails. Standard sizes of beds are: between headrails and footrails, 76″ for either twin or double beds; between siderails, twin 38½″, double 53½″. The headrails and siderails of any bed may be made of poplar to conserve more expensive wood, since they will be hidden by the bed covers.

———◆———

Plate 56 illustrates a Chippendale mahogany bed with graceful posts. The base is square, with a mitered molding overlaid on the bottom. The upper corners of the square are rounded. Above the turned rings the post tapers slightly toward the top, and is fluted for most of its length. The turned rings and plain

Plate 56

CHIPPENDALE BED

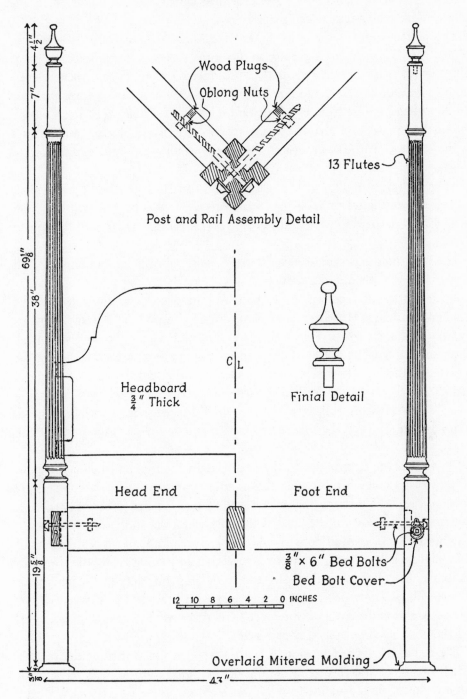

Wood Plugs

Oblong Nuts

13 Flutes

Post and Rail Assembly Detail

$69\frac{1}{8}''$

$4\frac{1}{2}''$

$7''$

38″

C L

Headboard
$\frac{3}{4}''$ Thick

Finial Detail

Head End

Foot End

$\frac{3}{8}'' \times 6''$ Bed Bolts

Bed Bolt Cover

$19\frac{5}{8}$

12 10 8 6 4 2 0 INCHES

Overlaid Mitered Molding

$3\frac{3}{8}''$

43″

131

tapered section above the fluting lend a nice balance to the whole, which is completed by the graceful urn-shaped finial.

The posts should be made first. The length of the post from floor to base of urn is 64⅝". A turning as long as this must run true in the lathe, or great difficulty will be experienced in the turning operation. If the stock is even slightly bowed, therefore, it may be wise to use two pieces, joining them at the top of the square base. For this joint, bore a 1¼" hole, 2⅛" deep, in the top of the square, and turn the upper section with a 1¼" by 2" round tenon at the lower end. Cut a groove in the tenon, to allow air and excess glue to escape.

After turning the posts (not including the finials), flute the upper section, cutting thirteen flutes on each post. Instructions for this process will be found in Chapter I, under "Fluting and Reeding of Turnings." Then sand the square surfaces.

The base moldings should next be made and applied. The molding on each post is joined with mitered corners.

Next, mortise the posts for the rails and headboard, as indicated in the head end drawing. Make the headboard, using ¾" wood. This may be shaped by band saw, after which a spokeshave or drawknife should be used to remove saw marks. In cutting the headboard, include two tenons at each end to fit the mortises in the headposts. The shape is shown in the half-drawing of the head end. Remember that the length of the headboard (and head- and foot-rails) must be increased if a full-sized bed is desired. Make a trial assembly of headboard and headposts to be sure the fit is perfect. No glue is to be used in these joints.

Cut the rails to length, round the upper edges slightly, and tenon the ends. Study the drawings for assembly details. After inserting the rail tenon in the post mortise, bore through the post into the tenon for the ⅜" by 6" bed bolt. Counterbore the post for the head of the bolt. Cut a slot in the rail for the nut. The headrail and footrail bolts should be placed slightly above center, siderail bolts slightly below center, to avoid interference in passing each other through the posts. After inserting the bolts and nuts, plug the slots in the rails with wooden plugs. Cover the holes in the posts with brass bed-bolt covers. Eight bed bolts and eight covers are required for this bed. By removing the bolts, the bed may be completely disassembled.

The finials are turned separately, with a wooden pin turned at the bottom which fits into a hole bored in the top of the post. If a canopy is to be used, a metal dowel should be used for greater strength. A tenpenny nail with the head cut off makes a dowel long and strong enough to pass through the finial stem and the canopy frame, and down into the post. In turning the finials (see detail drawing), note that the widest diameter of the urn does not exceed the diameter of the turned rings on the post. This is essential for good proportion.

The bed is now structurally complete. Remove the bolts and thoroughly sand all parts of the bed, apply finish, and reassemble.

———◆———

Plate 57 shows a more elaborately ornamented mahogany bedstead of the Hepplewhite period. The square base of the post is tapered below the rail and ends in a spade foot. The chamfered corners of the square may be done on the lathe, or they may be flat chamfers shaped by hand. The post is reeded, not fluted, and is further enriched by the water-leaf carving above the base. This carving is discussed in detail in Chapter I. Instructions for reeding are also given in Chapter I, under "Fluting and Reeding of Turnings."

The finial is unusual, the flame being tall in proportion to the urn, which has no neck. The carved flame strikes a nice balance with the carving lower on the post. The flames are first deeply outlined with a V-shaped gouge, then sloped off on one side with a No. 3 gouge.

Procedures required in making and assembling this bed are, in general, the same as those described in the preceding text, *Plate 56*. The square-tapered spade foot with its molded top is worked down by hand, after rough-shaping by band saw. The mitered molding of *Plate 56* is omitted in *Plate 57*. Reeding and carving take the place of fluting.

———◆———

Plate 58 shows a spool bed. We may imagine that the popularity of this style arose from the fact that its ornamentation was effective but easy to achieve, being a product of the lathe. Spool beds are usually of walnut, cherry, or maple. Most of the parts are straight pieces, turned in a spool design. Because of the length of the horizontal turnings, these beds should be made only in twin size.

Unlike four-poster beds, each end of a spool bed is glued into a single unit. Since head and foot are identical except in height, the procedure that follows will apply to both.

Plate 57

HEPPLEWHITE BED

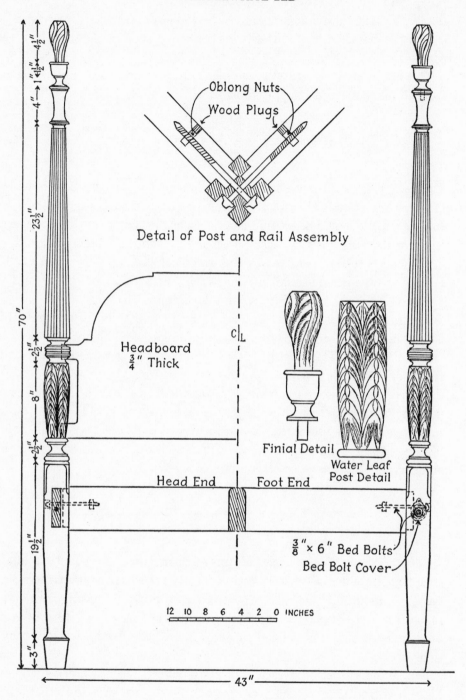

Oblong Nuts
Wood Plugs

Detail of Post and Rail Assembly

Headboard
$\frac{3}{4}$" Thick

C|L

Finial Detail

Water Leaf
Post Detail

Head End   Foot End

$\frac{3}{8}$" × 6" Bed Bolts
Bed Bolt Cover

12 10 8 6 4 2 0 INCHES

70"

23$\frac{1}{2}$"

4" 1" 4$\frac{1}{2}$" 4$\frac{1}{2}$"

2$\frac{1}{2}$"

8"

2$\frac{1}{2}$"

19$\frac{1}{2}$"

3"

43"

Plate 58

SPOOL BED

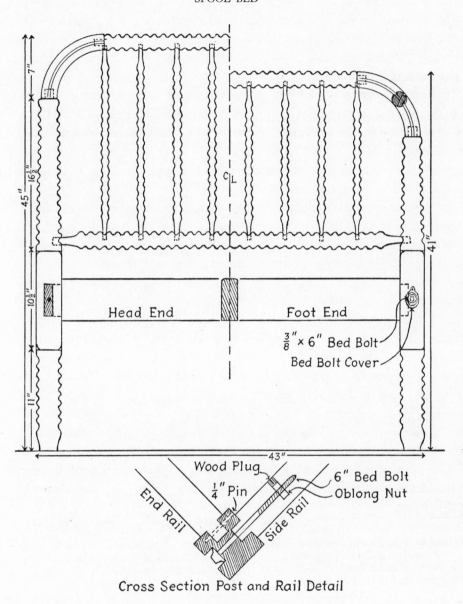

Head End   Foot End

$\frac{3}{8}'' \times 6''$ Bed Bolt

Bed Bolt Cover

Wood Plug

$\frac{1}{4}''$ Pin

6" Bed Bolt
Oblong Nut

End Rail

Side Rail

Cross Section Post and Rail Detail

12 10 8 6 4 2 0 INCHES

The first step is to turn the posts, including a ⅞" round tenon, 1" long, on the top of each post. Study the detail drawings of the post-and-rail assembly. Mortise the posts for the rails as indicated. Then make the rails, rounding the upper edges slightly, sand them, and tenon the ends.

Fit the posts and cross rail of one end together without glue, and measure for the lower cross turning. Turn this piece, with round ends to join the posts, and bore corresponding holes in the posts. Then glue the crosspiece and cross-rail to the posts. Bore through each rail joint and insert a glued ¼" tenon pin.

Next make the top corner pieces. These may be rough-shaped by band saw, then worked round by hand. Use a U-shaped gouge to cut three flutes the full length of each piece, on the top, front, and back. Bore a ⅞" hole, 1" deep, in each end. Sand to finish smoothness.

Place the corner pieces on the posts without glue, and measure between them for the top crosspiece. Turn this piece with a ⅞" round tenon, 1" long, at each end. Make a temporary assembly without glue, adjusting the joints if necessary for a perfect fit. With all parts in place, measure between the upper and lower crosspieces and turn the spindles to fit. Bore spindle holes in the crosspieces, positioning them accurately.

Now glue the spindles to the lower crosspiece, and glue the corner pieces to the upper crosspiece. Finally, apply glue to the spindle holes in the upper crosspiece, and to the lower holes in the corner pieces, and fit the top assembly in place on the posts and spindles. Repeat the procedure for the other end unit, making the posts and spindles of the head end longer, as indicated on the drawing.

When both end units of the bed are completed, fit the siderails into place and bore through each post into the tenon of the rail, for the ⅜" by 6" bed bolt. Counterbore the post for the bolt head, and cut a slot in the rail for the nut (see detail drawing). After inserting the bolt and nut, plug the slot with a wooden plug.

Remove the bolts and apply finish to the head, foot, and rails as desired. Reassemble, then attach a brass bed-bolt cover over the bolt hole in each post at the foot end. This bed requires four bed bolts and two bolt covers.

———◆———

In order to conserve space, it was customary in early times for children to sleep in trundle beds. These were made low to the floor, and were slid out of sight under the large beds when not in use. Since they were not on display,

Plate 59

TRUNDLE BED

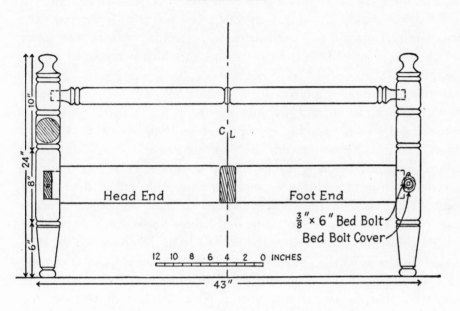

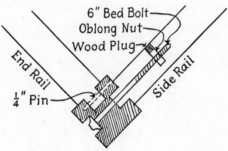

they were usually of simple design. In this less pretentious age they are ideal for nursery use.

The trundle bed in *Plate 59* is attractive and easy to make. The head and foot are identical, each being glued into a single unit.

The four posts should be turned first. The simple finial may be turned as part of the post, instead of being a separate piece as is usually the case. The sections mortised for the rails are square, with rounded corners. The lower end of the post is tapered, with a small bun foot which is turned as part of the post.

After turning the posts, mortise them for the rails and for the round ends of the turned crosspieces. Sand the square surfaces.

Next make the rails, rounding the upper edges slightly (see cross section of rail in drawing). Tenon the ends, and sand the rails.

Make a temporary assembly of one end (posts and rail), and measure for the crosspiece. In turning this piece, make sure the ends will fit the holes in the posts. Then assemble the complete end with glue, reinforcing the rail joints with tenon pins, as shown in the detail drawing. When both ends are completed, fit the siderails in place; and bore through each post into the side-rail tenon for the $\frac{3}{8}''$ by $6''$ bed bolt (see detail drawing). Counterbore the post for the bolt head. Cut a slot in the rail for the nut. After inserting the bolt and nut, plug the slot with a wooden plug. Remove the bolts for the finishing operation, then reassemble. Attach a brass bed-bolt cover over the bolt hole in each post. Four bed bolts and four covers are required.

CHAPTER VI

CUPBOARDS

Corner cupboards.   The corner cupboard is at once so useful and so decorative a piece that it seems strange its popularity has not been carried over into the modern period. Perhaps no other piece of furniture, with the exception of a grandfather clock, can add so much distinction to a room. Certainly no other piece is more adaptable, whether to a mansion or a small apartment, where usable space is at a premium.

Corner cupboards were made from about 1725 until nearly a century later. They were of two types: those built into a corner as part of the house, and those made as separate pieces to fit any corner. In either case the lines were usually architectural, the top being frequently molded to match the cornice of the room. Cupboards of less than ceiling height sometimes had scroll tops similar to those of highboys.

The interior of the top section was sometimes concealed with paneled doors, but more often was exposed, with glass doors or none. The shelves were cut in decorative shapes, and the top was often domed and carved to simulate a large shell. The lower section was always enclosed, with paneled wooden doors. In most cases the base rested directly on the floor; when feet were used, they were of the bracket type. The wood used varied with the purse of the user: those who could not afford mahogany or walnut had cupboards of cherry, pine, or other less expensive woods. Many of the latter were relatively plain, but others were decorated with fine moldings and/or other carvings, indicating that the corner cupboard was an object of pride in even the most modest homes.

139

The cupboard in *Plates 60* and *61* is an open-top design with ornamental HL wrought iron hinges. Knotty pine is decorative for this style, although plain pine was always used in authentic antiques.

This is a "one piece" cupboard, meaning that the back and side panels are each one piece from top to floor. The back panel is shaped at the top in a flattened arch. The side panels are cut back toward the top in a series of interrupted curves, so that the whole top section diminishes in width and depth from bottom to top.

The side and back panels are made first. The back may be a single board, but if composed of separate pieces these should be glued together before cutting to size. Each side panel is similarly joined and glued, and the front surfaces of all three panels are hand-planed. (Pine should always be planed, other woods sanded.) The panels are then band-sawed to shape. Since the side panels are to join the back at a 67½-degree angle, the side edges of the back panel and the back edges of the side panels are beveled to this angle, as shown in the detail drawing, *Plate 61*. A spokeshave or drawknife is used to remove the saw marks. The sides are then fastened to the back with long screws as shown in *Plate 61*. The sides are counterbored for the screw heads.

The shelves are glued with the grain running from side to side, not diagonally. The upper shelves are hand-planed on both surfaces. These open shelves are curved and graduated in size as indicated in the shelf plan, *Plate 61*. After band-sawing to shape, the edges are smoothed with a spokeshave. A ¼″ by ¼″ groove is then milled across the upper surface of each shelf, 1¼″ from the back edge, to hold plates. These shelves are fastened to the side and back with 1½″ No. 8 screws. Shelf No. 1 requires three screws at each side, Nos. 2 and 3 require two screws at each side.

The top, shelf, and bottom of the lower section are cut to the shape shown in the cross-section outline of the shelf plan. These are hand-planed on the upper surface. They are fastened to the back and sides in the same manner as the upper shelves, using four screws to each side.

The angle-front panels are cut from single boards, and hand-planed. The front edges are beveled to provide for miter-joining the front panels at a 67½-degree angle (see detail drawing, *Plate 61*). The angle-front panels are attached to the sides with wooden dowels as indicated in the drawing. They are also doweled to the top, bottom, and shelf (*Plate 60*). Panels may be held in place with brads while boring the dowel holes. Dowel ends are planed off even with the surrounding surface, and left exposed for their decorative effect.

The front panels are made in the same manner, with side edges beveled for the miter joint. They are doweled to the top, shelf, and bottom.

Plate 60

PINE CORNER CUPBOARD

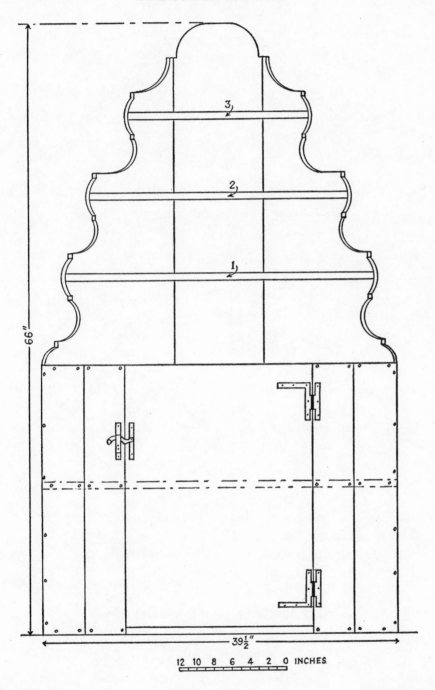

66"

3

2

1

39½"

12 10 8 6 4 2 0 INCHES

Plate 61

PINE CORNER CUPBOARD

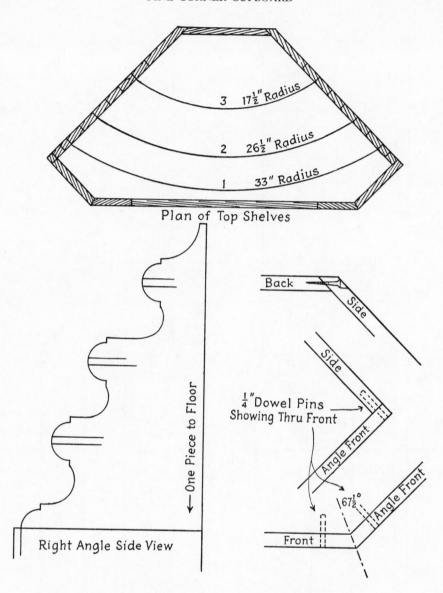

Plan of Top Shelves

3 $17\frac{1}{2}''$ Radius

2 $26\frac{1}{2}''$ Radius

1 33" Radius

Back

Side

Side

$\frac{1}{4}$" Dowel Pins
Showing Thru Front

Angle Front

$67\frac{1}{2}°$

Angle Front

Front

One Piece to Floor

Right Angle Side View

Hinges and Latch, 4" H.L. Wrought Iron

12 10 8 6 4 2 0 INCHES

The boards forming the door are then glued together, cut to length, and hand-planed. There are no cross members or battens. End grain is left exposed. The large hinges and latch of wrought iron are mounted on the surface, not recessed into the wood. They should be attached after final finishing.

The space below the door may be filled with a facing strip attached to the bottom with dowels. If preferred, this strip may be cut as part of the bottom itself, with shoulders at each side for the front panels.

When the above steps have been completed, the cupboard is ready to apply the desired finish. The natural color of the wood may be retained, or it may be darkened slightly for a mellow "antique" effect. After finishing, attach the door hinges and latch.

◆

Plates 62 and 63 illustrate the lower and upper sections of a mahogany cupboard in the Chippendale style. This is an exceptionally fine example, with a high scroll top, urn-and-flame finial, and interlacing arch doors. The mitered angles of the front are chamfered and covered with decorative pilasters. Door handles are small brass bails. Hinges are also brass, of the ornamental H type.

The upper section has a shelf behind each cross lattice of the door. The lower section has one shelf. Backs of both sections are of frame construction, with panels composed of random-width ¼″ thick boards, rabbet-joined without glue. This method of construction eliminates warping from shrinkage.

The four back panels (two upper, two lower) are made first. Random-width pieces of ¼″ boards are cut to length, rabbeted to fit together, and sanded. Frame members are cut, grooved for the ¼″ panels, and sanded. The stiles (vertical frame members) of the lower section continue to the floor. The frames are joined with mortise-and-tenon joints, the mortises cut in the stiles, and tenons on the ends of the crossrails. (See detail drawing of back panel, *Plate* 62.) In working out the dimensions, note that the front of the upper section is recessed slightly from the front of the base. The upper back panels must be correspondingly narrower. The two sections fit flush at the back.

After completing assembly of all back panels, the lower section of the cupboard is constructed first. Fasten together the two back panels with screws through the frames, as shown in the cross-section drawing, *Plate* 62. Then cut the top, shelf, and bottom, shaped to follow the interior outline of the case (see cross-section plan, *Plate* 62). The straight angle-back edges of the top and bottom will fit inside the back panel frames. The corresponding edges of the shelf are also cut straight, leaving a gap behind each edge because of the indented surface of the thinner panel wood. After attaching the shelf, these gaps are filled with horizontal strips, cut to fit. The top, shelf, and bottom are fastened to the panel frames with 1½″ No. 8 screws, driven through from the back of the frames.

Next, cut the extreme side panels of the front, floor length, with the inner edge angled for the 67½-degree miter corner. Attach the panels to the side frames with brads while boring and counterboring for wood screws. (See cross section, *Plate* 62.) After driving in the screws, plug the holes with wood plugs, matching the grain to the surrounding surface.

Cut the front stiles (also floor length), the top and bottom rails, and the vertical center door division. Angle the outer edges of the stiles for the miter corner. On the inner edges, cut the mortises for the rail joints. Cut mortises for the vertical center strip in the rails. Then cut the tenons on the ends of the rails and center strip, fitting each tenon to the corresponding mortise. Assemble the front frame with glue, and allow to dry before attaching it to the top, shelf, and bottom. The procedure for fastening the frame in place is a duplication of that used for attaching the angle-front panels: brad, bore, counterbore, screw, and plug. For screws which will be covered by the pilasters, plugging may be omitted.

Next chamfer the miter corners with a hand plane to provide a flat surface under the pilasters. Sand all front surfaces.

After cutting the pilasters to size (floor length) they may be reeded with a shaper, if one is available. A special-duty plane fitted with grooving blades may also be used, or the grooves may be cut by hand with a V gouge. The shaping is then finished with sandpaper. The cross section of the pilaster in *Plate* 62 will serve as a working guide. Attach the pilasters with glue and brads.

The base molding is one piece to the floor, forming a continuous foot across the front and angle-front, with mitered corners. The ogee top surface may be cut with a shaper, a special hand plane, or by repeated trips across a circular saw, readjusting the depth of cut for each trip. Smooth with hand tools and sandpaper. Cut the molded pieces to the proper lengths, mitering at different angles as required to fit around the floor-length pilasters. Attach to the case with glue and brads.

Select well matched ¼″ mahogany boards for the door panels, glue them together, and cut to size. Cut the doorframe pieces, and groove the inside edges to fit the panels. Cut mortises in the vertical frames, tenons on the horizontal pieces.

After gluing and assembling the doors, bore through each mortise for a tenon pin, as indicated in the front view. Glue the inside surfaces of the holes and insert the pins. Mortises for the locks should be cut after the doors have been fitted.

Procedure for constructing the upper section (*Plate 63*) is in general a repetition of that already described. Note that the horizontal dimensions are slightly less than those of the lower section. The angle of the recess across the front and angle-front is filled with an applied molding (*Plate 62*).

Before installing the shelves, cut a ¼″ by ¼″ groove for plates, 1¼″ from the back edge. Horizontal strips are used to fill the gaps behind the shelves, between the frames of the back panels.

The upper pilasters are narrower than those below, and are not reeded.

Instead of a top front rail, the upper section has an arched face panel. This is cut with horizontal grain. It does not continue to a feather edge under the applied molding at each side, but ends with a square edge. A piece with vertical grain is inserted to continue the curve under the molding. The face panel is joined to the stiles with tongue and groove, as shown in the cross-section plan, *Figure A, Plate 63*.

Make the arch molding in two sections, one for each side of the center block. Band-saw the curved strips, then shape the surface as indicated in the labeled cross section. The same cross section serves as the pattern for the straight moldings which join the lower ends of the arch molding, with mitered corners. These are also mitered at the angle corners to follow over the pilasters. A similar procedure is used for the scroll molding, using the labeled cross-section pattern. The arch molding is applied with glue and brads. The scroll molding may be attached with screws entered from the back of the face panel. Details of molding at the pilaster top are shown in the cross-section plan, *Figure A*. *Figure B* is a detail plan of the arch center block, which is turned separately and applied with glue and brads.

To finish the scrolls, turn plain round bosses and mount these with screws through from the back of the face panel. Turn the rosettes separately, shape them with a rounded sandpaper stick, and mount them on the bosses with a short ⅜″ dowel. Cut and glue a finial support block behind the central rise of the face panel, after boring a dowel hole in the top end of the block. Turn the urn-and-flame finial with a round pin at the bottom. Use a V gouge to cut the random wavy flame lines.

Cut the doorframe pieces, using separate pieces for the curved members. Join the frame with mortise and tenon through the full width of the frames, as shown in the detail drawing of doorframe joint construction. Reinforce the

Plate 62

MAHOGANY CORNER CUPBOARD (BASE)

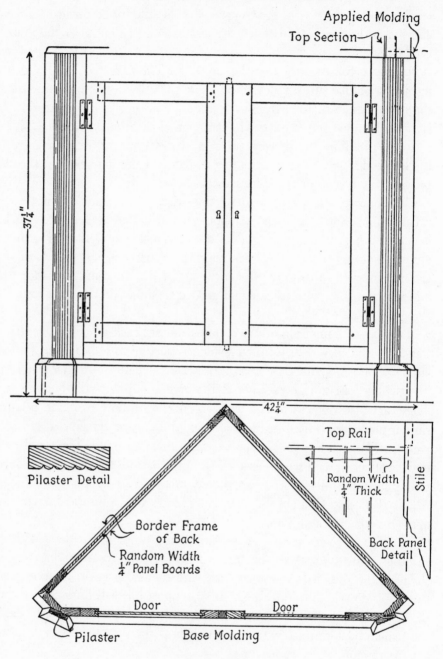

Applied Molding

Top Section

$37\frac{1}{4}''$

$42\frac{1}{4}''$

Pilaster Detail

Top Rail

Random Width
$\frac{1}{4}''$ Thick

Stile

Back Panel
Detail

Border Frame
of Back

Random Width
$\frac{1}{4}''$ Panel Boards

Door

Door

Pilaster

Base Molding

12 10 8 6 4 2 0 INCHES

3" Cast Brass H Hinges

146

Plate 63

MAHOGANY CORNER CUPBOARD (TOP)

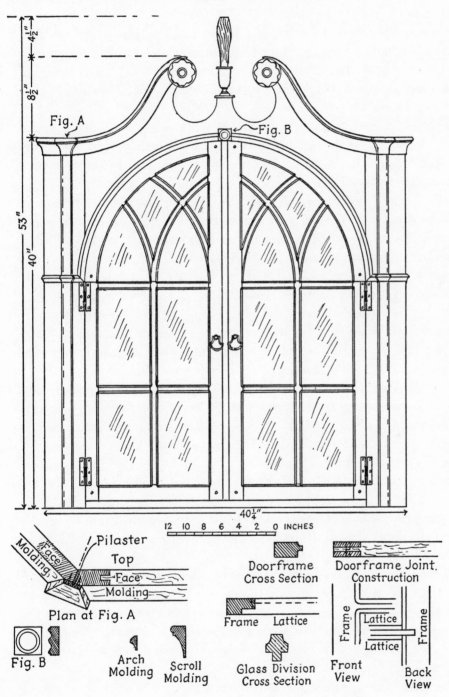

$4\frac{1}{2}''$

$8\frac{1}{2}''$

Fig. A

Fig. B

53''

40''

$40\frac{1}{4}''$

12 10 8 6 4 2 0 INCHES

Pilaster Top

Face Molding

Face Molding

Doorframe Cross Section

Doorframe Joint. Construction

Face

Molding

Plan at Fig. A

Frame Lattice

Fig. B

Arch Molding

Scroll Molding

Glass Division Cross Section

Frame

Lattice

Lattice

Frame

Front View

Back View

joints with tenon pins as in the lower doorframes. Rabbet the continuous inside edge for glass.

Cut the lattice pieces, rabbeting the inside edges as shown in the glass division cross section. Lap-join these pieces to each other and to the frames, using glue and brads (see cross section of frame and lattice). After complete assembly, cut the cove molding on the front inside edge of all openings (glass division cross section).

Mount the upper section on the lower; then cut, miter, and apply a simple molding to fill the angle formed by the slightly greater dimensions of the base. This molding is shown in *Plate 62,* front view, and follows the same mitering plan as the other moldings, to fit over the pilasters.

Finally, fit the doors, upper and lower, and the piece is ready for finish.

Welsh dresser. A type of cupboard which has become increasingly popular among lovers of antique styles is the long cupboard usually called a "dresser," though there seems to be no logical reason for the name. As these are usually of poplar or pine (though occasionally of walnut), with little decoration and without doors to protect the upper shelves from dust, it is evident they were originally used in kitchens or in the dining rooms of unpretentious homes. When well made, however, a dresser such as that in *Plates 64* and *65* is an impressive piece of furniture, and its long open shelves provide excellent display space for favorite pieces of glassware and china.

The scalloped cornice of this piece is unusually fine, as is the continuous foot. An ornamental molding applied just under the top of the lower section repeats part of the cornice design, and the upper side panels are cut in a pattern which harmonizes with the cornice scallop. The large wooden knobs and wrought-iron hinges are in the best tradition.

The dresser is made in two sections, the upper section being fastened to the lower with screws at the front (see cross section in *Plate 65*), and with sloping screws through the back. Quarter-round guide strips are fitted into the angles between the upper side panels and the top of the lower section, and held in place with brads.

Back panels of both sections are ½″ pine boards of random widths, with lap joints. Sides are of 1″ pine, grooved inside for the ends of the long shelves, which are also 1″ pine. The shelves are further supported by nails through the back boards at frequent intervals. Each upper shelf has a ¼″ groove for holding plates, 1¼″ from the back edge. Front edges of these shelves are frequently slotted to hold silverware.

When pine is used, smoothing of the wood surfaces is done with a hand plane. Walnut and other woods are smoothed by sanding.

Construct the bottom section in the following manner: Glue boards together to rough size for the sides, shelf, and bottom. Cut to size, making the sides floor length. Mill grooves in the sides at the proper positions to receive the shelf and bottom (cross section, *Plate 64*). Rabbet the back edges of the sides ½″ by ½″, for the back boards. If pine is used, hand-plane these panels; otherwise sand.

Assemble by coating the grooves with glue and inserting the shelf and bottom. At this stage the assembly has no rigidity, so care should be used in handling. Next cut a top horizontal rail, 1″ thick by 3″ wide, to extend across the back between the top corners of the sides. Rabbet the lower back edge of this rail, ½″ by ½″, for the back boards. Position this piece and bore two ¼″ dowel holes through each of the side panels into the horizontal rail for fastening. Glue and insert the dowels, and plane the dowel ends even with the surrounding surface. Exposed dowels form part of the decoration of the dresser.

Next, select random-width boards of ½″ pine to form the back. Cut these to length, to fit between the rabbeted edges of the top rail and case bottom. Rabbet the long edges of the back boards to fit together. Hand-plane the boards, then nail them in place, starting from one side and working to the other. Each board should be nailed first to the top rail, then to the shelf, and finally to the case bottom. At the start of this nailing process, the case assembly should be checked for squareness. It will be rigid after nailing.

Next cut all the pieces which form the front, except the doors and drawers. Cut back the lower inside corners of the floor-length stiles, to leave open space behind the curve of the foot. A tongue should be milled on the top end of each stile at *Figure A,* to fit into a matching groove in the horizontal panel containing the drawers. A groove is also milled on the lower inside edge for fastening the rail below the doors (*Figure B*). Fasten the stiles in place temporarily with brads, and bore for dowels to fasten them to the sides, shelf, and bottom. Glue and insert the dowels, then remove the brads. Plane or sand the dowel ends even with the surface.

The drawer panel is made of one piece of wood, with drawer openings cut out with a jigsaw or by hand. Grooves are milled at *Figure A* (both ends), and at C. The panel is then placed in position and doweled. The vertical center division between the doors is cut to length with a tongue at each end, to enter the grooves in the drawer panel and lower rail. Glue this piece in position, and dowel it to the shelf. Cut the lower rail with a tongue at each end and a groove for the center division panel. Glue in place, then dowel to the bottom at frequent intervals.

The base molding is cut along the top edge of the continuous foot. Cut the long front foot in one piece, and band-saw to the shape down in *Plate 64.*

Plate 64

WELSH DRESSER (BASE)

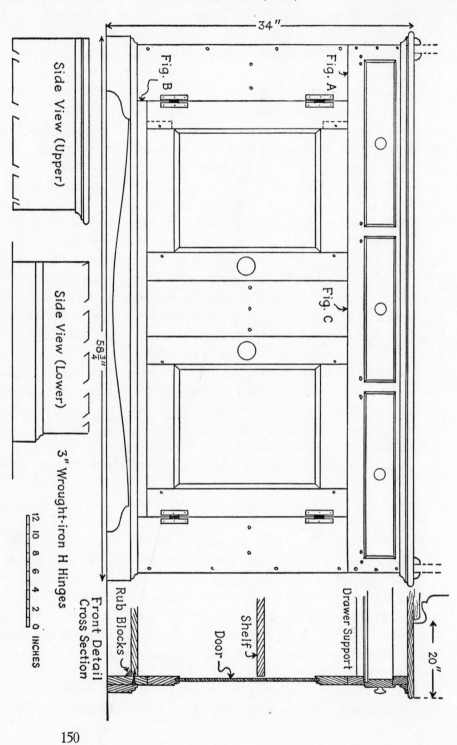

Side View (Upper)

Side View (Lower)

3" Wrought-iron H Hinges

12 10 8 6 4 2 0 INCHES

34"

Fig. B

Fig. A

Fig. C

58¾"

20"

Front Detail
Cross Section

Rub Blocks

Door

Shelf

Drawer Support

Plate 65

WELSH DRESSER (TOP)

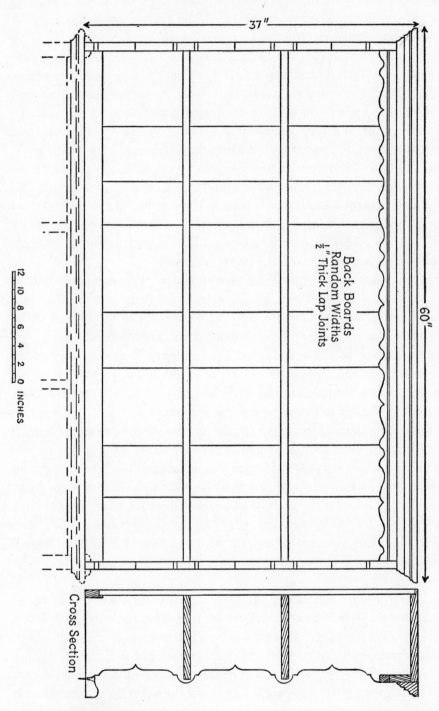

37"

60"

Back Boards
Random Widths
$\frac{1}{2}$" Thick Lap Joints

12 10 8 6 4 2 0 INCHES

Cross Section

Remove saw marks with a spokeshave. The lower edges of the side pieces are left straight (see lower side view). Miter the corners, and attach to the case with brads through the molding. Glue and screw rub blocks at frequent intervals in the angle formed by the foot and the case bottom.

Cut the top to size and plane (or sand). Round the projecting edges at front and sides. Attach the top with screws into the edges of the sides, back, and front. Where the screw heads will not be covered by the top section of the cupboard, counterbore and plug the screw holes. Cut the subtop molding (see cross section in the side view, *Plate 64*). Miter the corners and attach with brads.

After cutting the doorframe pieces, groove the internal edges to receive the $\frac{1}{4}''$-thick panels. Prepare mortise-and-tenon joints. Cut the panels to size, and plane or sand. Assemble the frames, inserting the panels at the same time, and reinforce each joint with a dowel as indicated in the front view, *Plate 64*. Apply a mitered molding around each panel for decoration. Fit the doors to the openings, then plane or sand the frame surfaces.

The drawer supports are cut next. These should be wide enough to extend under the drawers about $1''$. The length is measured to fit between the front panel and the backboards. They are fastened to the front by dowels and to the back by nails. Drawer guide strips are mounted on the drawer supports.

Make the drawers to fit the openings. The fronts are "lipped," with molded edges overlapping the openings all around, as shown in cross section, *Plate 64*. The drawer pulls are wooden knobs, slightly smaller than those on the doors. This completes the lower section, except for the finish.

The sides and shelves of the upper section may be made from single boards; if more are used, these should be glued together before cutting to size and hand-planing (or sanding). The sides are then band-sawed to the shape shown in the side view, *Plate 65*. Remove saw marks with a spokeshave or drawknife, then mill the grooves for the shelves, and rabbet the back edges for the back boards ($\frac{1}{2}''$ by $\frac{1}{2}''$). Mill plate grooves ($\frac{1}{4}''$ by $\frac{1}{4}''$) on the shelves, $1\frac{1}{4}''$ from the back edge. Cut slots for silverware along the front edges, if desired. Assembly procedure is similar to that described for the sides and shelves of the lower section.

Cut the top to size, and rabbet the back edge for the back boards (cross section, *Plate 65*). Then follow the same procedure as for the back of the lower section: cut, mill, plane, and attach a horizontal bottom rail; cut, mill, plane, and nail the random-width back boards to the bottom rail and shelves.

The cross section in *Plate 65* illustrates the construction of the cornice. A face board is fitted between the side panels, just below the top. This is fastened with screws through from the top and sides, the holes in the sides counterbored and plugged. The scalloped subcornice is band-sawed, spokeshaved, and planed, and attached to the face board with brads and glue.

The upper cornice should be molded to the shape shown in cross section. It is glued and bradded to the face board and side panels, with mitered corners.

The completed top section is placed on the base and anchored in place with long screws through the side panels, as shown in the cross section, *Plate 65*. Quarter-round guide strips are then fitted into the angles along the bottom edges of the side panels (see front views, *Plates 64* and *65*). The guide strips are held in place with long brads.

Hardware and knobs are not attached until the piece is completely finished, ready for use. The large H hinges may be either wrought iron or brass, and are mounted on the surface of the wood (not recessed). Rat-tail hinges would be equally appropriate. A simple turn latch, attached to each large wooden knob, serves to control the doors.

CHAPTER VII

CHESTS

PERHAPS THE earliest piece of furniture was a chest. As soon as man accumulated possessions, he required a place to keep them, and since early man was nomadic this receptacle was designed to be portable. Chests also figure prominently in early religious history. The Ark of the Covenant was a chest which transformed a tent, or even an open space, into a temple of worship.

The earliest chests were simply constructed boxes with lift lids. They were often elaborately carved. The addition of drawers began the evolution which eventually culminated in the tall chest of drawers, the chest-on-chest, the highboy, and the bureau.

Though we may be skeptical about much of the furniture supposedly brought to this country on the *Mayflower,* there is little doubt that that overloaded boat actually carried a large number of chests. Pilgrim families required some possessions with which to start life in the new world, and it is safe to suppose that the chest, crammed full, had first priority on baggage space. Like most English furniture of the time, these chests were usually made of oak, and many beautiful chests of this period still remain. The legs were simple extensions of the stiles, or sides of the frame. The fronts were paneled, and covered with flat relief carving. Construction was sturdy, with wide, deep mortise-and-tenon joints reinforced with wooden pins. Slightly later chests often had ball feet or bracket feet, and were made of various woods. No drawings of the earlier types have been included in this book, as such designs are not popular in reproduction.

154

Plate 66

PINE LIFT-LID CHEST

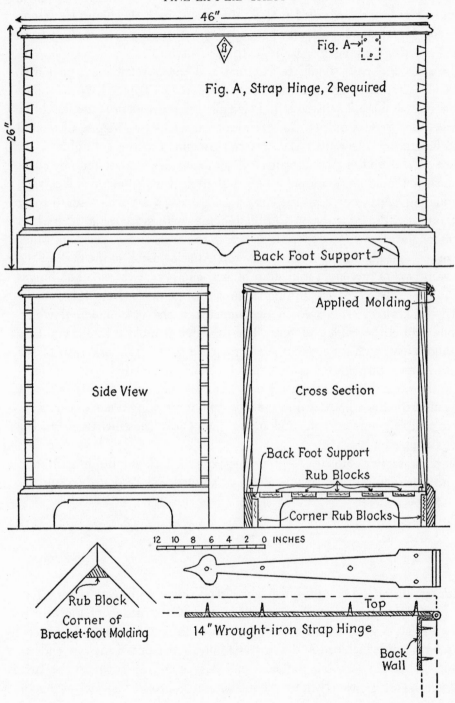

46"

26"

Fig. A→

Fig. A, Strap Hinge, 2 Required

Back Foot Support

Applied Molding

Side View

Cross Section

Back Foot Support
Rub Blocks

Corner Rub Blocks

12 10 8 6 4 2 0 INCHES

Rub Block
Corner of
Bracket-foot Molding

Top

14" Wrought-iron Strap Hinge

Back
Wall

The pine lift-lid chest shown in *Plate 66* is an eighteenth century design in which the ends are dovetailed into the front and back. Each surface: front, back, top, bottom, and ends, may be made from a single wide board, or from several boards glued together before cutting to size.

The sides and ends should be cut first and the dovetail joints prepared. Instructions for making these joints are included in Chapter I. Next, mill a groove in each piece for the bottom. Plane all surfaces smooth (pine should be planed, other woods sanded). Cut the bottom to size with a tongue all around to fit the grooves. Plane the inside surface. Assemble the case with glue.

Next cut the top to size, and plane. Mill a tongue on the front and side edges to attach the molding. Made separately and applied with tongue and groove, the molding helps to prevent warping of the lid, and also forms a lip to cover the meeting of the lid and case. Cut the molding with a groove at the back to fit the tongue. The surface shape is shown in the cross-section drawing. Miter the corners and glue the molding to the top. Attach the top to the back of the case with two 14" wrought-iron strap hinges, one near each end. The hinges are installed inside the back and lid as shown in the detail drawing.

The bracket feet are sawed in one piece with the base molding, which extends around the front and sides. The top edge is molded as shown. This continuous foot, with mitered corners, is attached to the front and sides of the case with brads through the molding. Rub blocks are glued at frequent intervals in the angle of the foot skirting and case bottom, and in the inside angles of the mitered feet, as indicated in the cross-section drawing. Plain brackets are used to complete support at the back of the chest. (See "Construction of Bracket Feet," Chapter I.)

The chest is now complete except for installing the lock and finishing. It may be left in the natural pine color, stained, or painted and decorated to suit the owner's taste.

———◆———

Plate 67 illustrates a beautiful mahogany lift-lid chest with two drawers. The ogee bracket feet are unusually fine for a chest. Construction of the case is similar to that of *Plate 66,* with the exception of the sub-bottom and drawers. The sub-bottom is included in the first assembly. The front of the case ends at the top of the drawers, but the sides and back continue down to the base molding, and are grooved both for the sub-bottom and for the bottom, as shown in the cross-section drawing.

Plate 67

MAHOGANY LIFT-LID CHEST

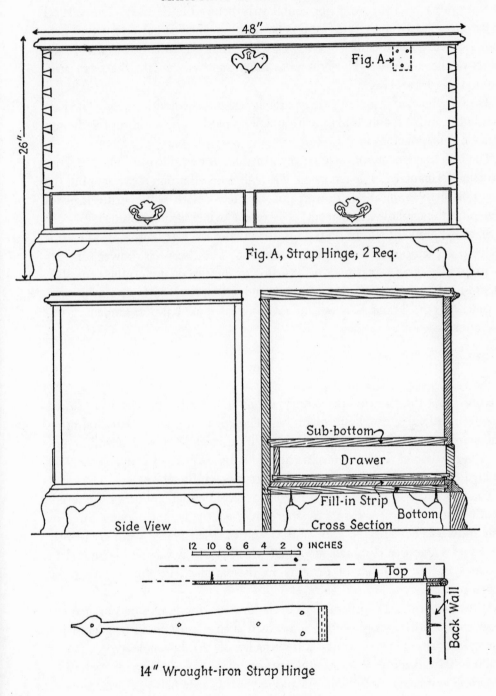

48"

26"

Fig. A →

Fig. A, Strap Hinge, 2 Req.

Sub-bottom

Drawer

Fill-in Strip

Bottom

Side View

Cross Section

12 10 8 6 4 2 0 INCHES

Top

Back Wall

14" Wrought-iron Strap Hinge

The lower front of the case consists of three vertical strips (cut with horizontal grain) and one long horizontal strip below the drawers. The vertical strips are tenoned into the front panel and the horizontal strip. The base molding will cover the horizontal strip, which may therefore be screwed to the edges of the case sides. The bottom is tongue-and-grooved to the front strip and to the sides and back.

The ogee bracket feet are made separately and attached with screws. The base molding is mitered and applied with glue and brads. The molding for the top is made and applied as in *Plate 66*.

The two drawers are of dovetail construction, as described in "Drawer Construction," Chapter I. The fronts are cut with a lip all around, overlapping the edges of the openings. The drawer pulls are brass, with willow-pattern plates matching the keyhole escutcheon. These are attached after finishing.

Since the drawer bottoms do not rest directly on the case bottom, fill-in strips are used at each side and at the center division. These serve as drawer supports or runners. A guide strip may be attached to the top of the center strip. The strips should be sanded smooth, as should all drawer surfaces, inside and outside. All outside and inside surfaces of the case should also be sanded during and after assembly.

Chests of Drawers

Until about the seventeenth century, clothing and other articles were stored inconveniently in great chests, or presses. Though well made of oak and often elaborately carved, these were usually mere boxes with lift lids. The addition of a drawer or two at the bottom of a chest added greatly to its convenience, and pointed the way to the evolution of modern storage furniture.

The first chests of drawers with fixed tops were developed during the seventeenth century. These were rarely more than 40" in height, having three or four drawers. Toward the end of the century, such chests were frequently placed on a stand to eliminate stooping. This form was further elaborated in America by the addition of drawers in the stand itself, thus creating the highboy.

At the same time cheaper methods of making looking glasses encouraged the popularity of low dressing tables, on which such glasses could be placed for convenient use. These lowboys were usually of the kneehole type, with a shallow drawer across the top and one or two small drawers at each side. American craftsmen made highboys and lowboys in matched sets for bedrooms. The beauty and adaptability of the lowboy, however, soon led to its use in other rooms as well. For such uses the kneehole was not required, and it was abandoned in favor of additional drawer space.

Highboys and lowboys were popular from about 1690–1790. Toward the end of this period, other forms also developed. These included the low bureau and the tall chest, as well as that rather amazing monument to the indefatigable energy of the early housewife, the chest-on-chest. This towering structure, whose drawers began just above the floor and continued to stepladder height, was inconvenient but beautiful with its gleaming, well polished brasses.

With the advent of Hepplewhite and Sheraton, the fashion swung to lighter, more graceful furniture. The all-purpose lowboy was replaced in its various uses by distinct dressing tables and other specific types. Highboys and tall chests yielded to the graceful bureaus of the new style.

Highboys and Lowboys. The popularity of highboys and lowboys began in the reign of William and Mary, and extended through the Queen Anne and Chippendale periods. Those of the first style were walnut. The stands had six turned legs, four in front and one at each back corner, with the trumpet turning characteristic of the William and Mary school. They were fitted with wide flat stretchers, close to the floor and forming an inward arc in traveling from one leg to another. The skirting was cut in plain or fancy arches between the legs. Drawer handles were of the early drop or bail types. Tops were flat, with heavily molded cornices.

During the Queen Anne period, the six legs were replaced by four cabriole legs, without stretchers. The arch shaping of the skirt was retained and elaborated, with acorns or other carved pendants sometimes used to complete the downward curves, which had formerly terminated in the two additional legs. The slender cabriole legs of this style sometimes appear too frail for the great weight of the highboy, and in the Chippendale period the cabriole legs became shorter and stronger, with the ball and claw replacing the Dutch foot. The scroll top appeared, with finials of the urn or urn-and-flame type. The elaborately shaped skirting was often decorated with carved designs and/or pendants. Shells or sunbursts were favorite designs for the top and bottom central drawers. Philadelphia highboys, particularly, were richly carved. The brasses were of the "willow" type, becoming more elaborate in the later styles. The wood was usually mahogany, though other woods, especially cherry and maple, were used.

Plates, 68, 69, 70, and *71* illustrate a Queen Anne lowboy and highboy designed as companion pieces. The curve of the leg is graceful but sufficiently modified for sturdiness. This curve is carried over to meet the skirting by means of a wing block. The Dutch or spoon foot is here used without a shoe.

The legs should be made first. The curved section of the leg pattern should be made to correspond with the leg cross sections in *Plate 69.* The upper section is a straight square post, forming the corner post of the lowboy. Cut and shape the legs as instructed in "Shaping a Cabriole Leg," Chapter I. Sand the shaped sections to finish smoothness.

Study the construction plan in *Plate 69,* and mortise the leg posts accordingly (see "Joinery," Chapter I). Note that the back panel is set flush with the back surface of the legs, which are rabbeted to receive it. The side panels are also set flush with the outside surface, but are joined with tongue and groove for greater strength. The front skirting is mortised into the legs, flush with the front surface.

The side panels are shaped at the bottom in cyma curves. These may be cut by band saw, after which a spokeshave or drawknife is used to remove saw-marks. Tongue the long edges to fit the leg grooves, and assemble with glue.

The top edge of the front skirting forms the lower edge of the bottom drawer openings, and is therefore higher at the center. The bottom edge is band-sawed to shape, including the lower outline of the sunburst carving, but not including the corner wing blocks, which are made separately and attached after assembly. The ends of this skirting are tongued to fit the leg grooves.

The full sunburst is carved directly on the skirting. Detail drawings of a cross section and surface segment of the design are included in *Plate 69.* Carving instructions will be found in Chapter I. After carving, glue the skirting to the leg-and-side assemblies.

The drawer partition frames should be made next. Study the open-front view and top-view plans in *Plate 69.* The frame immediately below the top is a plain four-sided rectangle. The front strip is made of the same wood as the other outside surfaces, and fits flush with the front leg surface. The two end pieces are cut to fit around the inside corners of the legs, and are tongued and grooved into the front and back pieces. They are bored and counterbored for 3″ screws to attach them to the side panels.

The second frame (from the top) is similar to the first, with the addition of two cross battens which are tongued and grooved into the front and back pieces at the drawer divisions. Assemble these two frames and attach them to the sides with 3″ screws, as shown in the open-front view.

The two lower side drawer frames should be made and attached next. These are similar to the corresponding end sections of the top frame, except that the front pieces fit behind the skirting and may be of cheaper wood. The inner end of each frame is formed by a cross batten. Attach these frames with screws into the side panels.

Next cut and install the vertical drawer partitions. These are placed just below the cross battens of the second long frame, to which they are attached with screws. At the bottom they are screwed to the inner edges of the lower side frames (open-front view). Cut a vertical strip of the case wood, with horizontal grain, and glue it over the front edge, joining the front surfaces of the horizontal frame and the skirting.

The short horizontal frame under the middle drawer is made to fit between the vertical drawer divisions, behind the skirting, and is attached to the vertical divisions with screws.

The thin back panel of the case should now be cut to size and nailed in place. Then cut the four leg wing blocks and glue them to the legs and skirting, as shown in the detail drawing, *Plate 69*. Use hand tools and sandpaper to dress down the surface after assembly. Sand all flat outside surfaces thoroughly.

Glue the top boards together, and cut to size. Note that the top extends over the back of the case about ½″ (*Plate 68,* side view). This practice is customary with lowboys but not with highboys. The front and side edges extend beyond the case, and are molded as shown. Sand and attach the top with screws from the underside of the top frame. Make the drawers as instructed in "Drawer Construction," Chapter I. Cut the drawer fronts with ¼″ molded lip edges (see cross-section side view, *Plate 68*). After final sanding and application of finishing material, install the locks and drawer pulls. The willow-pattern brasses shown in the front-view drawing are appropriate for this style.

The highboy stand in *Plates 70* and *71* is identical in structural features with the lowboy (*Plates 68* and *69*), with the top omitted. Dimensions are the same except for height, that of the highboy stand being 33″, and of the lowboy 29¾″.

For the upper section the side panels should first be cut to size. Since there are no corner posts, the front horizontal piece behind the cornice is tongued and grooved directly into the side, and the rabbets for the back panel are cut in the back edges of the sides. Grooves for the drawer partition frames are milled ⅟₁₆″ deep across the inside surfaces of the side panels.

From this point on, construction of this piece is largely the construction of the five drawer partition frames. These are similar to the upper frames used for the stand and lowboy. The front of the lower frame will be covered by an applied molding (see cross-section side view). This strip may therefore be made

Plate 68

QUEEN ANNE LOWBOY

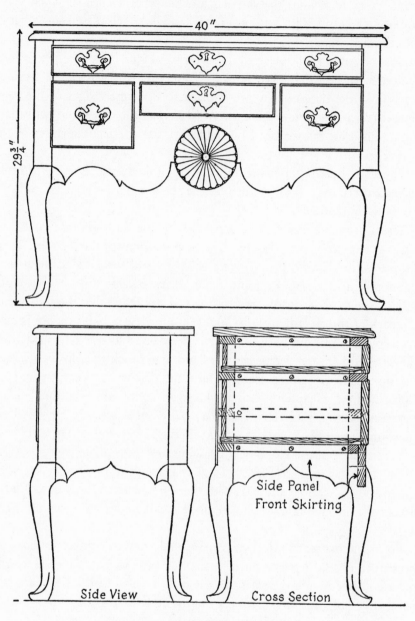

Side View   Cross Section

Side Panel
Front Skirting

12 10 8 6 4 2 0 INCHES

Plate 69

QUEEN ANNE LOWBOY

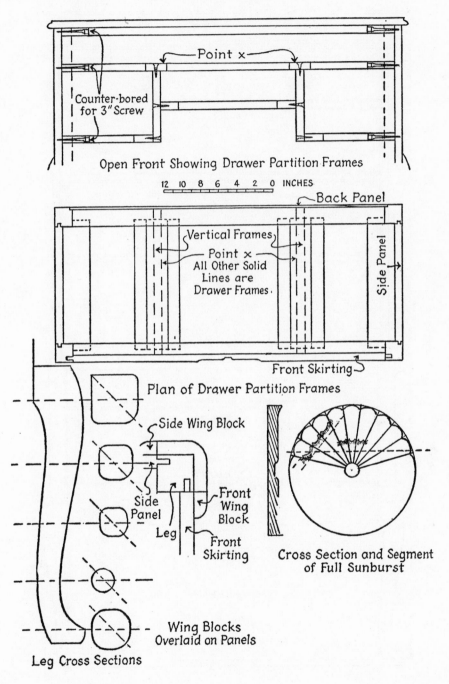

Point x

Counter-bored for 3" Screw

Open Front Showing Drawer Partition Frames

12 10 8 6 4 2 0 INCHES

Back Panel

Vertical Frames
Point x
All Other Solid Lines are Drawer Frames.

Side Panel

Front Skirting

Plan of Drawer Partition Frames

Side Wing Block

Side Panel

Front Wing Block

Leg

Front Skirting

Cross Section and Segment of Full Sunburst

Wing Blocks Overlaid on Panels

Leg Cross Sections

Plate 70

QUEEN ANNE HIGHBOY

70″

12 10 8 6 4 2 0 INCHES

40″

Plate 71

QUEEN ANNE HIGHBOY

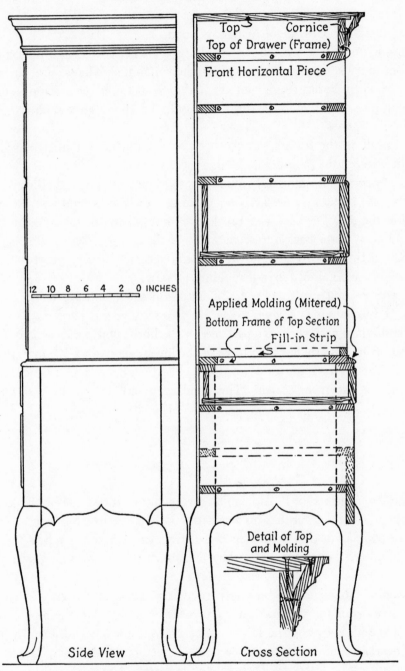

Top   Cornice
Top of Drawer (Frame)

Front Horizontal Piece

12 10 8 6 4 2 0 INCHES

Applied Molding (Mitered)
Bottom Frame of Top Section
Fill-in Strip

Detail of Top
and Molding

Side View   Cross Section

Construction Details Same as Companion Lowboy

165

of cheaper wood. Fill-in strips are used above the bottom frame, to raise the drawer level. The front fill-in strip forms a part of the front surface of the case, and must therefore be made of matching wood.

The frame under the two top drawers has a cross batten through the center from front to back, on which a drawer guide is mounted. The vertical surface partition between the drawers is cut to fit, and glued between the top and second horizontal frames. All outside surfaces should be thoroughly sanded after assembly.

After installing the frames, cut the back to size and nail it in place. This should fit between the rabbeted back edges of the sides.

The heavy cornice is not usually made of a solid piece of wood. As illustrated in *Plate 71,* the molding is worked on a piece ⅞" to 1" thick, and is tilted outward 2" at the top. The back is beveled to accommodate this tilt, and the top edge is cut away at the back to receive the lip of the case top, which is rabbeted to one half its thickness. The top is screwed to the cornice and to the front and side panels. (See detail of top and molding, *Plate 71.*)

The upper section should now be mounted on the stand. No fastening is necessary, but screws may be used to join the two sections if desired.

As is customary with such two-part pieces, the horizontal dimensions of the upper section are slightly less than those of the lower, allowing a ¾" margin at front and sides. The angle thus formed is filled with an applied molding, mitered at the two front corners. The molding is fastened to the base with brads.

———◆———

The master craftsmen of Philadelphia developed the art of furniture making to its highest peak of elegance. This was particularly true of the highboy, which was more popular in that area than elsewhere. An exceptionally fine Philadelphia highboy and matching lowboy are shown in *Plates 72, 73, 74, 75,* and *76.*

The wood is mahogany, which is particularly suited to the rich carving. Three variations of the shell design are used as ornament. On the top center drawer of the highboy and the lower center drawer of stand and lowboy, the shell is nearly round, with a rosette at the meeting of the rays. Graceful streamers suggesting leaf tendrils complete the design. The knee carvings suggest scallop shells. The center ornament of the skirting is unusual. The scallop shell is carved on a separate piece and applied, but the skirting itself is carved with curved lines forming "wings," which extend the design and bring its proportions into harmony with the pattern above.

The legs are cabriole, with realistically carved ball-and-claw feet. Brasses are "willow" pattern, more elaborate than those on the preceding pieces, as befits the change in style.

The lowboy (*Plates 72* and *73*) is similar in general construction to the preceding lowboy (*Plates 68* and *69*). The leg pattern must include the necessary thicknesses to allow for the carving. After rough-shaping by band saw, the legs should be carved with the knee shell and the ball-and-claw foot, while working down the leg shape with hand tools. The square upper sections of the front legs must be recessed to hold the quarter-columns, as shown in the detail drawing, *Plate 73*. They are then grooved for the side panels, as shown in the front corner assembly plan, *Plate 73*. Note that the side panel is to be tongued on the inside edge, to allow a thicker and stronger wall for the leg groove.

The top edge of the front skirting is cut lower under the deep center drawer, rather than higher as in *Plate 68*. The bottom edge is sawed to the shape shown in the front-view drawing. At the center the skirting includes the "wings" or corner extensions of the design, but does not include the shell. Cut the shell outline from a separate piece, fitting it exactly to the curves of the skirting. Carve the shell, following the procedures described in "Carving," Chapter I. Glue the shell in place, and complete the design on the skirting with a V gouge.

The vertical drawer partitions are also longer than in the preceding lowboy, to accommodate the drawer shape. In other respects the construction of drawer frames, front and back, is the same as in *Plate 68*. Strengthen the assembly by driving screws from the front leg post into each frame. These will be covered by the quarter-columns. Glue drawer guide strips to the frames at each side as shown in the open front view, *Plate 73*.

After assembling the case, make and flute the quarter-columns as instructed in Chapter I. Glue them into the recesses in the front legs, using screws (from the back) for added support (front corner assembly plan, *Plate 73*).

The drawers are constructed according to the procedure described in Chapter I. Cut the drawer fronts with molded lips as shown in the cross-section side view, *Plate 72*. Carve the front of the lower center drawer before assembling (see detail drawing, *Plate 73*).

Cut the top to size, and mold the edge. Indent the front corners as shown in the detail drawing, *Plate 73*. Sand, and attach with screws from the underside of the top frame. Cut a molding to fit the angle under the top, with mitered corners, and apply with glue and brads (see open front view, *Plate 73*).

Plate 72

PHILADELPHIA LOWBOY

42"

29½"

End Drawer Frame

Center Drawer Frame

Side View

Cross Section

12 10 8 6 4 2 0 INCHES

Plate 73

PHILADELPHIA LOWBOY

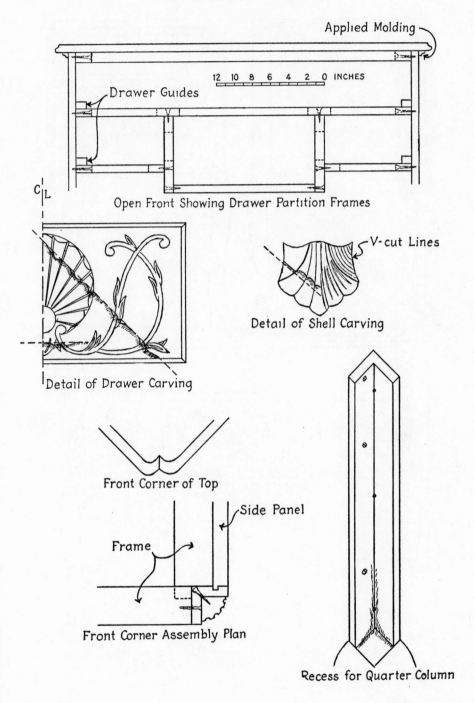

Applied Molding

12 10 8 6 4 2 0 INCHES

Drawer Guides

Open Front Showing Drawer Partition Frames

C L

Detail of Drawer Carving

V-cut Lines

Detail of Shell Carving

Front Corner of Top

Side Panel

Frame

Front Corner Assembly Plan

Recess for Quarter Column

169

Plate 74

PHILADELPHIA HIGHBOY (STAND)

End Drawer Frame
Center Drawer Frame

39"

33"

12 10 8 6 4 2 0 INCHES

Construction Details Same as Mahogany Lowboy

Plate 75

PHILADELPHIA HIGHBOY (TOP)

Fig. A

Face Panel

$52\frac{3}{4}''$

12 10 8 6 4 2 0 INCHES

Highboy Base

$37\frac{1}{2}''$

Face Panel
Turned Boss
Turned Rosette

Cross Section of
Arch Molding

Fig. A

171

Plate 76

PHILADELPHIA HIGHBOY (TOP)

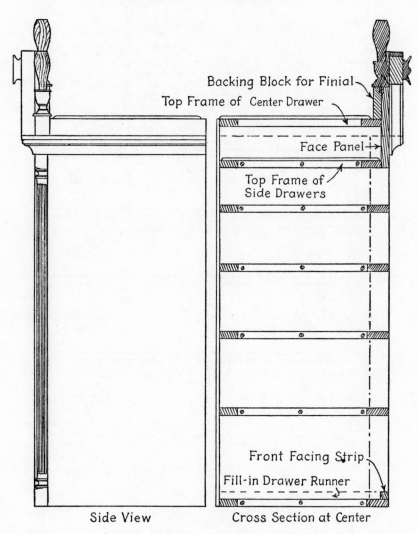

Backing Block for Finial
Top Frame of Center Drawer
Face Panel
Top Frame of
Side Drawers
Front Facing Strip
Fill-in Drawer Runner

Side View   Cross Section at Center

12 10 8 6 4 2 0 INCHES

The stand of the highboy is identical with the lowboy except in height (33″ instead of 29½″). The top is, of course, omitted. The angle molding which simulates the edges of the top is applied after the upper section is placed on the stand.

The construction of the upper section resembles that of the Queen Anne highboy, *Plates 70* and *71,* except for the front corner assembly. To provide for the quarter-columns, a recessed corner post is used at each front corner. This piece is L-shaped in cross section, the edge of the long arm forming the vertical side strip of the case front. The side arm is shorter by the thickness of the side panel, which completes the angle. A cross-section detail drawing of this corner construction is included in *Plate 78,* "Quarter-Column Chest."

The drawer partition frames are similar in construction to those of the lowboy. However, since the bottom frame rests on the stand, behind the applied molding, the front of this frame need not be of mahogany. Fill-in strips are used to raise the level of the bottom drawer, and a mahogany facing strip is glued and screwed in to fill the resulting gap in the front surface (*Plate 76*).

The drawer partition frames are supported in grooves $\frac{1}{16}$″ deep, in the side panels. Screws through the recessed corner posts into the frame edges give additional support. The screw heads will be covered by the quarter-columns.

The top-drawer partitions are constructed like those of the lowboy bottom drawers. The frame over the central top drawer is, of course, higher than the two side frames (*Plate 76*).

Procedures described in Chapter I are used in turning and fluting the quarter-columns. These are identical with those of the stand and lowboy, except in length.

The face panel of the highboy rises to a broken arch, or scroll, top. The panel may be shaped by band saw. It is attached to the corner posts by screws under the quarter-columns. The arch molding may be partly cut on a shaper and finished by hand, or cut completely by hand. The rosettes may be turned on the lathe and the outer edge scalloped with a rounded sandpaper stick. They are glued to turned bosses, which are attached to the face panel by screws from the back. (See cross section, *Plate 75.*)

The finial supports at each side are square blocks, with caps cut slightly larger and glued on. These blocks are fastened to the case by long thin screws entering diagonal top corners of the block. A backing block and cap are glued to the central rise of the face panel, to support the center finial (see cross section, *Plate 76*). A hole is bored in the center of each block for the finial dowel. Finials may be turned to shape, after which a V gouge is used to carve the flames.

The top of the case is made in three sections, that at the center being higher to accommodate the central drawer. Three-eighths-inch poplar may be used. Edges should be rounded, to give them a more finished look.

As in the case of stand and lowboy, the drawer fronts are lipped, and the top center drawer is carved with the same design (see detail drawing, *Plate 73*). The drawers are constructed as described in Chapter I. The brasses are attached after final sanding and finishing.

Bureaus. Chests of drawers without separate stands were also made in the late seventeenth and early eighteenth centuries, but were not widely used until about 1750. Various forms were developed, including the low chest or bureau, the chest-on-chest, the tall chest, and the desk.

Early low chests resembled well made modern bureaus in structure. The drawers were generally graduated in depth from bottom to top, and were usually surrounded by a small half-round or bead molding. On early pieces this molding was applied on the frame around the drawers, later upon the drawers themselves. In some cases the drawers were "lipped"; that is, the edges overlapped the opening.

The chests illustrated here are all of approximately the same period: the latter half of the eighteenth century. They differ, however, in important style features.

———◆———

Plates 77 and *78* illustrate a straight-front chest with a fluted quarter-column set into each front corner, as in the Philadelphia highboy previously discussed. General construction details of frame, drawer partitions, and so forth, are identical with those of the upper section of a highboy, but in this case the chest rests directly upon the bracket feet rather than on a stand.

The side panels should first be cut to size, and milled. Cut grooves $\frac{1}{16}''$ in depth to support the ends of the drawer frames. The positions of the grooves may be figured from the height of the frames shown in cross section, *Plate 78*. Rabbet the back edges to receive the back panel.

The modified front corner posts should next be cut to length and recessed for the quarter-columns as shown in the front corner detail, *Plate 78*. These are L-shaped in cross section. The long arm of the L extends to the front surface. The other arm is shorter to fit inside the side panel. Attach the posts to the side panels with glue and screws.

Next make the five drawer partition frames. Each frame is a simple four-sided rectangle. The front strip fits flush with the front edges of the corner

Plate 77

QUARTER-COLUMN CHEST

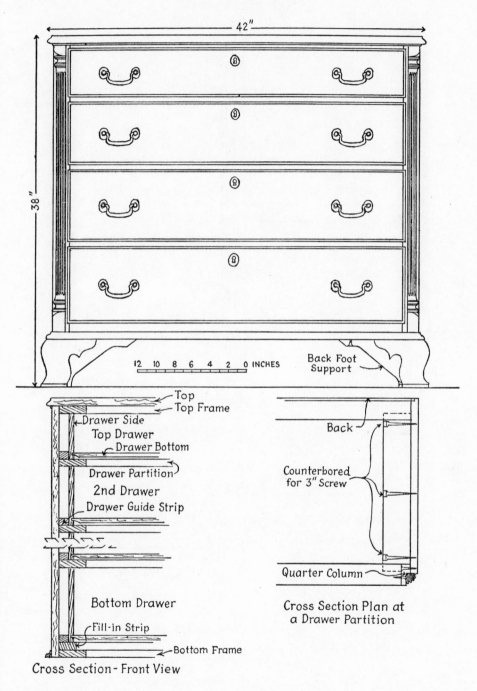

42"

38"

12 10 8 6 4 2 0 INCHES

Back Foot
Support

Top
Top Frame
Drawer Side
Top Drawer
Drawer Bottom
Drawer Partition
2nd Drawer
Drawer Guide Strip

Bottom Drawer

Fill-in Strip

Bottom Frame

Cross Section - Front View

Back

Counterbored
for 3" Screw

Quarter Column

Cross Section Plan at
a Drawer Partition

Plate 78

QUARTER-COLUMN CHEST

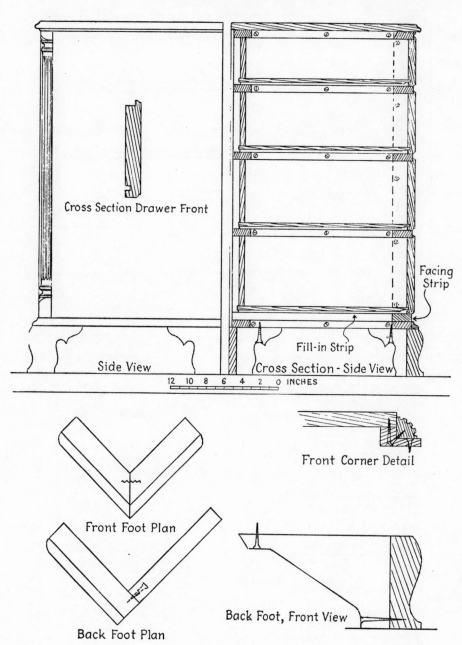

Cross Section Drawer Front

Facing Strip

Fill-in Strip

Side View

Cross Section - Side View

12 10 8 6 4 2 0 INCHES

Front Corner Detail

Front Foot Plan

Back Foot Plan

Back Foot, Front View

posts. This piece should be of the surface wood except in the bottom frame, which will be covered by the base molding. Cheaper wood may be used for the back and side strips, which fit inside the case sides. The side strips are tongued and grooved into the front and back pieces. The front corners are cut out to fit around the corner posts (see cross-section plan, *Plate 77*). The frames are screwed to the side panels with 3″ screws, as shown. Screws are also driven into the front corner edges from the recessed corner posts. These screws will be concealed by the quarter-columns.

The bottom frame fits flush with the bottom edges of the side panels and corner posts. Fill-in strips are glued above this frame to raise the level of the bottom drawer. A facing strip of the surface wood is fastened across the front with glue and screws passing up through the bottom frame (cross-section front view, *Plate 77,* and side view, *Plate 78*). After completing the above steps, sand all outside surfaces.

The top frame fits flush with the top edges of the sides and corner posts. As shown in the cross section, *Plate 77,* drawer guide strips are glued at each side, on all frames except the top.

The back may be made of random-width boards, milled for rabbet joints, and attached to the case with nails into each frame and the side panels.

Instructions for turning and fluting the quarter-columns are given in Chapter I. These should be attached with glue and with screws driven diagonally from the back of the corner post, as shown in the front corner detail, *Plate 78.*

Plans for the bracket feet are given in *Plate 78.* Construction of this type of foot is described in detail in Chapter I. The completed feet are attached to the case with screws.

Cut the base molding as shown in the cross-section side view, *Plate 78.* Miter the corners, and attach with glue and brads.

The boards for the top should next be glued up into a single piece, and cut to size. Note that the top projects slightly at front and sides, but is flush with the back of the case. Mold the front and side edges, sand, and attach with screws driven up through the top frame. Make, miter, and apply a small quarter-round molding in the angle under the top, at front and sides.

Make the drawers, following instructions in Chapter I. Cut the fronts with molded lips, as shown in the cross section drawer front, *Plate 78.* Sand all surfaces. Fit the drawers in place, and install the locks.

The chest is now complete except for applying the finish and attaching the drawer pulls. The front view, *Plate 77,* shows appropriate brasses. These are of an early type, with a small plate at each end of the bail rather than a single large plate. The small escutcheons match the plates.

Plates 79 and 80 show a fine four-drawer chest with serpentine front. The oval brasses and the use of line inlay on the drawers and feet suggest a slightly later design than that in *Plate 77.* The drawers are not lipped, but are surrounded by a small bead which is molded on the frame and inner front edge of the side panels (see *Plate 80,* detail *A*). The molded edge of the top and the molding at the base are chamfered on the front corners, as are the bracket feet, to follow the shape of the case. The reeded chamfers at the front corners of the case are created by applied strips (see detail *A, Plate 80*).

The side panels are first cut to size. Study the front corner detail, *Figure A* in *Plates* 79 and 80, to determine the shaping of the front edges. The back edges are rabbeted (see open top view, *Plate 79*). Grooves are milled $\frac{1}{16}''$ deep on the inside surfaces to support the drawer partition frames.

The five drawer partition frames are identical. The front piece of each frame is of the surface wood, and is cut to follow the serpentine shape shown in *Figure B, Plate 80* (same as drawer front). The back and side strips may be of cheaper wood. The side strips are joined to the front and back pieces with tongue and groove, as shown in the open top view, *Plate 79.* Each side strip should be bored and counterbored for three $3''$ screws, with which the frame is fastened to the side panels, as shown. Additional supporting screws are driven into the frame edges from the front corners of the side panels. These will be concealed by the reeded decorative strips (*Figure A*).

After completing the assembly of frames and side panels, rough-shape the front corner pieces (*Figure A*), and attach them with glue and screws from inside the side panels. Finish shaping with hand tools. A V-shaped gouge will cut the vertical grooves between the reeds.

Next, mark the outline of the bead molding on the frames, with pencil, completely around each drawer opening. Cut along the markings with a V-shaped gouge. Remove the wood between beads to a depth of about $\frac{3}{32}''$, forming a channel on the horizontal frames. Cut a sloping groove outside the single vertical bead on the front edge of each side panel, to give the bead relief. The result appears in cross section as a long-sided notch (detail of *Figure A, Plate 80*).

The base molding consists of one front and two side pieces. The front piece follows the serpentine shape. To make this, select a mahogany board of sufficient length, about $4''$ wide and $1\frac{3}{16}''$ thick, and place this in position under the front bottom frame. Mark the shape in pencil, continuing the line around the front corner to the back edge of the board. This method permits all of the curved portion to be cut on the front board. Next, measure at frequent intervals $\frac{3}{4}''$ out from the case line, and make a new pencil line for the start

Plate 79

SERPENTINE FRONT CHEST

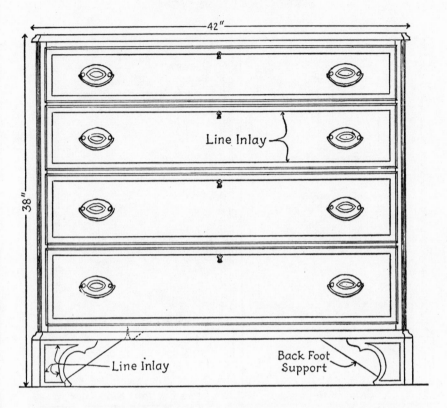

Line Inlay

Line Inlay

Back Foot
Support

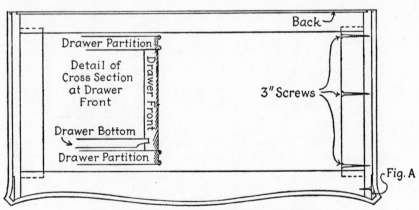

Drawer Partition

Detail of
Cross Section
at Drawer
Front

Drawer Front

Back

3" Screws

Drawer Bottom

Drawer Partition

Fig. A

Top Outline and Plan at a Drawer Partition

12 10 8 6 4 2 0 INCHES

179

Plate 80

SERPENTINE FRONT CHEST

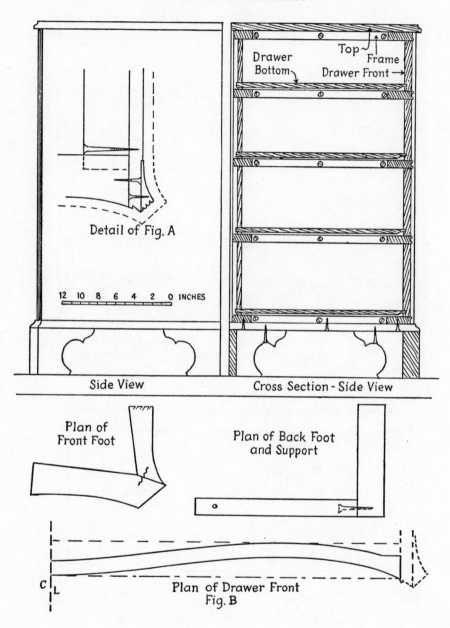

Detail of Fig. A

12 10 8 6 4 2 0 INCHES

Drawer Bottom

Top Frame
Drawer Front →

Side View

Cross Section - Side View

Plan of Front Foot

Plan of Back Foot and Support

C L

Plan of Drawer Front
Fig. B

180

of the profile shaping. Methods of cutting moldings are described in Chapter I. The side pieces are straight, with the edge molded to match the front. The molding is attached with screws from underneath, as shown in the cross-section side view, *Plate 80*. Side pieces are butt-joined to the front.

The front feet follow the shape of the front corner (see foot plan, *Plate 80*). They are shaped by band saw, after joining the mitered blocks with corrugated fasteners as instructed in Chapter I. The outside surface is then rough-sanded, after which line inlay is applied as shown in the front view, *Plate 79* (see "Inlaying," Chapter I). After finish-sanding, the feet are attached with screws. The back feet are not mitered, and after band-sawing the edges and finish-sanding, the feet are attached to the base molding with one screw through each foot. Plain support blocks are then attached, first to the feet, then to the bottom frame, as shown in the plan of back foot and support, *Plate 80*.

The top is cut to the shape shown in the outline drawing, *Plate 79*. The edges are molded. The top is attached to the top frame of the case, with vertical screws from underneath.

The drawer fronts are cut from thick wood, band-sawed to the serpentine shape shown in *Figure B, Plate 80*. The drawer bottoms are shaped at the front to correspond. Before assembling the drawers, work down and sand the band-sawed fronts to form a smooth surface with the front drawer division frames. Cut the inlay channels and set in the line inlay as shown in the front view, *Plate 79*. Finish-sand, assemble the drawers, and install the locks. The chest is now ready for the finishing operation, after which the brass drawer pulls are attached.

———◆———

Block-front chest. The chest in *Plates 81* and *82* is a block-front design. Block-front furniture originated and was made exclusively in New England, the style being generally attributed to two master cabinetmakers of Newport, Rhode Island: John Goddard and John Townsend. Considered by many the highest development of American furniture design, the original block-front pieces are rivaled only by "Philadelphia Chippendale" in the quality of workmanship and the excellence of the carving.

Block-front furniture was made only in the Chippendale period, and the style features of that era were naturally embodied in the designs. The favorite ornament was the shell carving. The feet were sometimes ball-and-claw, but more often a perfected form of the ogee bracket, known as the "Goddard foot."

Plate 81

BLOCK-FRONT CHEST

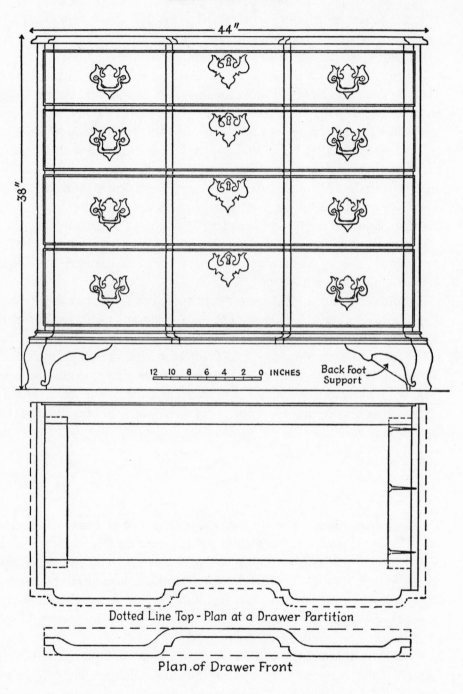

Back Foot
Support

Dotted Line Top - Plan at a Drawer Partition

Plan of Drawer Front

Plate 82

BLOCK-FRONT CHEST

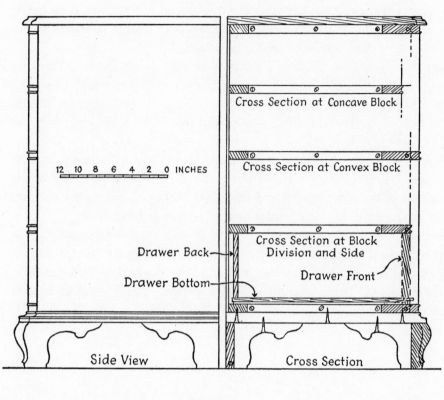

12 10 8 6 4 2 0 INCHES

Cross Section at Concave Block

Cross Section at Convex Block

Drawer Back

Drawer Bottom

Cross Section at Block
Division and Side

Drawer Front

Side View

Cross Section

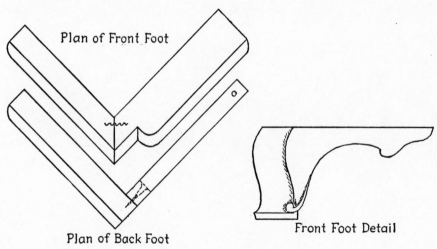

Plan of Front Foot

Plan of Back Foot

Front Foot Detail

183

This foot is distinguished by a small scroll, which provides a graceful termination for the raised or "block" portion of the foot.

The fronts of the drawers are cut from thick wood to form the block shape. Solid wood was always used, chiefly mahogany, occasionally cherry or maple. Block-front furniture was never veneered or inlaid.

In the foot plan, *Plate 82,* it will be noted that the block shape of the front is carried down onto the foot. The rough shape is band-sawed, after joining the mitered blocks from which the foot is made ("Construction of Bracket Feet," Chapter I). The raised portion of the foot is worked down into the scroll by hand.

Construction of this bureau is the same as that described in the preceding text (*Plate 79*), except that for all front pieces the block shape (*Plate 81*) is used instead of the serpentine. The front edges of the side panels are straight, since in this case there is no chamfer or applied corner piece.

The base molding is made and attached in the same manner as that in *Plate 79,* except that the front corners are mitered. The procedure for cutting the bead molding on the front frame, around the drawers, is also the same as that for *Plate 79.* There is no inlay. Willow-pattern brasses are used, as most appropriate for the style.

CHAPTER VIII

DESKS

THE WORD "desk" has been loosely used to describe any piece of furniture which contains writing facilities. Generally speaking, however, by "desk" we mean a low chest of drawers surmounted by a section of small drawers and pigeonholes, with a slanting lid or leaf which opens out to form a writing surface. Such a desk may or may not be topped by an additional section of shelves for books or bric-a-brac.

Slant-front desks were made throughout the eighteenth century, and partook of the same style variations as other furniture. They reached the height of elegance in design and workmanship in the Chippendale period, which included the block fronts of New England as well as the Philadelphia pieces. The lower parts of desks, like the bureaus of the period, were made in various shapes such as serpentine, oxbow, block front and straight front. The shell carving was a favorite form of ornament. Bracket feet were most popular. The ball-and-claw foot was also used and, more rarely, the Dutch foot. Desks with bookcases above often had scroll tops and finials, like the highboys of the same era.

———◆———

The desk in *Plates 83* and *84* is a straight-front design, with ogee bracket feet and an ornamental sunburst carving on the inside door. The brasses are

185

"willow pattern." The drawers are lipped, with the exception of the top drawer, which is made with the molded upper edge flush with the opening to avoid interference with the open leaf. This drawer is less wide than the others, to provide for a leaf rest at each side.

The sides of the desk are cut back at a slant above the drawer section. The top is beveled along the front edge to conform to the slant of the sides, to which it is attached by a series of dovetails.

The upper interior of the desk is divided into a central well and two side sections. Each side section contains four small drawers, with three pigeonholes above the drawers. Thin partitions are used to make these divisions. The top, sides, and subtop or bed are grooved for the partitions before the desk is assembled. A narrow wooden valance, cut in modified arches. decorates the top of each side section. Small brass knobs are used on the drawers.

The door of the central well is decorated with a carved sunburst. It is fitted with a lock, with a small brass escutcheon which harmonizes with the larger brasses on the lower drawers.

Construction procedure is as follows: Determine the measurements for the top, subtop, and sides, using bottom measurement for the width of the sides. Glue together well matched boards to form slightly oversize pieces, from which these members may be cut.

Saw the sides to length and width (bottom measurement), and rough-sand. On the inner surfaces mark the positions of the horizontal members: the lower-drawer partition frames, the subtop, and the horizontal divisions of the upper interior. Cut grooves for these cross members, $\frac{1}{16}''$ deep for the lower partition frames, $\frac{1}{4}''$ deep for the subtop and interior divisions. Rabbet the back edges of the sides to receive the thickness of the back boards.

The sides are to be joined to the top with a series of dovetails, as shown in the detail drawing, *Plate 83*. Instructions for making dovetail joints, as well as for other required processes, are included in Chapter I. Mark and cut the dovetail tenons on the top edges of the sides. Cut off the upper front corners of the sides to make the sloping front, and sand the edges.

Next make the four lower-drawer division frames indicated in the cross-section side view, *Plate 84*. Each frame is made of four pieces, cut to fit the inside measurements of the desk, with the front frame piece forming part of the desk front. This front piece must match the other surface wood, but the sides and back may be of cheaper wood. The sides are tongued and grooved into the front and back pieces. Assemble the four frames, then join them to the desk sides in the prepared grooves with $3''$ screws entered from the inside edges of the frames.

Plate 83

STRAIGHT-FRONT DESK

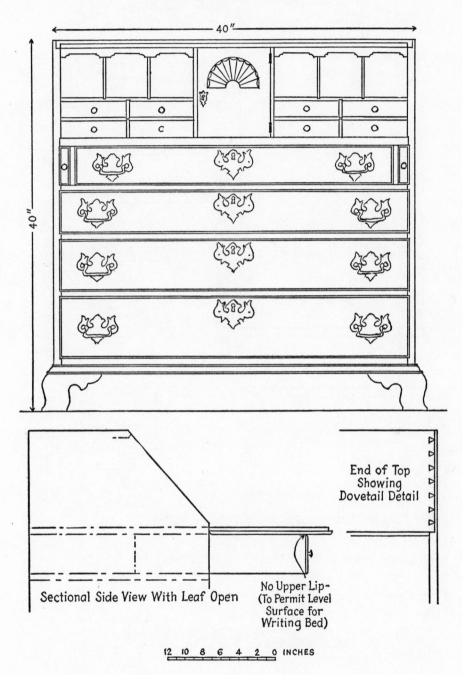

40"

40"

End of Top
Showing
Dovetail Detail

Sectional Side View With Leaf Open

No Upper Lip-
(To Permit Level
Surface for
Writing Bed)

12 10 8 6 4 2 0 INCHES

Plate 84
STRAIGHT-FRONT DESK

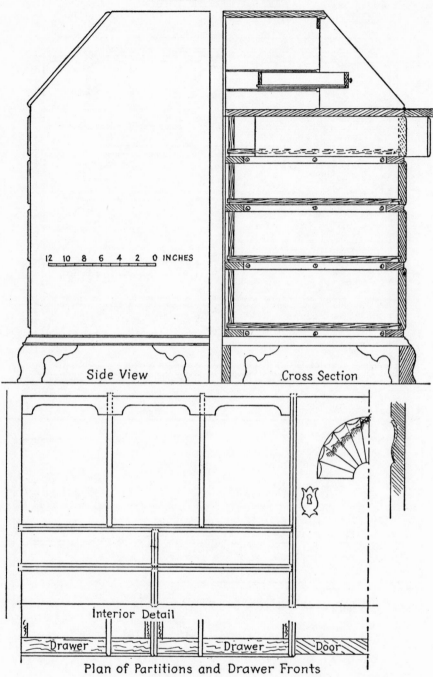

12 10 8 6 4 2 0 INCHES

Side View

Cross Section

Interior Detail

Drawer   Drawer   Door

Plan of Partitions and Drawer Fronts

Cut the subtop to length (measure exact distance between grooves in sides), and to width (from front edge of sides to back-edge rabbet. Then cut the top to size (outside measurement). Mark and cut dovetail mortises in the ends of the top to fit over the tenons on the desk sides. Rabbet the back edge of the top for the thickness of the desk back. Fit the top on the sides without glue, and mark the front bevel to continue the sloping line of the sides. Bevel the front edge of the top, following up with a clearance bevel underneath at right angles to the first (cross-section side view, *Plate 84*).

Study the half-plan of the upper interior, *Plate 84*. Lay out the required grooves for vertical partitions, on the underside of the top and the upper surface of the subtop, or bed. Mill the grooves $\frac{1}{4}''$ by $\frac{1}{4}''$, and completely sand these surfaces. Slide the subtop into the proper grooves in the desk sides, after preparing these grooves with glue. Then apply glue to the dovetails, and join the top to the sides.

The base molding is cut on the outer edge of a three-sided frame, which is attached under the front and sides of the desk, with the molded edge protruding. Use boards $1\frac{3}{16}''$ thick by $3''$ wide, of the same wood as is used for other surface pieces. Mold the edges as shown in the drawings, cut to length with mitered corners, and attach under the front and sides with screws from underneath.

The ogee bracket feet should be made next, following instructions in Chapter I. Attach the feet to the base frame with screws. The plain back-foot brackets should be screwed to the underside of the lower-drawer support frame.

The back of the desk is of frame construction, with two vertical panels separated by a central vertical frame strip. The over-all length of the back is measured from the rabbeted edge of the top to the lower edge of the bottom-drawer support frame. The width is measured between the rabbeted edges of the sides. After cutting the frame pieces to length, mortise the two horizontal strips, and tenon the three vertical pieces to fit. Groove all inside edges for the panels. Make the panels of thinner boards, random widths, rabbet-joined without glue. Assemble the frames and panels, gluing the frame joints; then nail or screw the frame to the desk sides and top, and to the drawer-support frames.

Refer to the half-plan of the upper interior, *Plate 84*. Cut the horizontal and vertical partitions to size, and prepare tongue-and-groove joints as indicated. Sand and glue in place. Cut the two continuous valance strips (one for each side section), with a band saw or jigsaw. Glue these to the underside of the desk top.

Make the door for the central well, and carve the sunburst design. Follow the surface and profile drawings in *Plate 84,* together with carving instructions in Chapter I. Fit and attach the hinges, and install the lock.

Both the small upper drawers and the large lower drawers should be constructed according to the directions in Chapter I. The fronts of the small drawers are plain. The large drawer fronts are cut with overlapping edges, or lips, at top and sides (see cross-section side view, *Plate 84*). All four edges are molded. The top edge of the upper large drawer is not lipped, but is molded to simulate a lip (*Plate 83,* sectional side view). This drawer is shorter than the others, to provide space for the leaf supports at each side, as shown in the front view, *Plate 83.* Two vertical strips, with horizontal grain, should be cut to fit between the subtop and the first partition frame, to divide the drawer opening from the leaf supports. These are attached with glue.

The leaf supports are plain rectangular pieces, of the same wood as the surface members. They should be about ⅝″ thick, long enough to extend from the front surface to just inside the back panel, and wide enough to slide easily between the subtop and the first partition frame. The front edge of each support should be covered with a face panel ¼″ thick, with vertical grain. This should fit flush at top and bottom but extend ¼″ at each side, forming a lip. Mold all four edges to match the molded drawer fronts. Glue these face panels to the leaf supports, then cut and glue a strip of felt along the top edge of each support, to protect the surface of the writing leaf when in use.

The side pieces of the first partition frame will act as runners for the leaf supports and drawer. However, guide strips are required to keep them running true. These strips should be mounted on the side frame pieces, directly behind the vertical front division strips.

It is desirable to install a stop for the leaf rests, to keep them from pulling out farther than necessary to support the leaf. A simple device for this purpose is made by screwing a small block of wood to the inner surface of the leaf support. The block must be placed high enough to clear the drawer guide strip, and in such a position that it will catch on the vertical front division when the leaf support is extended the desired distance.

The leaf is formed of a central panel tongued and grooved into a three-sided mitered frame, as shown in *Plate 86,* detail drawing. This method of construction prevents warping and insures rigidity when the open leaf is used for writing. Panel and frame are of the same thickness, $1\frac{3}{16}″$. A single board, 10¾″ wide, may be used if available for the panel. Two boards may be glued together if necessary to obtain this width. Cut to length with a tongue ¼″ thick by ½″ wide at each end. Next cut the long top frame piece 3″ wide. Miter the ends, measuring carefully to make the inside corners of the miters exactly meet the corners of the panel. Mill a groove in each miter edge, ¼″ wide by ½″ deep. Glue this piece to the panel.

Now prepare the end frame pieces, also $^{13}\!/_{16}″$ thick by 3″ wide. The top end of each is mitered to join the long frame piece; the lower end is cut off flush with the lower edge of the panel. Groove the miter ends ¼″ wide by ½″ deep, and continue this groove along the inside edge to engage the tongue on the panel end. Make hardwood splines, with diagonal grain, to join the mitered ends of the top and end frame pieces. Glue and insert the splines, glue the tongues and grooves, and clamp in position until the glue has thoroughly dried.

The top and end edges of the writing leaf should next be rabbeted to fit inside the front opening of the desk, leaving a lip on the outside surface to overlap the opening, as shown in the sectional side view, *Plate 83*. Then sand both surfaces thoroughly.

Attach the leaf to the desk with two desk hinges. Then install the lock, and cut the necessary groove under the bevel of the desk top, to engage the tongue of the lock. Install locks on the four large drawers.

The desk is now ready for finish-sanding, followed by application of the desired finish. Finally, mount the brass drawer pulls and keyhole escutcheons. The "willow" brasses shown in *Plate 83* are appropriate for the style of this desk.

———◆———

The desk in *Plates 85* and *86* has a reverse serpentine, or oxbow front. The style is of the same general period as that of *Plate 83*, but may be slightly earlier. This is suggested by the early-type brasses, and by the bead molding cut on the frame, instead of on the drawer fronts. There is no carving, but an ornamental pendant is suspended at the center front of the base molding. The feet are ogee, with gracefully scalloped wings. No other ornament is needed, since the shape of the front is highly decorative.

Construction procedure is so nearly identical with that described in the preceding text, *Plate 83*, that repetition is unnecessary. Points of difference are as follows:

The front strips of the drawer partition frames are shaped as shown in *Figure A, Plate 86* (same as lower drawer fronts). The shape may be cut with a band saw.

The molded base frame should be cut from strips about 4″ wide. Hold the

Plate 85

OXBOW-FRONT DESK

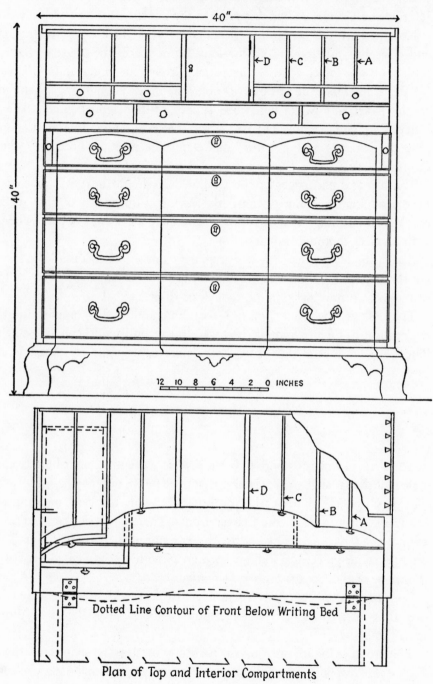

12 10 8 6 4 2 0 INCHES

Dotted Line Contour of Front Below Writing Bed

Plan of Top and Interior Compartments

Plate 86

OXBOW-FRONT DESK

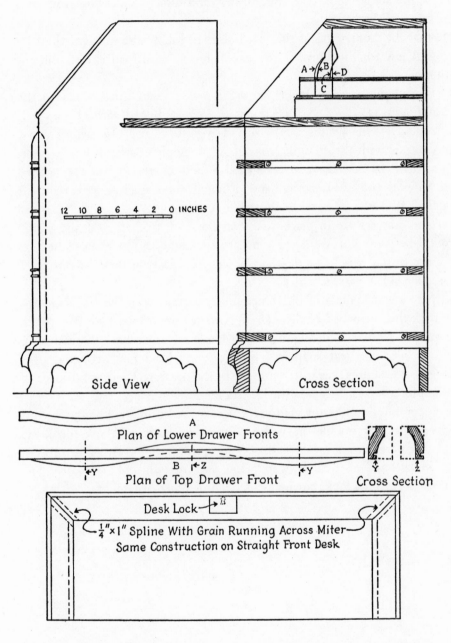

12 10 8 6 4 2 0 INCHES

Side View

Cross Section

A

Plan of Lower Drawer Fronts

B   Z

Y

Y

Plan of Top Drawer Front

Cross Section

Y   Z

Desk Lock

$\frac{1}{4}$"x 1" Spline With Grain Running Across Miter—
Same Construction on Straight Front Desk

strips in place under the desk assembly, mark the shape in pencil on the wood, then measure and draw a parallel outline for the outside edge of the molding. Band-saw the shape, mold the edge, miter, and attach under the front and sides of the desk with screws.

Note that the front wing of the foot bulges to follow the shape of the base molding. Allow for this bulge in the size of blocks used for the feet, and cut accordingly.

The three lower drawer fronts are band-sawed from thick wood to the shape in *Figure A, Plate 86.* The upper drawer is shaped vertically as well as horizontally. This heightens the decorative effect, and also avoids a too abrupt contrast with the straight front above it. A plan of the shape is given in *Figure B, Plate 86.* The points marked Y and Z are also shown in cross section. Shaping must be done by hand, although some stock may be removed with a circular saw or drill, with adjustable depth gauge.

After the drawers are in place, mark on the desk front the outline of the half-round beads. Use a V-shaped gauge to cut along the markings, then remove stock with a chisel to a depth of about $\frac{3}{32}''$, leaving the beads in relief (cross-section side view, *Plate 86*).

There are several points of difference in connection with the leaf supports. In this desk the end wood of the leaf supports is not covered by a face panel, but is simply sanded well and finished. There is no vertical division strip between drawer and leaf support. The bordering bead for the top drawer also encloses the support, as if it were part of the drawer. There is no space in this design for a forward stop on the leaf support.

The upper interior has three drawers across the entire width, the central drawer being nearly double the width of the side drawers. Above these, the usual plan of partitioning is followed, with a central well and two side sections, each of which has two small drawers below and four pigeonholes above. The door of the well has a lock, but no escutcheon or other ornament.

CHAPTER IX

MIRRORS AND
DRESSING GLASSES

THE DEVELOPMENT of styles in mirrors, or "looking glasses," as they were usually called, was greatly affected by technological developments in the manufacture of glass. Early mirrors were handmade; the glass was thin and irregular, and silvering was done by the mercury process. The quicksilver tended to adhere unevenly to the surface, resulting in the blotched appearance of many old mirrors. Beveling was difficult, usually done while the glass was molten, and at so slight an angle it can often be barely seen. Risk of breakage during manufacture was great, and increased when large pieces were attempted. For these reasons mirror glasses were costly, and usually small. Where large mirrors were desired, they were made in small sections, joined with a butt bevel, metal ribbing, or decorative molding. Not until the time of Sheraton did improved processes of manufacture bring large glasses within reach of fashion.

In the colonies mirror frames were made from about 1710, but the glasses were imported. The English luxury tax was fixed according to the size of the glass, adding a further reason for using small mirrors. The frames were large and often ornate to compensate for the small area of the glass. Wooden frames, when not gilded or otherwise covered, were generally made of the same wood as other furniture of the time: walnut in the period of Queen Anne, mahogany

195

in that of Chippendale or later. Gilded, painted, or lacquered mirrors were usually made of pine.

Early American craftsmen copied English mirror styles closely, but made one notable improvement in construction. Whereas English frames were made with the backboard cut to fit against the glass inside the frame, American makers cut the backboard larger and nailed it to the frame. This provided a space between the glass and the backboard, thus protecting the silvering.

The Queen Anne style of mirror was popular in America beyond the middle of the eighteenth century. The glass was usually in two parts, both beveled, with the upper part cut to follow the curves of the frame. An ornamental design was often cut on this upper section, which overlapped the lower one without any concealing trim. The upper portion of the frame was usually arched or curved, and surmounted by a cresting.

———◆———

Plate 87 illustrates a crested Queen Anne mirror. The cresting may be either of solid wood or veneered. It is mounted in a groove, ¼″ wide by ⅛″ deep, cut into the top of the frame, and is supported by rub blocks, as shown in the cross-section drawing.

The frame itself consists of four straight pieces molded to the shape shown in cross section on the drawing. The molding may be cut with a shaper, if available. An alternative method is to loosen the stock by repeated trips across a circular saw, readjusting the depth gauge for each cut. The stock may then be removed with a sharp chisel. Work the molding down to a smooth finish with sandpaper.

Next, cut two rabbets in the back of each strip, as shown in the cross section. Cut the strips to length, with mitered corners, and glue. Reinforce the joints with splines, as described in "Miter Joints," Chapter I.

Lay the assembled frame flat, with molded surface up, and mark the straight edges of the top corner inserts (*Plate 87,* front view). Cut away the corner surface between the markings to a depth ⅟₃₂″ above the spline. The undersurface must be flat and smooth (see detail drawing, *Plate 87*). Cut two inserts to fit the corner space, with diagonal grain. Glue in place, and work the double curves and molding by hand to match the frame surface.

Cut the cresting with a jigsaw or coping saw. Remove saw marks from the edges with sandpaper, and sand the front surface. If veneer is used, it is applied next. In any case, both the cresting and frame should be finished

Plate 87
QUEEN ANNE MIRROR

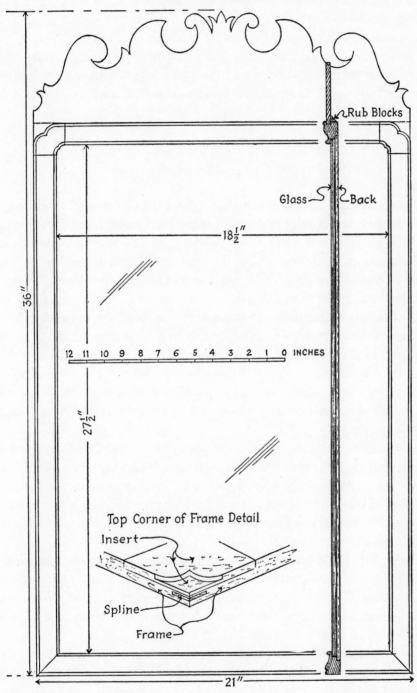

Rub Blocks

Glass

Back

$18\frac{1}{2}''$

36"

12 11 10 9 8 7 6 5 4 3 2 1 0 INCHES

$27\frac{1}{2}''$

Top Corner of Frame Detail

Insert

Spline

Frame

21"

197

before they are joined. Groove the top of the frame to a depth of ⅛″, and glue the cresting in the groove. Make several small triangular rub blocks, and glue these in the angle behind the cresting (see cross section, *Plate 87*).

The backboard may be made of masonite or thin plywood. It should be cut to fit the outside rabbet on the frame back. After mounting the mirror glass in the inside rabbet, attach the backboard to the frame with brads or screws.

◆

Plate 88 illustrates a typical mirror of the Chippendale period. The elaborate decorative panels are of solid mahogany, which was just coming into general use in Chippendale's time. The new availability of this very workable wood probably accounts, at least in part, for the exuberant decoration of late eighteenth century furniture. Veneering was temporarily abandoned for carving and intricate shapes. The C curve was used as a basic principle of design. Variants of the curve are combined to make up the panel shapes in *Plate 88*.

The frame is constructed of four straight strips of mahogany, molded to the shape shown in cross section on the drawing. The molding may be cut with a shaper, or with a circular saw and hand tools as described in the preceding text (*Plate 87*). Two rabbets are cut in the frame back (see cross section). The strips are then mitered and joined with splines, as described in "Miter Joints," Chapter I.

The top corners of the assembled frame are then marked and cut out for the corner inserts (see detail drawing, *Plate 88*). The top surface should be cut down to a depth ⅟₃₂″ above the spline. The undersurface must be flat and smooth. Cut two inserts to fit the openings. The grain of these pieces should run diagonal to the frame. Glue in place, and mold the surface by hand to match the frame.

The decorative panels may best be cut with a jigsaw. Top and bottom panels are of different design, and must be cut singly unless two frames are made at one time. Leave the side edges wide enough to protrude slightly from the frame. The protruding edges will be sanded down after the panels are glued in place, to insure an even joint.

The two identical side panels at the top may be cut in a single operation, using two layers of wood. The same method may be used for the two lower side panels. Smooth the edges and front surfaces of all panels with sandpaper.

Groove the frame to a depth of ⅛″ for mounting the top and bottom

Plate 88
CHIPPENDALE MIRROR

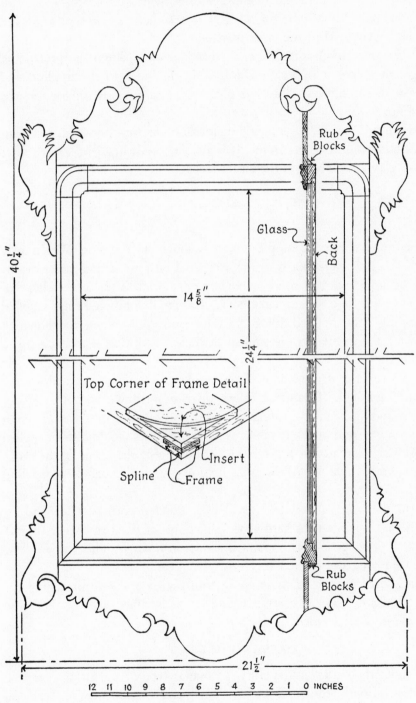

Rub
Blocks

Glass

Back

$14\frac{5}{8}''$

$40\frac{1}{4}''$

$24\frac{1}{4}''$

Top Corner of Frame Detail

Insert

Spline   Frame

Rub
Blocks

$21\frac{1}{2}''$

12 11 10 9 8 7 6 5 4 3 2 1 0 INCHES

panels. Glue the top panel first, and reinforce with rub blocks (see cross section, *Plate 88*). Allow time for the glue to set, then reverse the frame and mount the lower panel in the same way.

When the glue has thoroughly dried, plane or sand down the protruding side edges to obtain a smooth surface. Glue the side panels in place and reinforce with rub blocks. Allow the glue to dry thoroughly, then apply the desired finish.

The backboard is a plain rectangle of masonite or thin plywood, cut to fit inside the outer rabbet of the frame. It is attached with brads or screws, after the mirror glass is mounted in the inside rabbet.

———◆———

A wide-frame mirror of simple design is shown in *Plate 89*. While early frames of this type were nearly always veneered on pine, a nice effect can be achieved by using selected solid mahogany or walnut. The surface shape of the frame proper is a simple ogee curve, further decoration being supplied by protruding strips applied along the inner and outer edges. As shown in the drawing, the inside strip is applied in such a way that it forms a lip to hold the glass.

Shape the surface of the frame pieces in rough length, using methods described in "Moldings," Chapter I. Work this surface down with hand tools, and finish sanding before attaching the inner and outer strips (also in rough length) with glue and brads. If veneer is to be used, this should also be applied before the strips are attached. Note the positioning of the strips in the cross-section drawing, *Plate 89*. Allow time for the glue to set before proceeding further.

Next cut the frame pieces to length, with mitered corners. Glue and reinforce the miter joints with hardwood splines, as described in "Miter Joints," Chapter I. A cross section of the joint is shown in *Plate 89*. The frame is now ready for applying the desired finish.

The backboard may be of masonite or thin plywood, cut to fit behind the glass on the frame edge (see cross section). It is attached with brads driven at an angle into the frame.

DRESSING GLASSES

Throughout the eighteenth century, a popular type of mirror for personal use was that variously known as the "dressing glass," "toilet glass," or "shaving stand." Used by both men and women, these mirrors were designed to stand

Plate 89

WIDE-FRAME MIRROR

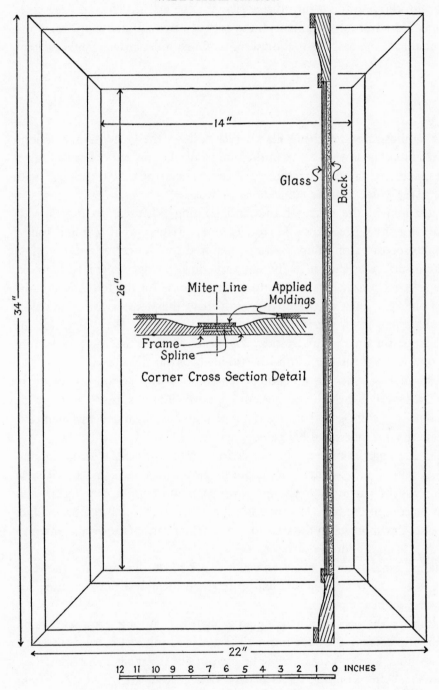

Glass

Back

Miter Line   Applied Moldings

Frame
Spline

Corner Cross Section Detail

14″

26″

34″

22″

12 11 10 9 8 7 6 5 4 3 2 1 0 INCHES

201

atop dressing tables or chests of drawers. Their shapes and decorative details varied with the prevailing furniture styles, but the essential features remained the same. They were small mirrors hung between two upright supports, which were mounted on a box of small drawers in which toilet articles could be kept.

———◆———

Plate 90 illustrates a dressing glass which follows the Queen Anne style in the crested top, the inward curve of the case front, the tiny curved brass drawer handles, and the dainty miniature ogee feet. The standards are topped with small finials, which may be either brass or wood.

Construction of the mirror frame and cresting is similar to that already described for the Queen Anne Mirror, *Plate 87*. Refer to that text and follow the same procedure, omitting the steps required for the corner inserts. Mold the frame surface as shown in the cross-section drawing, *Figure F, Plate 90*.

Glue selected boards together to the proper widths for the top, bottom, and sides of the case, then cut them to length. Saw the front edges of the sides to the shape shown in the side-view drawing. Rabbet the back edges for the case back, as shown in cross section, *Figure G*. Groove the top and bottom from front to back for the vertical partitions between the drawers.

Cut dovetail mortises in the ends of the case top and bottom as shown in *Figure H*. Dovetail the top and bottom edges of the sides to fit the mortises. Instructions for cutting and fitting dovetail joints are included in Chapter I. Assemble the top, sides, and bottom of the case.

The drawer partitions are solid wood from front to back, with grain running vertically. Band-saw the front edges to the shape shown in the side-view drawing. Fit the partitions to the grooves in top and bottom, apply glue, and slide in place. Cut the back to size, and glue it inside the rabbeted back edges of the case. Cut mortises in the case top for the standards (see detail drawings *G* and *H*). Sand all outside surfaces.

Miniature bracket feet for dressing glasses are made the same for the back corners as for the front. The method differs considerably from that used for bracket feet on larger pieces.

Molding for the ogee feet in *Plate 90* is shaped in a long strip, with hand tools. Eight pieces are then cut to rough length and mitered at one end (four rights and four lefts). A jigsaw may be used to cut the wing shape shown on the drawing. After sanding, the two parts of each foot are glued to the case bottom simultaneously, with glue applied to the top edge of each foot piece

Plate 90

QUEEN ANNE DRESSING GLASS

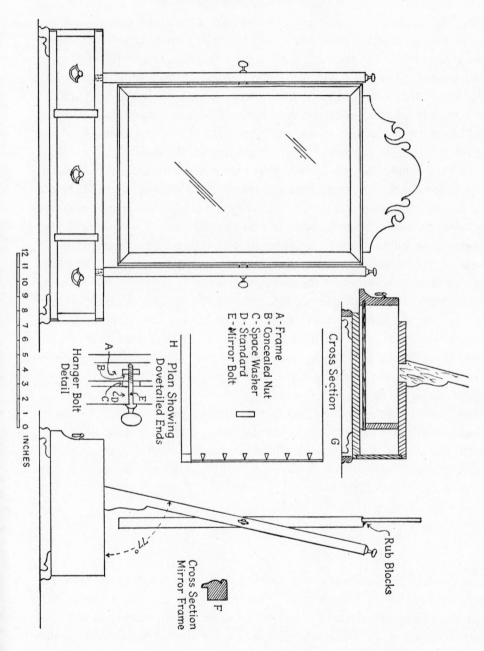

A - Frame
B - Concealed Nut
C - Space Washer
D - Standard
E - Mirror Bolt

Cross Section

G

H Plan Showing
Dovetailed Ends

Hanger Bolt
Detail

Rub Blocks

Cross Section
Mirror Frame

F

12 11 10 9 8 7 6 5 4 3 2 1 0 INCHES

and to the mitered ends. Use a quick-setting hot glue, and "rub" the pieces into position. Glue is the only fastening agent required.

The shape of the two upright standards is shown in the front and side views. The corners are left square. If wooden finials are desired, cut the standards long enough for these to be turned on the top ends. In band-sawing these pieces, allow for the backward angle, 77 degrees, and for the tenon (see *Figure G*). Cut the tenons to fit the mortises in the case top, and make a saw cut in the bottom of each, from front to back, for wedging. Turn the finials or, if brass finials are to be used, bore a hole in the top of each standard to fit the finial pin or dowel. Bore the holes for the hanger bolts. Sand the standards, then glue and wedge them in position on the case.

The brass hanger bolt assembly is shown in a detail drawing. The position of the hole in each side of the mirror frame is slightly above center. Bore the hole in the frame edge, then mortise from the back of the frame so that a concealed nut can be slipped into place in the bolt hole. Insert the bolt end through the standard, through the space washer, then into the frame edge and concealed nut. Make a wooden plug to fit each nut slot, and glue it in place. Sand the plug even with the surrounding surface.

Drawer construction is explained in Chapter I. Use $\frac{3}{8}''$ wood for the drawer sides, $\frac{1}{4}''$ for the bottoms. Select a piece of mahogany long enough for the three drawer fronts, and rough-cut this to the shape shown in cross section, *Figure G*. A circular saw may be used for this, as in cutting a molding. Dress down the surface with hand tools, and cut the proper lengths. Sand all drawer surfaces, and assemble.

Construction is now complete. Remove the hanger bolts to detach the frame, then apply the desired finish to frame and case. After finishing, attach the drawer pulls. Small brass bails like those illustrated are most appropriate for this style. Insert the glass and backboard in the frame, and mount it on the case with the hanger bolts.

———◆———

The dressing glass in *Plate 91* features the shield shape and serpentine front which were typical of Hepplewhite. The feet are miniature brackets of the shape commonly called the "French foot." The finials, drawer pulls, and hanger bolts are brass. The diamond-shaped inlay around the keyhole of the center drawer may be of lighter wood, or ivory.

Construction of this mirror frame differs from others in that there are no

Plate 91

HEPPLEWHITE DRESSING GLASS

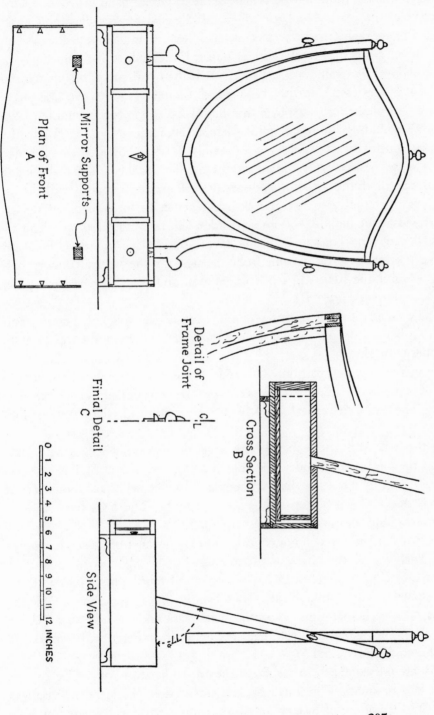

Plan of Front
A

Mirror Supports

Detail of
Frame Joint

Cross Section
B

Finial Detail
C

C.L

Side View

0 1 2 3 4 5 6 7 8 9 10 11 12 INCHES

mitered corners. The frame is formed of three pieces, band-sawed to follow the curve of the glass. The back edges are rabbeted for the glass and backboard. Similar rabbets may be seen in cross section in *Plate 87*. Rabbets on these curved pieces may be cut with a shaper, if available, or by hand.

The ends of the frame top are mortised to fit over tenons cut on the top ends of the sides (see "Mortise and Tenon," Chapter I). The two side pieces are joined at the bottom ends by a thin hardwood spline (grain running horizontally) extending into each frame member approximately ½". This is the strongest construction possible. It may readily be seen, however, that a frame of this shape is necessarily somewhat fragile. The backboard may be made of masonite or thin plywood, band-sawed to shape and attached with brads.

To construct the case, first glue boards together to form pieces of the required widths for the top, bottom, and sides. Cut these to the proper lengths. Shape the top and bottom according to the outline in *Figure A, Plate 91*. Groove the inside surfaces from front to back for the vertical drawer partitions. Rabbet the back edges of top, bottom, and sides for the back panel (see cross section, *Figure B*).

Prepare small dovetail mortises in the ends of the top and bottom, and matching dovetail tenons on the sides (*Figure A*). Assemble the top, bottom, and sides with glue.

The vertical drawer partitions are solid wood from front to back of the case. Measure accurately to fit between the grooves milled in the top and bottom, and cut with vertical grain. Apply glue, and slide the partitions into place.

Cut the back to fit the rabbeted back edges of the case, and join with glue. Mortise the top for the standards as shown in *Figures A* and *B*. The mortises should be slightly narrower than the standards, which will have shoulders cut on each side to form a stop and increase rigidity. The backward angle is 77 degrees. Sand all outside surfaces.

The four miniature feet are identical, and may be cut from a single strip of wood. Each foot is composed of two pieces. Cut the eight strips roughly to length, and miter one end of each (four lefts and four rights). Jigsaw to the shape shown on the front and side views. Sand to finish smoothness. Glue the two parts of each foot simultaneously to the case and to each other. Use a quick-setting hot glue, and "rub" into position with mitered ends joined. No other fastening is required.

Band-saw the standards to the shape shown in the front view. The corners should be left square. The finials are not included in the standard measurement. Cut the bottom of each standard to fit the mortise in the case top, leaving a shoulder at each side as shown in the front view. The bottoms of shoulders and tenons must be cut at a slant to provide for the 77-degree backward tilt of the standard. Make a saw cut from front to back of the tenon, for wedging. Bore a hole in the top of each standard for the finial pin, and bore the holes for the hanger bolts. Sand the standards, glue and wedge in place. Bore a hole in the center top of the mirror frame for the third finial.

The brass hanger bolt assembly is illustrated in *Plate 90,* and the required procedure is explained in the accompanying text.

Make the drawers as instructed in Chapter I, using $\frac{3}{8}''$ wood for the sides and $\frac{1}{4}''$ for the bottom. The drawer fronts must be made from thicker wood, band-sawed to match the serpentine shape of the top and bottom. Sand all drawer surfaces. After assembly, install the lock on the center drawer, and inlay with wood or ivory in a diamond pattern.

Remove the hanger bolts to detach the frame, and apply finish to frame and case. After finishing, install small brass knobs on the case drawers, and mount the brass finials on the standards and frame. Insert the mirror glass and backboard in the frame, and attach with brads. Mount the frame on the case with the hanger bolts.

CHAPTER X

CLOCK CASes

PERHAPS IN no other field of antiques does so much confusion exist, when one attempts to relate styles to dates, as in that of clock cases. Since the essential features of the case are largely governed by the requirements of the movement, little creative originality is possible except in superficial decoration. It is perhaps partly for this reason that makers of one period copied those of another. However, certain general conclusions are possible.

The short bob pendulum was invented about 1640, but was not generally used until about 1675. It was replaced by the long pendulum about 1680. At this early date the movements were housed in metal frames, often ornate, with the pendulum swinging free below (wag-on-the-wall clocks). Volumes have been written on the history of clockmaking, but our concern is with clock cases. We begin, therefore, with the reign of William and Mary in England, when the grandfather clock came into being.

A few fully enclosed tall clocks were made by 1665, with short pendulums, but these were rare. Generally speaking, the grandfather clock developed from the long-pendulum wag-on-the-wall, and this development began at the top. Hoods of fine woods were used first, and the extension of casing to enclose the pendulum followed. The evolution occurred in America at the same time as in England, but most American tall-clock cases followed the English styles. William and Mary, Queen Anne, and Chippendale style features are duly found in their respective periods, but by no means *only* in their periods. Pleasing lines and types of ornament were carried over and mingled with those of a later day. Clocks have been found whose styles were as much as one hundred years old when they were made.

If confusion exists as to styles, it is even greater as to makers. A few great names stand out: the Willards, the Terrys, and others; but although an expert may be able to identify the maker of a particular clock, the task is hopeless for an amateur. The name on the dial may tell the story, but more likely it tells only a part of it. Early makers frequently imported either parts or complete movements, and printed their own names on the dials. Many early clocks were made on order, and the name on the dial may be that of the customer, or of the dealer who sold it, rather than that of the maker either of the movement or of the case. The following comments, therefore, will apply only in the most general sense, bearing in mind the great prevalence of exceptions.

From 1680 to 1710, cases were simple. Doors were sometimes paneled, sometimes plain. Hoods were plain, or with twist-turned or twist-carved pillars. Bottoms stood flat on the floor, without feet. From 1700 to 1710, we find "bell tops," twist pillars, bottoms resting on the floor or on bun feet. These features were typical of the William and Mary style.

The Queen Anne period introduced arched tops and rounded tops, generally finished with molding. Pillars on hoods were turned or carved. Feet were bun or ball type, a few were ogee brackets. Doors were paneled, sometimes carved with sunburst or shell. Marquetry and lacquer were also used. From about 1725 on, hood tops were increasingly elaborate. Arched tops were often ornamented with fretwork, and the broken arch made its appearance, to develop later into the popular scroll top. Finials of brass or turned wood were used, and ogee feet became popular. Carving was sometimes used on the hood face panel as well as on the door panel.

From 1750 on we find the Georgian influence (including Chippendale) in scroll tops, fine carving on the hood fronts, carved finials, shell-carved and block-front doors, inlay, fluted pillars.

Most American tall clocks were made between 1760 and 1840, although some were made as early as 1740, especially in the Philadelphia and Boston areas. Chippendale, Adam, Hepplewhite, Sheraton, and Directoire styles are all found, and usually mixed. A clock case true to a single period in every detail is rare. By 1800, wooden clock movements were widely used, and these, being infinitely cheaper, brought clocks within the reach of a much wider market. Often such movements were bought and used for many years before the owner could afford to have a case made by a local or itinerant cabinetmaker. Woods used included pine, cherry, maple, and fruit woods, as well as walnut and mahogany. Poplar was sometimes used, veneered or painted. Veneer was also occasionally applied over fine woods; one clock known to the author is of fine tiger maple overlaid with mahogany veneer. Presumably the cabinet maker happened to have the maple on hand, while his customer preferred a mahogany finish.

This was the golden age of fine cabinetwork, and many famous furniture makers made clock cases. The Philadelphia masters, including Savery and Gostelow; the Newport Goddards and Townsends; Duncan Phyfe of New York, Chapin of Connecticut, and the fine craftsmen of Boston and Salem, all made cases which are eagerly sought and treasured today. In addition, the famous clockmakers often designed and made their own cases, or had them made by employees.

While most tall-case clocks were of the size known as "grandfather," some clocks were made ranging from three feet to sixty-four inches in height. These are called "grandmother clocks," and are highly prized for their rarity. Unfortunately, this scarcity has led to a wide variety of fake "grandmother clocks," including cut-down "grandfathers."

There have been numerous types of wall and bracket clocks, but the banjo clock is by far the most popular today, as it was in its own day. Banjo clocks first appeared about 1800, and were made by Simon Willard, his relatives and associates, and a host of imitators. The best of these clocks were expensive, and true originals are rare. So many reproductions have been made, however, that essential parts may easily be purchased.

In addition to the banjo clocks for which they became famous, and grandfather clocks, the Willards also made fine shelf clocks, notably the type called the Massachusetts shelf clock. These were of fine workmanship, and made to sell to the rich, as were all clocks up to this time. In the early 1800's, however, a young clockmaker named Eli Terry conceived the idea of making attractive shelf clocks by mass-production methods, to sell at the unheard-of low retail price of $15. After considerable experiment, Terry developed the pillar-and-scroll shelf clock which became popular for its beauty as well as for its practicality. Terry-type clocks were made by many copiers, including Seth Thomas, an employee of Terry's who later became a famous clockmaker in his own right. Terry's Patent Clock is prized by collectors and by lovers of beauty in antiques, but his great claim to fame is as the father of mass production in the clockmaking field. Before his time, only one family in ten in the United States owned a clock. Terry led the way in making good timepieces available to all.

Early shelf clocks usually had glass doors covering the base, or pendulum box, as well as the dial. The lower sections of these doors were decorated with landscapes, portraits, or other designs painted in reverse on the back of the glass. Sometimes the art work was very fine, but in many cases it has not survived the wear of years and excessive housewifely zeal. Old clocks with damaged paintings are frequently restored by specialists in the art of reverse painting on glass.

The advent of cheap mirror glass had profound effects upon furniture forms and decoration. As might be expected, mirrors were used on clock cases in a number of ways. Often the mirror was placed in the lower door, as substitute for a painting. Other makers ambitiously combined both a painting and a mirror, in a space not overlarge for one. Hanging clocks sometimes included so much mirror that it is a question whether they should be classed as clocks with mirrors, or as mirrors with clocks. Like all fads, this one died out, and mirror clocks are now seldom seen. Original wall-type examples are rare and much sought after by collectors, particularly the New Hampshire mirror clocks, one of which is illustrated in *Plate 102*. Cases of this type are relatively easy to make, and combine double utility with decorative effect.

There are, of course, innumerable types of antique clocks other than those mentioned here. Many volumes have been written on clocks alone, and we have not attempted to do more than to skim the cream of the subject. The clocks illustrated in the following pages are the best examples (we believe) of types which are not only beautiful in themselves but also lend themselves particularly well to reproduction.

———◆———

Plates 92 and *93* illustrate a tall clock which in most features is characteristic of the William and Mary style. It is appropriate for a brass-dial movement. The top is flat, with a heavy mitered cornice. Mitered moldings are also used at top and bottom of the waist, and at the base.

The hood columns are of a simple pattern, with a turned center section and hand-shaped double blocks at each end. Instead of detached full columns, such as were used on later clocks, the front columns are cut so as to fit around the edges of the door (see *Figure A, Plate 93*). Quarter-columns are used at the back corners.

The waist is plain except for the mitering of the front frame, the arch of the door, and the elaborate brass escutcheon. The base is perfectly plain and rests on a continuous foot. Clocks of this early period were usually of walnut or of cherry.

All tall-clock cases are constructed in two sections. The base and waist form one section, with a one-piece back which extends to the hood top. The shelf which supports the clock movement rests upon the top edges of the side panels, which extend above the upper waist molding, or apron, far enough for this purpose. It is anchored with screws. The hood is a separate removable section which is not attached to the case in any way. It has no back and no bottom panel.

The base (except for the back) should be made first. This section is marked *Figure D* on the side-view drawing, *Plate 92,* and also on the cross-section plan, *Plate 93.* Cut the front and sides to size, then mill a ⅛″ by ⅛″ tongue on the front edge of each side, and a corresponding groove in the inside surface of the front ("Tongue and Groove Joints," Chapter I). Rabbet the back edges of the sides to receive the thickness of the backboard (½″). Glue the tongue-and-groove joints, and reinforce them with rub blocks glued into the inside angles at close intervals. Sand the outside surfaces of the base. Make and insert the bottom, supporting it with rub blocks inside the case.

Make and attach the continuous foot, which includes the base molding. Instructions for making bracket feet and for cutting moldings will be found in Chapter I. In this case the two operations are combined to make a single piece. A full-size cross-section pattern is marked *M4, Plate 93.* Sand the foot and molding, then attach to the base with glue and brads, placing a corner block in the angle of each front foot, and a supporting block on the inside surface of each back foot. The main support of the case is provided by these blocks rather than by the feet themselves.

Cut the four pieces of the waist front frame with mitered corners as shown in the front-view drawing, *Plate 92.* The lower edge of the top piece should be band-sawed to the arch shape. The door opening should be ¼″ narrower and ¼″ shorter than the door to allow for an overlap of ⅛″ at each edge. Join the mitered corners with glue, and reinforce with splines (see "Miter Joints," Chapter I).

The waist sides should be cut longer than the front, since they extend up inside the hood to support the movement shelf. The required length may be determined by the height of the movement support indicated in the cross-section side view, *Plate 92.* Mill the sides and front for ⅛″ by ⅛″ tongue-and-groove joints. Rabbet the back edges of the sides. Assemble the front and sides with glue, and reinforce with rub blocks closely spaced (see cross-section *C, Plate 93*). Sand the outside surfaces of the waist.

Measure the waist (outside measurement) and the base (inside measurement) at front and sides. Make a frame to fill the space between the lower

Plate 92

FLAT-TOP GRANDFATHER CLOCK

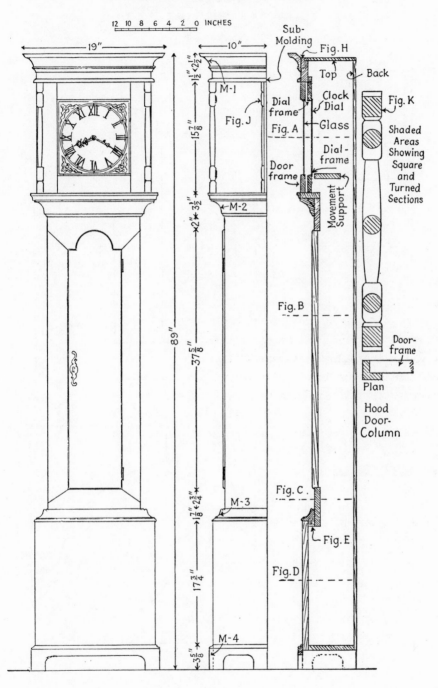

12 10 8 6 4 2 0 INCHES

19"

10"

Sub-Molding

Fig. H

Top

Back

$1\frac{1}{2}" \langle 2\frac{1}{2}" \rightarrow$

M-1

Fig. J

Dial frame

Fig. A

Clock Dial

Glass

Fig. K

Shaded Areas Showing Square and Turned Sections

$15\frac{7}{8}"$

Dial-frame

Door frame

Movement Support

$\leftarrow 2" \rightarrow 3\frac{1}{2}"$

M-2

89"

$37\frac{5}{8}"$

Fig. B

Door-frame

Plan

Hood Door-Column

$\frac{7}{8}" \leftarrow 2\frac{3}{4}" \rightarrow$

M-3

Fig. C

Fig. E

$17\frac{3}{4}"$

Fig. D

$\frac{3\frac{5}{8}"}$

M-4

213

Plate 93
FLAT-TOP GRANDFATHER CLOCK

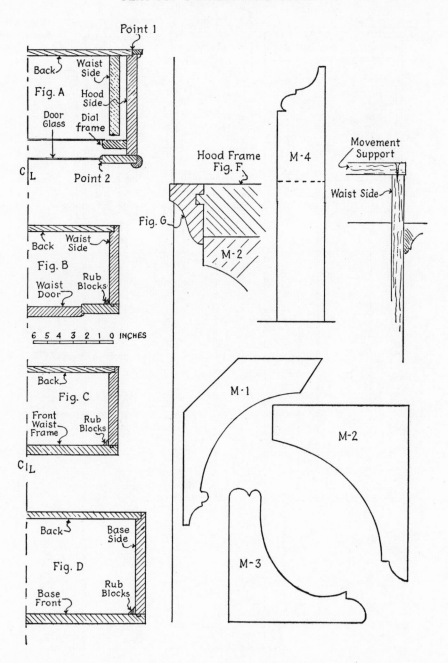

Point 1

Back

Waist Side

Fig. A

Hood Side

Door Glass

Dial frame

C L   Point 2

Back

Waist Side

Fig. B

Waist Door

Rub Blocks

6 5 4 3 2 1 0 INCHES

Back

Fig. C

Front Waist Frame

Rub Blocks

C L

Back

Base Side

Fig. D

Base Front

Rub Blocks

Hood Frame Fig. F

M·4

Movement Support

Waist Side

Fig. G

M·2

M·1

M-2

M-3

214

edge of the waist and the upper edge of the base (see *Figure E* in the side-view cross section, *Plate 92*). Attach this spacer frame inside the base top with screws. Insert the waist and fasten it with screws from the inside into the spacer frame. Use care to align the waist properly, so that it will stand even and straight above the base when in upright position.

Make the molding for the angle between waist and base (*M3, Plate 93*). Attach this with screws from inside the waist, and with brads through the molding into the base. The corners are mitered.

Next, make the molding for the waist top (*M2, Plate 93*). This molding serves as the platform or support for the hood, in addition to its decorative function. It is usually called the "apron." It should be securely fastened by screws from inside the waist, as well as by glue.

The hood, or bonnet, is constructed next. Its base is formed by three frame pieces (front and sides) which are designed to fit over and rest upon the apron. Three-quarter-inch wood is usually used. The sides of the frame are not shortened to fit inside the case back, but extend through the back, ending flush with the lip edge of the rabbeted sides. Openings will be cut in the back for the frame ends. This provides a stop against tilting of the hood when it is in position on the case. Assemble the base frame with tongue-and-groove joints, cutting the tongues on the side pieces, the grooves in the inside edge of the front strip. Make the frame $\frac{1}{8}''$ larger than the apron (upper waist molding), then cut a $\frac{1}{8}''$ tongue on all three sides of the outside frame edge (see *Figure F* in the molding cross section, *Plate 93*).

Next make the trim molding (*Figure G* in the molding cross section). This molding is $\frac{5}{8}''$ wide and $\frac{7}{8}''$ thick ($\frac{1}{8}''$ thicker than the frame). Groove the back of the molding to fit the tongue of the frame, placing the groove so that the molding will fit flush with the frame top, with a $\frac{1}{8}''$ lip projecting below the bottom frame edge. This lip will cover the division between hood and waist when the hood is in position on the case. Miter the corners, and attach the molding to the hood base frame with glue and brads.

Now make the hood sides, using $\frac{3}{4}''$ wood. Study the cross-section plan marked *Figure A* in *Plate 93*. The rear edges of the two sides must be rabbeted to receive the $\frac{1}{2}''$ thickness of the back when the hood is mounted on the case. A part of this rabbet will be formed by the vertical rear corner piece at each side of the hood (*Point No. 1* in *Figure A*). Mark the position of the hood sides on the hood base frame; cut grooves in the frame and corresponding tongues on the sides. Glue the sides in place on the base frame. Screws may be driven from the bottom of the frame up into the sides for added strength, although this was not usually done on antique clocks.

Next, measure and install the front panel marked *Figure H* on the cross-section side view, *Plate 92*. This piece is ¾″ thick by 3½″ high. The length is determined by the width of the hood before the upper moldings are applied. Rabbet the top edge of the strip for the ½″ top or roof board, as shown in *Figure H*. Cut recesses in the front edges of the side panels to receive the ends of the front panel (¾″ by 3½″). Attach the front panel to the sides with screws, placing the screws so as to be later covered by the decorative moldings.

Cut the ½″ top board to size. This piece projects ⅜″ beyond the back edges of the sides, to cover the thickness of the corner pieces and corresponding extensions of the moldings (see next paragraph). Attach the top to the sides and the front panel with screws. Sand all outside surfaces.

Now refer to *Point 1* on *Figure A,* and note the corner piece which projects at each side to form an angle for the quarter-column. This vertical piece is ⅜″ thick by ⅞″ wide. Its length is the distance from the hood base to the underside of the quarter-round submolding. Cut the two pieces (one for each side), sand them, and attach to the rear edges of the sides with glue and brads. This will leave a space ⅜″ wide above each corner piece, which must be filled. Part of this will be covered by the submolding and the cornice; the remaining gap may be filled with a close-fitting strip, fastened with glue.

The cornice molding (*M1, Plate 93*) should next be made to fit the top of the hood at front and sides. The sides extend to cover the thickness of the corner pieces, as explained in the preceding paragraph. The front corners are mitered. Attach the molding with glue and with screws from inside the hood. Make the quarter-round submolding, miter the corners, and attach with brads at the bottom edge of the front panel and across the sides (*Plate 92,* all three drawings).

The hood doorframe is made of ⅝″ wood, with tongue-and-groove construction. Refer to *Point 2, Figure A*. Note that the inner edge of the frame has a molded lip which projects over the edge of the glass pane on the outside, while the inside is rabbeted to receive the glass and putty.

The front columns are part of the door assembly. A detail drawing of the column, *Figure K,* is included in *Plate 92*. Turn the front columns and the back quarter-columns by the same pattern (see Chapter I for quarter-column procedure).

The quarter-columns are glued into the angles formed by the rear corner pieces and the hood sides (*Figure J, Plate 92,* side view). The front columns are turned as full columns, after which a quarter or pie slice is cut from each. This forms a right-angled opening which fits around the side edges of the door frame (*Figure A, Plate 93*). Attach the columns to the frame with glue and brads. Install hinges at the back of the right-hand column as indicated in *Plate 92,* side view. No knob is required to open the door, since the left-hand column provides a handhold. A simple brass latch may be placed on the left side to hold the door closed.

Every grandfather clock must have a dial frame, which is seen only when the hood door is opened. Its purpose is to serve both as a stop and as a decorative frame for the clock dial. In appearance it is a duplicate of the hood doorframe, and it is constructed in exactly the same way, except for its dimensions. Since the dial frame fits inside the hood sides, its width is determined by the inside measurement of the hood width. Its height must be sufficient to project upward beyond the lower edge of the hood front panel (cross-section side view, *Plate 92*). The frame should be glued to the front panel, and attached to the sides with rub blocks. It may be made and placed before the front panel is attached, or inserted and attached after assembly.

The waist door should be made of $\frac{7}{8}''$ wood, cut to the shape shown in the front view, *Plate 92.* The door should be $\frac{1}{4}''$ longer and $\frac{1}{4}''$ wider than the opening in the case, so as to overlap the edge of the opening $\frac{1}{8}''$ all around.

Refer to *Figure B, Plate 93.* Note that the door edge is rabbeted on the inside to fit the door opening, leaving a $\frac{1}{8}''$ lip all around. Cut a small thumbnail molding on the lip. Sand the door, fit the hinges, then install the lock.

The back of the case is a solid piece from the bottom of the base to the underside of the hood top. It may be made from a single board, or from several boards glued together. One-half-inch wood should be used. Lay out the outline in pencil to conform to the varied measurements of the base, waist, and hood. The finished back should fit inside the rabbeted back edges of the side panels. An opening must be cut at each side for the hood base frame. Attach the back to the case with screws or nails. Place the hood in position, and work down the edges of the back, if necessary, to achieve a smooth fit. Apply the desired finish to the entire case, then permanently attach the hardware, including the brass escutcheons shown in the front-view drawing.

The movement support shelf usually comes with the movement, or is made to fit it. It is installed by resting the ends on the upper edges of the case sides (see detail drawing, *Plate 93*). Screws may be inserted if desired.

———◆———

The grandfather clock in *Plates 94* and *95* has a beautifully proportioned mahogany case, with fine fan inlay in the panel corners of the waist door and base. The top is arched for a moon-dial movement, and is ornamented with fretwork. The finials are of brass, mounted on wooden finial blocks. The hood front columns and the waist quarter-columns are stop-fluted, with ⅛″ brass rods forming the stops. These are shown in detail drawings in *Plate 95*. Brass caps and bases are used on all columns. Door hinges and escutcheons are also of brass.

Unlike those of the preceding clock, the hood front columns are full detached pillars, set between the cornice and the base molding of the hood. Quarter-columns are set into angles between the hood sides and back corner strips.

The arch shape of the top, cornice moldings, front frame, and hood door conforms to that of the moon dial. A similar arch is cut over the small window in each side panel.

Construction of tall-clock cases is discussed in detail in the preceding text (*Plates 92* and *93*). Details will not be repeated here, but points of difference will be noted.

Construct the base as described for *Plates 92* and *93*. After assembly, inlay the base front with line and fan inlay as shown in the detail drawing, *Plate 95*. Inlaying procedure is discussed in Chapter I. Sand the outside surfaces.

The base molding is the same as that in *Plates 92* and *93*, without the foot. Make and attach the ogee feet as instructed in "Construction of Bracket Feet," Chapter I.

Procedure in making the waist is similar to that for *Plates 92* and *93*, except for the front corner assembly, which is shown in a detail drawing, *Figure D, Plate 95*. This corner assembly differs from that used for ordinary quarter-columns. In this case the fluting must extend to the bottom of the column, to permit insertion of the brass rods. Square blocks are then inserted to complete the corner above and below the column.

Prepare all the members of the waist (except moldings) before starting assembly. The waist front frame is made with perpendicular tongue-and-groove joints rather than mitered as in *Plate 92*.

Instructions for making and fluting quarter-columns will be found in Chapter I. Study the detail drawings of the columns in *Plate 95*. Use the measurements given on the waist-column drawing.

Rabbet the back edges of the sides for the ½″ back. Make the bracing strip shown in *Figure D, Plate 95*, to run the full length of the waist.

Assemble the sides, front, and fluted quarter-columns * with the bracing strip, as shown in *Figure D*. Use screws (placed as shown), as well as glue. Insert

---

* If preferred, the quarter-columns and lower end blocks may be prepared but not assembled until after the finish has been applied.

Plate 94

ARCHED TOP GRANDFATHER CLOCK

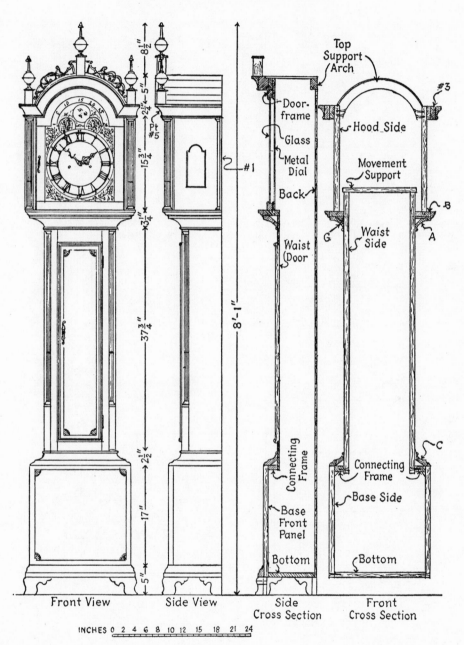

Front View   Side View   Side Cross Section   Front Cross Section

INCHES 0 2 4 6 8 10 12 15 18 21 24

Plate 95
ARCHED TOP GRANDFATHER CLOCK

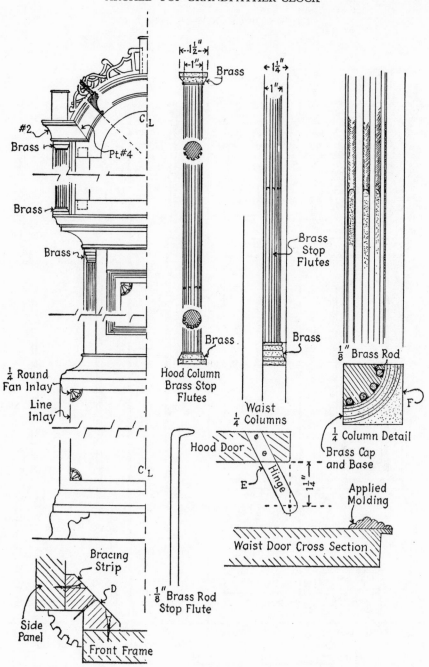

#2
Brass

Brass

Pt.#4

C_L

Brass

Brass

¼ Round
Fan Inlay

Line
Inlay

C_L

Brass

$1\frac{1}{2}''$

$1''$

Brass

Hood Column
Brass Stop
Flutes

Brass

$1\frac{1}{4}''$

$1''$

Brass
Stop
Flutes

Brass

Waist
¼ Columns

$\frac{1}{8}''$ Brass Rod

F

¼ Column Detail

Brass Cap
and Base

Hood Door

E

Hinge

$1\frac{1}{4}''$

Applied
Molding

Waist Door Cross Section

Bracing
Strip

D

Side
Panel

Front Frame

$\frac{1}{8}''$ Brass Rod
Stop Flute

220

the ⅛″ brass flute stops from the bottom, as indicated in the column-detail drawings. Fit brass caps at top and bottom of each quarter-column (*Figure F*).

Measure the open corner spaces above and below the columns, and make square blocks to fit these spaces, completing a perfect corner. Attach the blocks to the sides and bracing strip with glue and screws, in the same manner as the quarter-columns. Sand all outside surfaces.

Fit the waist into the base top as described for *Plate 92*. Since the connecting frame for this case is wider, strengthen the assembly with rub blocks glued and screwed in the angle as shown in the cross-section front view, *Plate 94*. Make, miter, and apply the molding shown in *Figure C, Plate 94*.

The apron (upper waist molding) may be a solid piece, as shown in *Plate 93*, *M2*, or it may be constructed as shown in *Figure A, Plate 94*. In the latter case the upper edge of the surface molding is rabbeted, and a flat strip, ½″ thick, is inserted to fill the gap between molding and case. The strip is fastened to the waist with screws from the inside, and to the molding with small screws driven down through the strip into the molding.

With the lower case complete except for the door, the next step is to construct the hood. Study the cross-section drawings in *Plate 94*. The hood base frame is indicated at *B*. This frame (front and two sides) is constructed first. The mitered frame molding is next made and applied, after which the hood sides are milled and joined to the frame. Follow the detailed instructions for these members in the preceding text (*Plate 92*), with the following exceptions:

The hood sides have small arched windows, as shown in the side view, *Plate 94*. The window openings must be cut out and rabbeted on the inside edge for glass and putty, before assembly. The outside surface of the lip around the opening should be cut with a narrow thumbnail molding, or rounded.

The fluted columns at the front of the hood are not attached to the door, but are set apart. Therefore, the outside front edges of the hood sides are exposed. These should be cut with a thumbnail molding before assembly. The inside front edges should be rabbeted to receive the door. The rabbet is ½″ deep by ⅜″ wide; thus the ⅞″ door frame will protrude ⅜″ from the front line of the molded lip. Sand all outside surfaces, then assemble the base frame, frame molding, and sides.

The dial frame should now be made, sanded, and attached. The purpose and construction of this frame are explained in the preceding text. In this case the inside measurements of the frame (including the arch) duplicate the inside measurements of the hood door, while the outside must be ⅜″ narrower to fit inside the hood sides, and the height is the full height of the hood. It is of mortise-and-tenon construction, and is attached to the sides with rub blocks.

The next step is to construct the front arch frame. This does not include the molding. It is economical and practical to glue pieces of mahogany together to form a rough arch, then cut the arch frame, rather than to cut it from a single large piece. The horizontal ends at each side of the arch (*Point No. 2, Plate 95*) are cut in one piece with the arch. When completed, with molding, the arch must project forward from the dial frame a distance slightly greater than the depth of the hood base frame and molding. On this clock the arch frame (without the arch molding) projects 2⅝″ from the dial frame. The horizontal extensions at the sides (built out with filler strips behind the solid ends, as shown at *Point 3, Plate 94*) correspond to the width of the base frame. After cutting and sanding the arch frame, attach it to the dial frame and the front edges of the hood sides with glue and screws. Then make and attach the filler strips at the top of the side panels, behind the horizontal extensions of the arch frame (*Point 3*).

The top support arch at the rear of the hood is of ⅞″ wood. It should be cut with the same outside radius as that of the front arch, but with an inside radius 2″ less, to fit over the back of the case when the hood is mounted on the clock. There are no horizontal side extensions on this piece. The ends are cut to fit into the rabbets on the back edges of the hood sides. Attach this arch with screws into the sides, as shown in the cross-section front view, *Plate 94.*

Now determine the measurement for the top from front to back (outside measurement across both arches), and cut strips of ⅜″ wood to this length. Build the top on the supporting arches, using glue and small screws or nails. Bevel the edges of the strips as required to make a perfect fit. Plane and sand the surface to a smooth curve.

The arch molding may, of course, be cut from solid wood, but a more economical method is to glue up a perfect circle from pieces of 1″ mahogany. The radius of the circle should be not less than the outside radius of the front arch on the hood. Mark the arch radius on the circle, and band-saw the correct outline. Then attach the circle to the face plate of a lathe, and turn the molding to the pattern indicated in cross section on the detail drawing, *Plate 95.* When finished, cut the required arc from the circle, sawing the ends at the proper angle for the miter joint (*Point 4, Plate 95*). Attach the molding to the arch frame with glue and brads. Shape enough straight molding for the horizontal sections on the front and sides (*Point 2, Plate 95,* and *Point 5,* side view, *Plate 94*). Cut these pieces with mitered corners, and attach with glue and brads.

The finial blocks should be made next. These are plain rectangular blocks, grooved for the ends of the fretwork. The central block has a vertical groove on each side; the end blocks are grooved only on the inside. Make square wooden caps, glue and brad them to the blocks, and drill a small hole in each for the screw shafts of the brass finials.

Make a pattern for the fretwork. This may be drawn on paper and pasted to the wood, or it may be drawn directly on the wood. Saw the two fretwork pieces at the same time, using two layers of wood with the pattern uppermost. Use a jigsaw or coping saw to cut the design, then smooth it with small files and sandpaper.

Sand the finial blocks, bore a dowel hole in the base of each block, and glue in a ⅜″ dowel. Bore matching dowel holes in the top of the front arch frame. Correct positions for the finial blocks are shown in the drawings. Glue the central block in place, insert the fretwork, then glue the end blocks.

Make the hood doorframe with mortise-and-tenon joints, as shown in *Plate 95*. The frame should be ⅞″ thick, the top piece being arch-shaped to fit the opening. Rabbet the inner edges for glass and putty, and mold the lip to a quarter-round. Install the lock.

Hood doors on grandfather clocks are usually attached with brass strips at top and bottom rather than with hinges. These strips may be cut from brass to the shape shown in *Figure E, Plate 95*. Drill screw holes in the strips and attach them with small brass screws, diagonally across the door edges as shown: one at the top right-hand corner and one at the bottom. Set the door in place and mark the position of the screw hole on the hood frame. The upper hanger will be screwed to the underside of the applied molding, the lower to the hood base frame. These screws should not be driven in too tightly, since the hangers must pivot on them when the hood door is opened. After fitting the door in place, mark the position of the lock and cut a groove on the inside edge of the door opening to engage the tongue of the lock.

Now make the two vertical back-corner strips for the hood. These pieces project from the sides between the top molding and the base frame, forming the angles for the quarter-round pillars at the back of the hood. Each piece is 1½″ wide by ⅜″ thick. The length is determined by measurement between the underside of the top molding and the base. Similar strips are described in the preceding text, and illustrated in *Figure A, Point 1, Plate 93*. In this case, however, the strips are glued to the hood sides flush with the back edge, rather than behind the edge.

Turn the hood columns to the measurements given in the detail drawing, *Plate 95*. Flute them a little more than halfway around, as shown in cross section on the drawing. The flutes run the full length of the column. Determine the length by accurate measurement between the underside of the top molding and the base frame. Turn the ends to fit the openings in the brass caps to be used. The back quarter-columns on the hood are plain turnings (see side view, *Plate 94*).

Cut the waist door panel ¼″ wider and ¼″ longer than the opening in the door frame, to allow for a ⅛″ overlap all around. Rabbet the inside edge to fit the door opening, as shown in the waist door cross section, *Plate 95*. Inlay the panel with line and fan inlay (*Plate 94,* front view). Sand to finish smoothness, then make and apply the edge molding shown in the waist door cross section, *Plate 95*. Cut as required to install the brass hinges and lock.

Make and attach the case back as described in the preceding text, then apply the desired finish to the case, hood, and columns. After finishing, complete the hood columns by inserting the brass flute stops and mounting the brass caps and bases. Holes are provided in the brass castings for small screws, to attach the columns to the hood. Waist quarter-columns may be attached with screws from the inside, after finish, and the flute-stop rods inserted as the next operation. Cap and base castings are fastened with screws. The end blocks below the quarter-columns are then attached with screws from inside. Hinges, locks, and escutcheons are permanently attached after finishing. Brass ball finials are equipped with screw shanks for mounting.

———◆———

A fine mahogany grandfather clock in the Philadelphia Chippendale style is shown in *Plates 96* and *97*. The hood top is a scroll, or broken arch, and is unusually well proportioned. The finials are of brass, mounted on fluted wooden blocks. The center finial block tapers gracefully toward the arch cornice. The hood front frame and door are arched, like the cornice, to conform to the shape of a moon dial. The hood columns are slender turned posts without fluting. Waist and base quarter-columns are fluted, with turned rings above and below the fluting, and the ends left square. The waist door and base panel are shaped at the top in an attractively modified arch.

Construction of this clock follows the procedures described in the preceding text (*Plates 94* and *95*), except for the following points of difference:

The front of the base is composed of a frame (tongue-and-groove joined) with a molded panel set over the opening. A cross section of the panel is shown in *Plate 97*. The panel overlaps the opening ⅜″ or more all around. There is no inlay.

Quarter-columns are used both on base and on waist, requiring special front-corner assembly. In the case of the preceding clock waist, the assembly was complicated by the sectional construction of the columns, a necessary provision for inserting brass stop flutes. On this clock, however, brass stop flutes are not used, and the quarter-columns are solid from top to bottom, including the square ends as well as the turned and fluted sections. They can therefore be used as corner posts, with tongue-and-groove joints for the sides and front, as shown in the corner cross section, *Figure C, Plate 97*. The outside corner is shown in *Figure D*.

The hood top, or roof board, is flat rather than arched. There is therefore no top support arch. The upper section of the hood is built out to overhang the lower at front and sides, so that the outer edge of the scroll molding extends slightly beyond the outer edge of the hood base molding.

Follow the instructions in the text for *Plates 94* and *95* to make the hood base frame, molding, and sides. (The overhang will be added later.) All dimensions must be figured from *Plates 96* and *97*.

The dial frame is shown in *Figure B, Plate 97*, and also in the detail drawing of the hood door. Note that the dial opening is slightly smaller than the glass opening in the door. Both openings are arched. The top outside edge of the dial frame does not follow the arch shape, however, but is cut straight to fit under the flat roof board. The width is measured to fit between the hood sides. Assemble the dial frame with mortise-and-tenon joints, sand to finish smoothness, and attach to the hood sides with rub blocks.

The face panel of the hood is set forward, so that the applied molding at its lower edge will be in line with the molded edge of the hood base frame. This creates a gap between the face panel and the dial frame. A piece called the arch facing (*Figure B, Plate 97*) is made to fill this gap. The top and side edges of this piece are identical with those of the dial frame, but the lower edge follows the shape of the face panel. Sand this piece and attach it in front of the dial frame.

The overhanging upper section of the hood is made next. On this particular clock the overhang is not great, and may therefore be accomplished by attaching the upper side panels directly to the hood sides. Where the design of a clock requires a greater depth of overhang, a spacing strip is first attached to the hood sides, and the outer panels are then attached to the spacer. The lower edge of the spacer is sometimes molded, to project and form part of the decorative scheme of the hood.

The front face panel of the hood is band-sawed to the shape indicated in the front view. Its lower edge is cut out for the arch above the door; the upper edge is shaped to form a backing for the scroll molding (including rosettes) and

Plate 96

SCROLL-TOP GRANDFATHER CLOCK

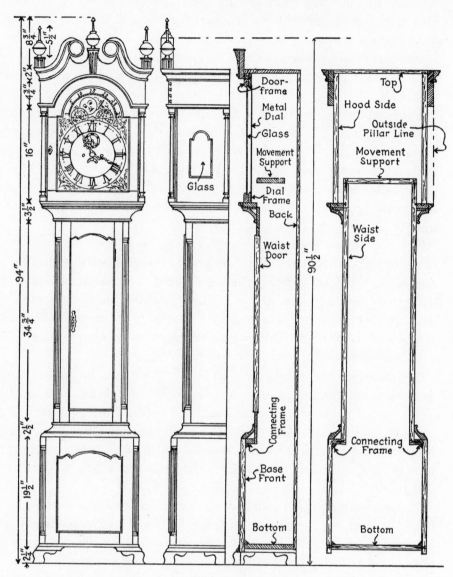

INCHES 0 2 4 6 8 10 12 15 18 21 24

226

Plate 97

SCROLL-TOP GRANDFATHER CLOCK

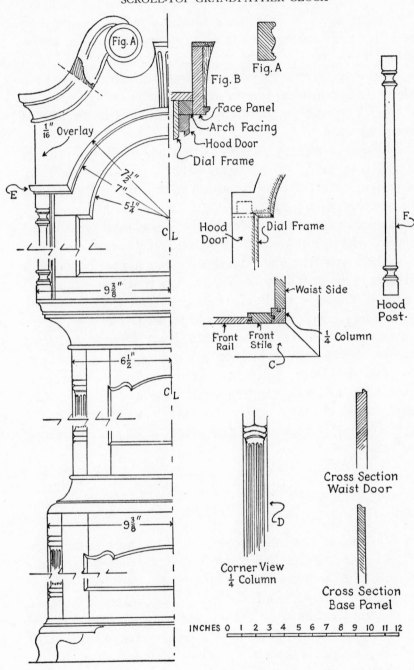

Fig. A

Fig. B

Fig. A

Face Panel

Arch Facing

Hood Door

Dial Frame

$\frac{1}{16}$" Overlay

E

$7\frac{1}{2}$"

7"

$5\frac{1}{4}$"

C L

Hood Door

Dial Frame

Waist Side

Front Rail

Front Stile

$\frac{1}{4}$ Column

C

$9\frac{3}{8}$"

$6\frac{1}{2}$"

C L

$9\frac{3}{8}$"

F

Hood Post.

Cross Section Waist Door

D

Corner View $\frac{1}{4}$ Column

Cross Section Base Panel

INCHES 0 1 2 3 4 5 6 7 8 9 10 11 12

227

the center finial support. The side edges are dovetailed on the back surface, and the front edges of the upper side panels are dovetailed to fit (see side view, *Plate 96*). Instructions for making dovetail joints are included in the section "Joinery," Chapter I.

The lower edge of the overhang (sides and front, including the arch) is trimmed with an applied molding, shown in cross section in *Figure B*. The corners are mitered. The outer edge of this molding is in line with the molded edge of the hood base frame.

The scroll molding may be partly cut with a shaper and finished by hand, or it may be cut entirely by hand. The rosettes are turned (cross section in *Figure A*). They are doweled (one dowel in the center) to turned bosses, which are screwed to the face panel from the back.

The side finials are mounted on wooden blocks. These are first made and fluted, then covered with square wooden caps bradded on. They are attached to the hood with ⅜″ dowels. The center finial support is formed by gluing a shaped, fluted piece to the central rise of the front face panel (cross-section *B*, *Plate 97*). The top of each block is drilled for the screw shank of the brass finial.

The hood pillars are plain turnings, as shown in *Figure F*. The same pattern is used to turn the quarter-pillars at the back of the hood. These are quartered from the same diameter as that of the front posts (see quarter-column procedure, under "Half- and Quarter-Columns," Chapter I). Brass caps and bases are not used; the pillars are cut to exact length and glued in place.

After finishing, attach the hood door as described and illustrated for the preceding clock (*Plate 94*). Permanently attach hinges, locks, and escutcheons, and mount the finials.

———◆———

The clock in *Plate 98* is an unusually fine example of the rare type known as "grandmother." Its style is of the Chippendale period. Carving details of the wooden finial and of the exceptionally beautiful shell decoration on waist and base are characteristic of John Goddard, the master cabinetmaker of Newport, Rhode Island. The feet are dainty ogee brackets, but without the scroll typical of the later Goddard foot. (A brief discussion of Goddard may be found under "Block-Front Chest," Chapter VII.)

The hood pillars and the waist quarter-columns are stop fluted. Unlike *Plate 94*, the flute stops are not brass, but are carved in the wood. This process is described in Chapter I. Half cross sections of the pillars are shown in a detail drawing, *Plate 98*. The front corners of the base are chamfered, with a finely molded taper at the lower end of the chamfer and over the mitered molding at the top. Mitered moldings are also used at the bottom of the base and at the top of the waist.

Read the text and study the drawings in *Plates 92* and *93*, for general tall-clock construction. Follow the procedures described except for modifications required by the different design of the clock, as follows:

The base front is of frame construction, with a wide top piece as shown in the front view, *Plate 98*. It is tongue-and-groove joined. The panel overlaps the frame opening not less than ¾" all around (see cross-section *A*). It may be attached by screws (no glue) from the inside of the base front frame. The shell design is carved in one piece with the panel (see "Carving," Chapter I). *Figure E* shows both surface and cross section of the shell. After assembling the base, chamfer the front corners as shown in the front and side views.

The feet are made separately from the base molding ("Construction of Bracket Feet," Chapter I).

The front-corner assembly of the waist is shown in cross-sections *B* and *C*, *Plate 98*. The quarter-columns are first turned, fluted, and stop fluted as shown in cross-section *D*. Instructions for these processes are given in Chapter I, in the sections on quarter-column procedure, fluting and reeding, and stop fluting. Square sections are left at top and bottom of the columns as shown in the front- and side-view drawings, *Plate 98*. The sides and front are joined to the quarter-columns with tongue and groove, reinforced with rub blocks glued into the inside angle at frequent intervals.

This clock has a groove milled across each side of the waist, to receive a tongue cut on the inner side edges of the hood base frame, as shown in *Figure K*. This method of construction ensures rigidity of the hood on the case. The tongue and groove must be sanded for a smooth, easy fit, to permit sliding the hood in place. The groove must be milled before assembling the waist. The side pieces of the hood base frame must be cut from wood wide enough to allow for the tongue, which is cut before assembling the frame.

The hood base frame and trim molding are constructed as for *Plate 92*. The hood sides, however, differ in two respects. Since the pillars are not attached to the door, the front edges of the sides must be milled for the door opening. The inside front edge is rabbeted to a depth of ½", so that the ⅞" doorframe will protrude ⅜" from the lip of the opening. The rabbet is ⅜" wide. The lip is molded as shown in cross-section *H*, *Plate 98*. Arched windows are cut in the sides, as shown in the side view. The window openings are rabbeted on the inside for glass and putty. The outside lip is molded.

Plate 98

GRANDMOTHER CLOCK

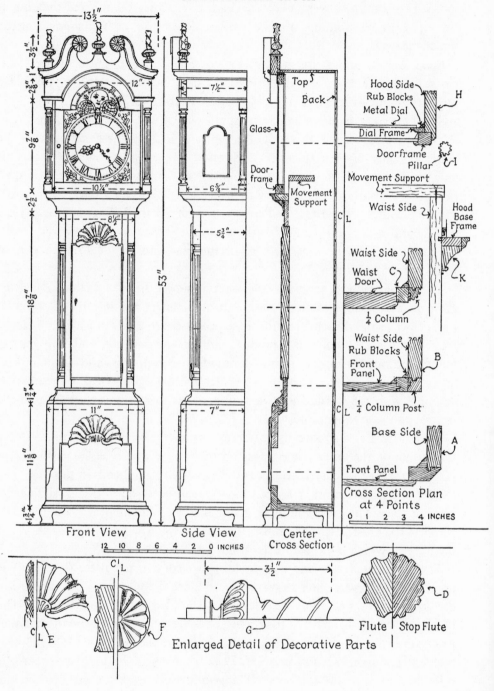

Front View   Side View   Center Cross Section

Enlarged Detail of Decorative Parts

The dial frame is made and attached as described in the preceding text, *Plates 96* and *97*, except that in this case the dial opening is exactly the same size as the glass opening in the hood door.

The construction of the overhanging upper sides and front is also described in the preceding text, *Plates 96* and *97*.

The profile shape of the scroll molding may be seen in the side view. The rosettes are carved after turning, as shown in the cross section and surface drawings, *Figure F*.

The side finial blocks are not fluted, but are otherwise made and attached as for *Plate 96*. The central block, however, is built out behind the facing panel rather than in front (see side-view cross section, *Plate 98*). The finials are of wood, turned and then carved (*Figure G*). A ⅜″ dowel is turned on the base of each finial to fit corresponding dowel holes in the finial blocks.

The four hood columns are full detached pillars, fluted all around, as shown in *Figure I*. The end blocks are left square. The length should be measured accurately to fit between the hood base frame and the overhanging upper section. They are attached with glue.

The hood doorframe, like the dial frame, is arched to expose the moon dial. The joints are mortise-and-tenon. Refer to the text and illustrations on *Plate 95* for details of fitting and attaching the door.

The waist door is similar to the base panel, except for its dimensions. The edges are rabbeted on the inside to fit the door opening, leaving a ⅛″ molded lip all around. This rabbet includes the half-circle outline of the shell, which laps an average of ½″.

All hardware is permanently attached after finishing. The hinges and the small knob on the hood door are brass. The waist door lock may be covered with ivory, brass, or wood inlay, or with a brass escutcheon.

———◆———

Plate 99 illustrates a Willard-type banjo clock and a suitable bracket. The finial is turned in the form of an acorn. This was a popular ornament, although many banjo clocks had brass finials of spire, urn, or eagle design, particularly of the latter after the War of 1812. The naval scene on the base is also a typical postwar motif. This is a reverse painting on glass, as is the waist decoration. Such paintings are made by artists who specialize in this type of work. Names of suppliers of these and other special clock parts and ornaments may be obtained from the American Clock and Watch Foundation, Box 881, York, Pennsylvania.

The back of the case is a single panel, cut to the banjo shape and with rounded edges projecting slightly beyond the top and sides. The round top, or drum, is usually cut from two blocks of wood and joined at the top center with glue, reinforced with a piece of closely woven cloth glued over the joint. It is fastened with screws through from the back, as are the other side panels. The front of the top is a round pane of clear glass set in a round frame, or bezel, which is usually of brass. Wood bezels were used on some early examples. Clocks with brass bezels frequently have a wooden ring, slightly larger than the bezel, attached to the front of the drum. A gap is left at the bottom of the ring to permit inserting the pendulum when the clock movement is installed. The bezel is hinged to one side, to form a door for winding and setting the clock.

The finial base is made separately from the case. It may be turned as part of the finial, but better procedure is to attach a separate base and mount the finial with a dowel.

The sides of the waist project slightly into the drum at the top. Rub blocks are used to reinforce the joining of drum and waist. The sides also project into the base, where they are similarly reinforced. Cheaper wood may be used to continue the side panels to the bottom inside the base, forming partitions for the weight channel. A tin-plate cover is attached across these partitions to separate the weight from the pendulum (see cross section). Note that the waist is slightly less deep than the drum and base (side view).

The sides, top, and bottom of the base are mitered together and reinforced with rub blocks, as shown in the open front view.

The front panels of both waist and base consist of frames enclosing the glass paintings. The frame strips are grooved for the rope molding, which may be purchased ready to use. The strips are joined to the frame corner blocks with tongue and groove. The base front is hinged to one side, forming a door. The waist front is fastened to the waist sides by means of small screws driven through lips projecting up behind the bezel and down into the base. These lips may be made in either of two ways. The top corner blocks of the waist front may be made from pieces with slightly larger vertical measurement, so that when the front surface is cut away to fit the curve of the bezel, a lip is left projecting up at the back. The lower corner blocks are similarly made with lips projecting downward. An alternative method is to cut the corner blocks to exact size, then recess the backs and attach wood or metal strips to form the lips.

The side arms are of brass, and may be purchased ready to attach. They are

Plate 99

BANJO CLOCK

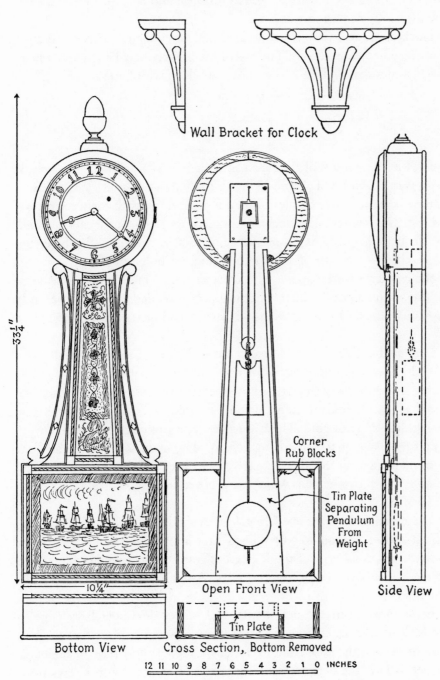

Wall Bracket for Clock

Corner
Rub Blocks

Tin Plate
Separating
Pendulum
From
Weight

Open Front View

Side View

$33\frac{1}{4}$"

$10\frac{1}{4}$"

Bottom View

Tin Plate

Cross Section, Bottom Removed

12 11 10 9 8 7 6 5 4 3 2 1 0 INCHES

233

fastened with thin brass nails. The desired finish should be applied to the wood before brass and glass parts are attached.

The bracket top, or platform, is molded and ornamented with small balls, which are attached with dowels. The rest of the bracket may be made in one or two pieces, as desired. Fluting and molding are done with hand tools.

----◆----

The clock in *Plate 100* is of the type usually called Massachusetts shelf clock. This style was a favorite of Aaron Willard, the famous Boston clockmaker.

Structurally, this clock resembles a miniature tall clock, with the waist section omitted. For this reason such clocks are sometimes erroneously called grandmother clocks. The hood is a separate unit, not attached to the base, but mounted securely by means of a sliding dovetail, as shown in *Figure D*.

Patriotic emblems were popular as decorative motifs after the War of 1812, and for this reason an eagle finial is not inappropriate, and may be more easily purchased than the authentic brass urn. Turned wood urns or acorns were also used.

The glass of the door is a single pane, but is divided into two sections by a painted gold line. The upper section is decorated with patriotic emblems and gold leaves, with a circle of clear glass in the center to expose the clock face. The lower section has the maker's name painted in gold on a henna-red oval. The scallops and leaves are of gold. These are all reverse paintings on glass.

The entire outside of the case is mahogany. The hood top projects at front and sides and has a rounded edge, veneered over the end grain. It is surmounted by a cresting, cut in two sections which are grooved into the central fluted finial block.

The base should be constructed first. Cut the sides to size and rabbet the inside front and back edges to a depth equal to the thickness of the false front and the back, respectively. Cut the false front from cheaper wood, sizing it to fit between the rabbeted edges of the sides. Assemble with glue and brads. Sand the sides.

Cut the bottom (from cheaper wood), and rabbet the upper back edge to take the back panel (see cross-section side view, *Figure B*). Note that the bottom projects beyond the false front to provide a supporting ledge for the outer front panel. Attach the bottom to the sides and false front with screws from the underside.

Next, glue up the backboards into a single piece, and cut to size. The back should run the full height of the case (including the hood), and fit between the rabbeted back edges of the sides. Since the hood will be narrower than the base, the width of the back must be cut to correspond. The top inside edge should be rabbeted to receive the hood top. The bottom edge should be cut to fit the rabbeted back edge of the case bottom, as shown in *Figure B*.

The size of the top opening in the base must now be reduced to provide a platform for the hood. This is done by making a frame which fits inside the base sides and on top of the false front. The front frame piece may be seen in *Figure B*.

Now make dovetail-shaped guide strips and mount these on the side pieces of the frame with glue and brads, as shown in *Figure D*, sliding hood detail. These will prevent the hood from lifting up or tipping forward.

Cut the hood sides, and rabbet the back edges for the case back. Study the sliding hood detail in *Figure D*, and shape the bottom edges of the sides as shown. Then cut the case top, sizing it to project at the front and sides as shown in the drawings. Round the front and side edges. Mark the back edge of the top for the position and width of the case back. Cut a rabbet on the underside, between the markings, to fit the rabbeted top edge of the back (*Figure B*). Sand the outside surfaces, and attach the top to the sides with glue and rub blocks.

Slide the hood assembly into position on the base, and check the fit. Cut a filler strip to fit across the front below the hood door (*Figure B*), and screw this to the sides. The screws will be covered by the molding.

Instead of a dial frame made like the door, such as is used on grandfather clocks, the Massachusetts clock hood has an inner front with the dial circle cut out. The dimensions of this piece are determined by inside measurement between the sides, and between the top and bottom of the hood. It is attached to the sides and the hood top with rub blocks, and to the bottom filler strip with screws (see *Figure B*).

The hood base molding should be made next (see cross section, *Figure B*). Methods of cutting moldings are described in Chapter I. Miter the corners of the molding, and attach it to the sides and to the front filler strip with glue and brads.

Cut a filler strip to fit across the front of the base, below the decorative panel and behind the wide oval base molding (*Figure B*). Attach this to the false front with glue and brads. Make the oval base molding and attach it to the filler strip and sides, with mitered corners. Sand thoroughly.

Next make the decorative panel for the base front. The exact structure of the frame will depend on the type of decorative panel to be used. This may be a

Plate 100

MASSACHUSETTS SHELF CLOCK

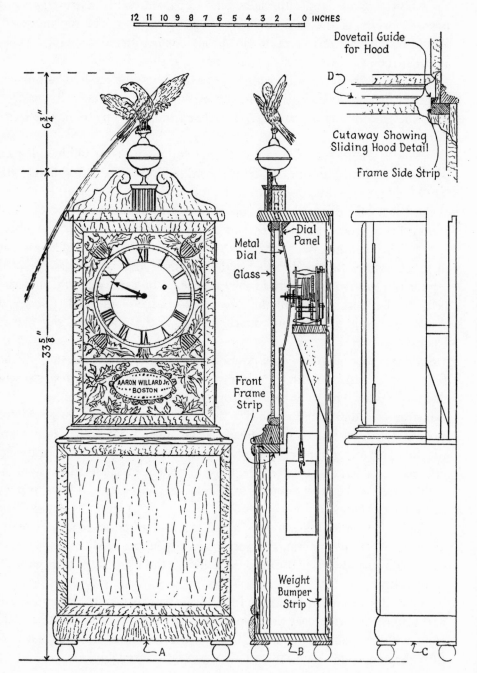

12 11 10 9 8 7 6 5 4 3 2 1 0 INCHES

Dovetail Guide
for Hood

Cutaway Showing
Sliding Hood Detail

Frame Side Strip

D

Dial
Panel

Metal
Dial

Glass

Front
Frame
Strip

AARON WILLARD Jr.
BOSTON

Weight
Bumper
Strip

$6\frac{3}{4}$"

$33\frac{5}{8}$"

A   B   C

reverse painting on glass, a mirror, or a panel of richly grained mahogany, as shown in *Figure A*.

If a wood panel is used, this is cut full size, and a frame is simulated by glued-on strips of oval crossbanded molding, with mitered corners. If glass is used, a simple mitered frame is constructed of mahogany $\frac{9}{16}''$ by $\frac{9}{16}''$, and the crossbanded oval molding, $\frac{3}{4}''$ wide, is glued on the face of the frame. This provides a lip to hold the glass, which is inserted from the back and puttied. Spline construction is used for this and the upper doorframe ("Miter Joints," Chapter I). The frame (without molding) must be the same thickness as the filler strip below the frame (*Figure B*).

The decorative front is usually attached to the base in such a manner as to be easily removed and replaced. This is accomplished by embedding two vertical pins in the bottom edge of the frame, one near each corner. Corresponding pin-holes are made in the top edge of the filler strip, behind the oval molding. At the top of the frame, two horizontal hooked pins are embedded in the back edge, one near each corner. A groove for each pin is cut in the top surface of the base top frame, with a hole at the back to catch the hook. The panel is then easily mounted on the base by inserting the lower pins in their holes first, then pushing the upper edge against the case until the hooks catch. The pins are indicated by heavy black lines in *Figure B*. The hood must be removed before the panel can be lifted off.

The ball feet may be turned on a lathe, with a round tenon turned on the upper side to be glued into a corresponding hole in the case bottom. The tenon also passes through a thin square piece of mahogany, similar to a finial block cap. The edges of this square are slightly rounded.

The finial block should be first cut to size, then fluted on the front surface as shown in *Figure A*. Cut a vertical groove in each side for the cresting (see *Figure B* for position). The square cap is cut slightly larger, and beveled so that its lower edge fits the top of the block (*Figure B*). The cap is then glued and bradded to the block, and a hole is prepared for the screw shank of the brass finial (or for a dowel, if a wooden finial is used). The finial block is attached to the hood top with a $\frac{3}{8}''$ dowel. Refer to *Figure B* for position.

Next make the cresting of $\frac{3}{8}''$ wood, veneered with vertical-grain figured mahogany. Shape both pieces in a single operation, cutting the double thickness with a scroll saw or jigsaw. Remove saw marks with a small file, and sand smooth. Glue the cresting in place, inserting the inner edges in the finial block grooves. Glue rub blocks in the angle formed by the back surface of the cresting and the case top.

The hood door is constructed in the same manner as the frame for a glass

base panel, described above, except that in this case the frame mahogany is
⁹⁄₁₆″ wide by ⅝″ thick. The frame is hinged to the right side of the hood
(*Figures A* and *C*).

The movement support is constructed last. Study your movement to determine the exact position of the movement shelf, then construct brackets as
shown in *Figure B*. Attach these to the back of the case with glue and screws.
Make and attach a bumper strip to protect the back from damage by the heavy
weight if the clock is moved or tilted (*Figure B*). However, the weight should
always be taken out of the case if it is to be moved more than a few inches
for adjustment of position.

The clock in *Plate 101* is an excellent example of the Terry pillar-and-scroll
shelf clock. This was the first clock ever made by mass-production methods,
cheaply enough to find a market among people of moderate means. Since it is
also one of the most beautiful clocks ever made, it was justly popular in its day
and is now valued by collectors. Because of the fragility of some of its parts,
original cases in perfect condition are rare.

Unlike the preceding clocks, this case is partitioned to separate the weight
channels from the central space which accommodates the movement, dial, and
pendulum. The shape of each partition, or guide batten, is shown in the side-
view cross section. Small holes are made through the battens for the insertion
of pins into the wood framework of the movement. The exact placing of the
pinholes will be best determined from the particular movement to be used. A
narrow strip to support the dial is nailed across the battens (see *Figure B*, cross-
section side view), with vertical holes for pins to be inserted into the lower edge
of the dial. A wooden pulley above each weight channel is mounted in the top
of the clock, which is cut out for this purpose.

The structure of the case may be best understood by study of the cross-section
plan. The two end sections of this drawing show the extension of the case top,
bottom, and back beyond the sides, with cross sections of the turned pillars.
The other sections are labeled.

The first step is to prepare the baseboard. This may be of solid mahogany, but
the usual and economical procedure is to use pine, with strips of mahogany
glued on to form the exposed ends and front edge. These strips are not mitered.
For greater strength, a single solid strip is applied along the entire front edge,
its width being the depth of the front from the outer edge of the molding to

just inside the doorframe. Behind this strip at each end, a rectangular piece of mahogany completes the exposed section from the molded edge to the case side. Most antique clocks of this type show the end division plainly, in difference of grain or color.

After gluing up the baseboard, cut it to over-all dimensions and lay out the interior plan in pencil on the upper surface. Use the cross-section plan as a guide. The case sides will be tongue-and-grooved to the base board (see "Joinery," Chapter I). The grooves for the guide battens should be sized for the width of wood to be used (⅜″ or less). Cut the required grooves, then mold the front and side edges to the shape shown in the drawings (see "Moldings," Chapter I).

The top board is usually of pine, with crossbanded mahogany glued on to form the edges. Since the top projects only slightly beyond the cresting, ¼″ mahogany may be used at the front. The side pieces should be wider, because of the exposed undersurface (from case side to edge). After gluing, mold the edges to the half-oval shape shown in the drawings.

Lay out the groove plan on the underside of the top board, and cut grooves for the sides and battens. These are placed to correspond exactly with those on the baseboard. Since the top is both thinner and narrower, however, the saw setting for depth of cut, and the fence adjustment, must be changed. Cut slots for the two weight-support pulleys. These should be placed so that each weight cord will be centered in its channel, in line with the drum on the movement (back of center). Study the movement for position. If a spring-driven or electric movement is used, the weight-support pulleys are not required.

The case sides are of solid mahogany. Measure the required width (from inside the case back), and cut the board ¼″ narrower. Glue ¼″ crossband mahogany over the end grain on the front edge, and mold the half-oval shape. Cut the sides to length, with a tongue at each end to fit the grooves in top and bottom. Sand all outside surfaces, and assemble the sides, top, and bottom with glue.

Cut the battens from thin soft wood (⅜″ or 5⁄16″), shaping them as shown in the cross-section side view. These pieces separate the weight channels from the movement and pendulum. Note that the upper section is cut out to permit minor adjustments to the clock movement. The length should be accurately measured to fit into the grooves previously cut in the case top and bottom. (If desired, battens may be installed with glue and brads, omitting the grooves). Slide the battens into place from the back.

Next, glue the back boards together, and cut to size. The length is determined by inside measurement between top and bottom of the case. The width

Plate 101

ELI TERRY PILLAR AND SCROLL CLOCK

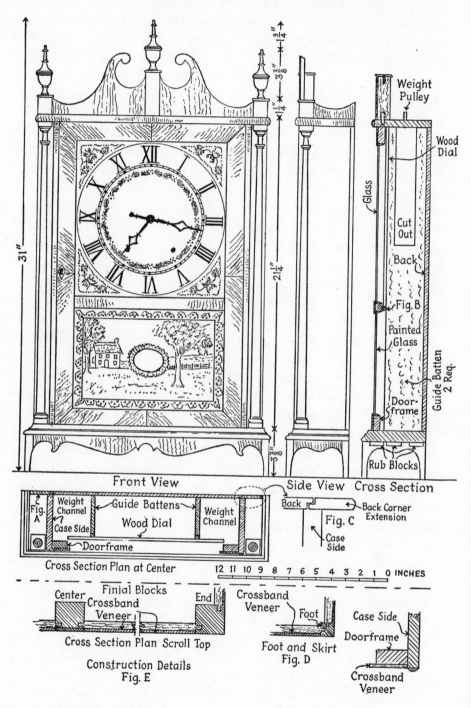

Weight Pulley

Wood Dial

Glass

Cut Out

Back

Fig. B

Painted Glass

Guide Batten 2 Req.

Doorframe

Rub Blocks

31"

21¼"

3⅜"

3¼"

3¼"

3⅜"

Front View   Side View   Cross Section

Fig. A

Weight Channel

Guide Battens

Weight Channel

Case Side

Wood Dial

Doorframe

Back

Back Corner Extension

Fig. C

Case Side

Cross Section Plan at Center

12 11 10 9 8 7 6 5 4 3 2 1 0 INCHES

Center

Finial Blocks

Crossband Veneer

End

Crossband Veneer

Foot

Case Side

Doorframe

Crossband Veneer

Cross Section Plan Scroll Top

Foot and Skirt Fig. D

Construction Details
Fig. E

must include a rabbet edge at each side to join the back corner extension (*Figure C*). Attach the back to the case with small nails.

Cut the two back corner extensions (*Figures A* and *C*) from solid mahogany. These pieces extend the back to the full width of the case top and bottom. The outer edges are molded in a half-oval. The inner edges are rabbeted to join the back behind the case sides. Sand and attach with glue and brads.

Turn the pillars as shown in the front and side views. These are cut accurately to fit between the case top and bottom, at the front corners. Glue the ends and set in place, then drive two thin nails into each pillar end, through the top and bottom of the case.

Next, cut panels slightly larger than required for the front and side skirting. Thin pine may be used. Veneer the panels with crossband mahogany, as shown in *Figure D* (see "Veneering," Chapter I). Cut to length, with a tongue at each end to join the feet. Shape the skirting pieces as shown in the front and side views. The curves may be cut with a band saw, or jigsaw. Remove saw marks with a small file, and sand smooth.

Cut the four feet to length from ½″ by ½″ mahogany. Each foot should be 2½″ long. Shape the feet to follow the curve downward from the skirting (see front and side views). Cut grooves in the foot tops to fit the skirt tongues (*Figure D*).

Assemble the feet and skirting with glue, then glue the assembly in place on the case bottom. Make rub blocks to fit the angle between skirt and bottom, and glue these at close intervals (see cross-section side view).

The cresting is also made of pine, veneered with crossband mahogany. The front cresting is made in two pieces, tongued at each end to join the finial blocks (*Figure E*). The side cresting is similarly tongued at the front edge. The required shapes are shown in the front and side views. Procedure is the same as that for the skirting, described above.

The finial blocks may be made of mahogany, or of bird's-eye or curly maple for contrast. The central block is taller, as shown in the drawings. All three are square in cross section, and are grooved for the tongues of the cresting (*Figure E*). A slightly larger square mahogany cap is then glued and bradded to the top of each block.

The finials may be of brass or turned wood. In either case, they are attached with dowels. A hole for the dowel is bored in the top of each finial block.

Dowel the central block to the case top, insert the front cresting, then glue on the side blocks and insert the side cresting. Glue rub blocks in the angles formed by the back bottom edges of the cresting and the case top.

If desired, ordinary butt-joint construction may be used, instead of tongue-

and-groove joining, for legs and finial blocks. The procedure described is preferred, however, for greater strength.

The doorframe is of soft wood, with mahogany veneer. The soft-wood frame should be made complete before veneering. It is of ordinary frame construction, with a crosspiece separating the two glass panes. Joints are tongue-and-groove. Inside edges need not be rabbeted for the glass and putty, since the veneer used is ⅛″ thick and is cut so as to form the required lip.

After assembling the soft-wood frame, cut the ⅛″ mahogany veneer as shown in the front view. Note that the sides, top, and bottom of the frame each have two pieces of veneer, cut at an angle to form a herringbone-grain pattern at the butt joint. The corner joints are mitered. The crosspiece veneer is cut with perpendicular grain.

The dial support is a narrow strip of thin soft wood (⅜″ or ⁵⁄₁₆″) nailed across the guide battens. Its position is shown in *Figure B*. Make a small vertical hole near each side for inserting a long pin into the lower edge of the dial.

The two weight pulleys are small circles of hardwood, about 1¼″ diameter by ⅜″ thick, grooved around for the weight cords. Bore a hole through the center of each for a steel pin, on which the pulley will turn freely. Slide the pulley onto the pin, and lay it across the slot in the case top so that the pulley will be centered in the slot. Groove the case top slightly for the ends of the pin, and drive a small staple to anchor each end.

Hold the movement in place to determine the position of the required pin-holes in the guide battens for anchoring the movement. These will be placed to correspond with the holes in the movement frame. After anchoring the movement in place with four pins (one at each side corner), run the weight cords up through the pulley slots, over the pulleys (in the grooves), and down into the weight channel. The weights are attached by hooks on the cord ends.

———◆———

The New Hampshire mirror clock in *Plate 102* is a type also popular in the first half of the nineteenth century. It is designed to hang on the wall. Two flat brass hanger plates are screwed to the top edge of the back (see side-view drawing, *Figure A*).

The case is a simple rectangular box. The top, bottom, and sides are joined with tongue and groove. The back may be fitted into rabbets in the side edges, or it may be made with rounded edges to show behind the sides. Rabbeted support strips for the dial are screwed to the top and sides, as shown in the detail

Plate 102

NEW HAMPSHIRE MIRROR CLOCK

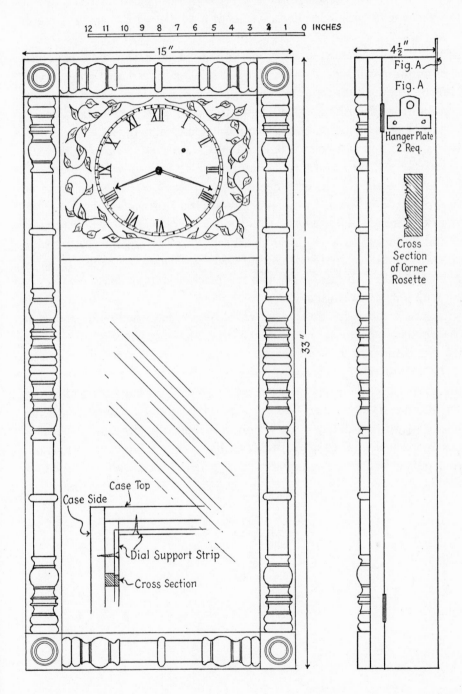

12 11 10 9 8 7 6 5 4 3 2 1 0 INCHES

15"

33"

4½"

Fig. A

Fig. A

Hanger Plate
2 Req.

Cross
Section
of Corner
Rosette

Case Top

Case Side

Dial Support Strip

Cross Section

243

drawing. The dial is attached to these strips with turn pins or screws, two at the top and one at each side. The movement is supported by screws through from the back.

The door forms the entire front, and is composed of a frame with one cross-piece, enclosing two panes of glass. The upper glass is decorated with reverse painting around the clear center which exposes the clock face. The large lower pane is a mirror. The frame is made with tongue-and-groove construction.

The turned ornamentation of the frame is made separately and applied with brads and glue. Top and bottom half-columns are turned as one column, the two sides as one. Procedure for half-column turning is discussed in Chapter I. There are four corner blocks ornamented with applied rosettes, which may be of brass, plaster, or of turned wood as shown in the cross-section drawing.

The cases were usually of pine, with mahogany veneer. The plain sections of pillars and corner blocks were painted black, and turned rings and rosettes were covered with gold leaf. Bulges were burnished to a high brilliance. In some cases the flat frame surfaces were painted black and the pillars completely gilded, with burnished rings and rosettes.

Original movements for this type of clock usually have the winding post at ten o'clock. The movement shown in the drawing, with winding post at two o'clock, is a banjo-type movement which is more easily obtained in reproduction. The weight cable is carried up over a grooved wooden roller mounted directly above the cable drum, on a shaft which runs from the back of the case to the dial frame. It then passes over a second roller similarly mounted near the left side of the case. A pulley is hung from this cable, the free end of which is then anchored at the top corner of the case. The weight is suspended from the hanging pulley. When the winding post is at ten o'clock, only one roller is required at the top.

CHAPTER XI

PERIOD CHARACTERISTICS
OF ENGLISH AND AMERICAN
FURNITURE

An INTEREST in fine furniture carries with it, necessarily, some interest in the style characteristics of different periods. The amateur cabinetmaker enjoys his hobby more when he understands the significance of each bit of shaping or decoration. The professional cabinetmaker finds that such knowledge improves his salesmanship. The housewife, whether she is selecting furniture for her own home or intelligently observing that of her friends, finds her judgment and appreciation increased as she learns to recognize what she sees. In addition, there are many for whom the study of period styles is, in itself, a fascinating hobby.

The busy man or woman, however, is often dismayed by the sheer abundance of information offered on this subject. He is confronted by an embarrassment of riches, a mass of verbiage in which the essential facts are scattered like precious nuggets through a mountain of ore. The mining process is rewarding, but requires a discouraging amount of time.

It is not our purpose to compete with those who have written so fully and, indeed, so interestingly on the subject of period furniture. We do not offer the brief historical notes in this volume as a magical substitute for more extensive

245

reading. We do, however, attempt to offer the salient facts, arranged for easy reference.

For the reader's convenience we have arranged these facts in two forms. The first is a Chronological Key, designed to answer the question: What were the chief distinguishing characteristics of furniture during a certain period? The second is a Subject Key, designed to answer the question: In what particular period did a certain characteristic occur?

If the reader desires, for example, to make or purchase a piece of furniture appropriate to the period of his own or a customer's home, the Chronological Key will quickly identify the suitable style. He may then turn to the Subject Key for amplification of details. If, on the other hand, he has in mind a specific piece of furniture, he may use the Subject Key to identify its period from a prominent characteristic. For example, if the piece has a distinctive type of foot, turn to the section headed "Feet," identify the period in which that foot was popular, then turn to the Chronological Key and compare the other salient characteristics of that period with those of the particular piece.

These Keys are necessarily brief; indeed, that is their chief merit. They are designed for quick reference rather than for a full treatment of the subject. The characteristics mentioned for any period, therefore, are only those which predominated; the omission of other features does not imply their nonexistence. It must be remembered that style developments and transitions were gradual; there was considerable mingling and overlapping of characteristics from one period to the next. Those of our readers who desire fuller information on any point will, perforce, seek it in the abundance of material mentioned above. For them the Keys in this chapter will make the task easier, by first identifying the particular point of interest.

CHRONOLOGICAL KEY

Jacobean: 1603–1688

Heavy, massive oak furniture decorated with all-over relief carving and split turnings; low chests and large press cupboards; canopied beds; chairs straight, uncomfortable, and scarce; stools commonly used for seating. Upholstery used only by the rich: needlepoint, velvet, leather, brocades, Turkey work, rush. Development of gate-leg table.

William and Mary: 1688–1702

Dutch influence, tending toward greater comfort and lighter, more graceful styles; curved lines, hood tops, shaped stretchers, ornamental turnings; walnut supplanted oak; veneering, especially on mirror frames; marquetry; lacquer;

increasing use of upholstery. Drawer pulls: brass or pearl drops, some bails. Development of grandfather clock, tall chest on stand. American developments: highboy, butterfly table.

Queen Anne: 1702–1714

Cabriole leg, Dutch foot, fiddleback chair splat; walnut chief wood; increasing use of veneer; some carving; lacquer and decorative painting; marble tops. Upholstery: needlepoint, chintzes, damask, leather; development of drop-leaf tables without gates.

Georgian: 1715–1800

Reigns of three Georges. "Georgian" usually refers to early half of this period; later furniture styles named for the great designers. Transition period: gradual development from Queen Anne to later styles. The late Georgian period, called the Golden Age of furniture making, began about the middle of the century, when the influence of Chippendale was at its height, and continued through the Hepplewhite and Sheraton periods.

Chippendale: 1710–1779

First to use mahogany to great extent; chief ornament was carving. In early years developed and elaborated Queen Anne features: cabriole leg; Dutch, ball-and-claw, and ogee foot, with variations; pierced splat; serpentine-front cabinets; fine carving, emphasis on C curves. Chinese influence in later years: square, fluted legs; pagoda motifs; fret-back and ladder-back chairs. Upholstery: brocades, needlepoint, leather. Drawer pulls: brass bails, "willow pattern" plates.

Adam Brothers: 1760–1792

Light, graceful, classical; slender straight lines; tapering legs, often fluted; flat surfaces. Ornamentation: painting, gilding, inlay. Vase and urn favorite designs. Mahogany, maple, pine, painted or gilded. Upholstery: French brocades, moire.

Hepplewhite: 1765–1795

Delicate lines; straight, square-cut, tapering legs, plain or with spade foot. Chair backs: shield or interlacing hearts. Bureaus and tables: concave curves. Ornamentation: inlay, some carving, including wheat ears, Prince of Wales plumes, bellflower husks. Dining tables frequently had two slender legs at each corner rather than one heavier leg. Mahogany, satinwood, rosewood, solid or veneer. Upholstery: light brocades, damask, haircloth. Drawer pulls: brass, bails on stamped oval plates.

Sheraton: 1751–1806

Borrowed and altered designs of Hepplewhite, also French Louis XVI. Delicate, simple styles; straight lines, convex curves, geometric forms. Tapered legs, usually round, sometimes square, often reeded. Chair backs: square, lattice or other openwork, narrow top rail with wider central panel. Ornamentation: turning, reeding, inlay, painted furniture; tambour work on cabinets. Mahogany, rosewood, satinwood, veneer. Upholstery: plain or patterned silks, gold and silver brocades, haircloth. Drawer pulls: brass, bails or rings on stamped plates, oval or other shapes; brass knobs.

Early American Styles

Earliest influence was Jacobean, followed by Queen Anne and other English styles. In New York and Pennsylvania the English influence was mingled with Dutch Colonial and Quaker. Maple, white pine, and fruit woods; in New York, Pennsylvania, and in the South: walnut, then mahogany. In addition to copying English styles, Americans developed some distinctive forms not previously known in England: butterfly tables (1700-1725), highboys (1690-1790), block-front furniture (1750-1780), rocking chairs (from about 1725), some forms of cottage furniture such as slat-back chairs (from about 1650), and Hitchcock chairs (1826-1843).

Philadelphia Chippendale: 1725–1790

Walnut and mahogany; fine, realistic carving of ball-and-claw feet, urn-and-flame finials, shells and other designs on knees and rails of chairs, drawer fronts, and so forth.

Block-Front Furniture: 1750–1780

Originated by Goddard and Townsend of Newport, Rhode Island; also made in Connecticut. Mahogany, sometimes cherry or maple; fine carving, shell design most popular. Goddard foot: a perfected form of bracket foot, following the block-front shape, with bulge ending in carved scroll.

Federal: 1790–1825

This period epitomized by Duncan Phyfe. Styles influenced by Hepplewhite, Sheraton, French Empire. Mahogany, veneer; reeding, carving; lyre design very popular. Upholstery: brocades, satin, damask, haircloth, frequently in striped patterns. The later years of Phyfe's influence showed a gradual deterioration in furniture design. Slender, graceful lines gave way to the heavy, ungainly forms of the Empire period. Drawer pulls: brass, bails or rings on fancy stamped plates; knobs of brass, glass, and wood.

Empire: Early Nineteenth Century

Trend toward French influence in United States following Revolutionary War. Architectural forms used in furniture; large plain surfaces; legs and brackets thick, with elaborate but coarse carving; marble tops. Mahogany, burl veneers, gilding, painting, stenciling. Development of power lathe influenced use of cheap ornamental turnings, as in spool beds, and mass production of "fancy chairs," such as the Hitchcock chair. Massive bureaus, heavy pedestal tables, scroll sofas, sleigh beds.

Victorian: Middle and Late Nineteenth Century

Elaborate curves; search for novelty in furniture forms and decoration led to caricature revivals of ancient styles. Mahogany, black walnut; marble tops; horsehair upholstery, coarse carving, fads and fripperies.

SUBJECT KEY
(Dates are approximate)

Feet

TURNED: *ball, bun, melon, onion.* Chiefly late seventeenth and early eighteenth century; also used in later periods.

STUMP: leg ends without feet; used on back legs in America.

STUB: feet with no legs.

SCROLL: *Flemish scroll,* carved, used on scroll leg, may curve in or out, seventeenth century. *Spanish foot,* possibly a later variant of the Flemish, is usually constructed with two glued-on blocks for the outward sweep of the scroll. Used on straight legs, except for a variant with a cuff at the top of the scroll, which is found on cabriole legs.

DUTCH: also called *club, pad, spoon.* Variations: *drake, Dutch grooved, slipper, snake.* With or without shoe, Queen Anne and Chippendale periods, early and middle eighteenth century.

BALL AND CLAW: Chinese origin, dragon claws grasping pearl. Variations: animal claw, bird claw, rat claw. Favorite foot of Chippendale period, middle eighteenth century.

PAW: animal paw with no ball, wood or brass. Late Empire, nineteenth century.

BRACKET: used without legs. Made of two blocks joined with mitered corners; wings cut in cyma curves or scrolls; profile straight or ogee; occasionally carved. Chippendale period, early and middle eighteenth century. *Goddard foot:* perfected form developed by John Goddard for block-front furniture, with carved scroll ending the bulge, 1750–1780. *French foot:* slender bracket with miter corner straight or slightly concave, inner curve simple. Much used by Hepplewhite, late eighteenth century.

SPADE: a square, tapered foot used on square, tapered legs. Adam, Hepplewhite, Sheraton, late eighteenth century.

ROUND OR MOLDED TAPER: used on round, tapered legs. Typical of Sheraton, late eighteenth century.

BRASS FOOT: often found on curved legs of tables, 1800–1825, and on Empire sofas. Plain, or animal paw. Brass paw feet also popular on French furniture, notably Louis XVI.

Finials and Drops

FINIALS: used on scroll-top pieces, such as clocks, highboys, cabinets; also on bedposts; occasionally found on very early chairs and settees. Usually of wood, turned and/or carved. Urn shapes most popular, with or without flame; cartouches (fanciful designs), also bird shapes, animal heads, human busts. Turned finials without carving used in all periods, but particularly on William and Mary styles; carved finials most popular in Chippendale period. Brass finials used by Hepplewhite and Sheraton; also on Willard and Terry-type clocks, and some tall clocks. (See also *Supplement* at end of chapter.)

DROPS: reverse finials, hanging down from curved apron, often found on highboys and lowboys of the William and Mary and Queen Anne periods.

Hardware

DRAWER PULLS: 1690–1720: small brass bail drops, tear drops, pearl drops, either solid or hollow; small brass plates with hand-stamped designs, attached with wire cotter pin, bent over inside and driven into wood. Some bail handles used, with cotter pin at each end of bail. 1720–1780: brass bails, brass plates with stamped designs; early bails attached with cotter pins, later with bolts or posts and nuts. "Willow pattern" brass plates cut by hand or cast in a mold, edges beveled; elaborate pierced designs in latter part of period. Some bails had no large plates, but a small round or oval plate at each end of bail. 1780–1820: Hepplewhite: bails on large oval plates, hand-stamped designs; stamped from thin brass, not cast or cut; some small plates. Sheraton: same, also round or oval ring handles attached at top of plate; "lion and ring" (mouth of lion holds ring); octagon plate and ring; brass knobs. 1815–1830: Early Empire:

same as above, but more often knobs of brass, glass, or wood. Usually round, projecting about one inch from surface. Brass knobs stamped with designs, often patriotic. Two types of glass knobs: pressed glass, attached by screws, either formed as part of the knob (glass), or separate metal screws set into knob with plaster of Paris; cut-glass knobs, backed with foil and sunk into brass cup with screw attached. Wood knobs seldom used on good furniture except on early chests, sometimes on bureaus or other pieces in late Sheraton and late Empire styles. (For additional details see *Supplement* at end of chapter.)

ESCUTCHEONS: brass keyhole plates, usually matching plates of drawer pulls.

HINGES: concealed unless ornamental. Brass or wrought-iron ornamental hinges: *H, HL, rat-tail,* used on eighteenth century cupboards; *strap,* chiefly on chests; *butterfly,* on gate-leg and butterfly tables.

NAILS AND SCREWS: used from early times, handmade of iron. After 1790, nails made by machine; upholstery nails with large round heads used for ornament. Screws made by machine after 1820, screws with pointed ends after 1850.

CASTERS: used in 1700 with leather rollers; in Chippendale and later periods with metal rollers.

Legs

TURNED: inverted cup, trumpet, spool or knob, ball, sausage, vase, spiral, bulbous: seventeenth and early eighteenth centuries.

FLEMISH SCROLL: carved, seventeenth century.

CABRIOLE: believed to be of Chinese origin; plain or carved: Queen Anne, Chippendale, early and middle eighteenth century.

SQUARE: fluted or fretted, inside corner chamfered: Chinese Chippendale, middle and late eighteenth century.

CLUSTER OF COLUMNS: Chinese Chippendale, middle and late eighteenth century.

TAPERED: round or square; reeded, fluted, or inlaid; taper often on inside surfaces only: Adam, Hepplewhite, Sheraton, late eighteenth and early nineteenth centuries.

SPLAYED OR RAKED: used on stools, Windsor chairs, seventeenth and eighteenth centuries.

CURULE: crossed half-circles: Adam, Sheraton, Duncan Phyfe, late eighteenth and early nineteenth centuries.

CONCAVE: Sheraton, Federal, Empire, late eighteenth and early nineteenth centuries.

WINGED LION: Empire sofas, nineteenth century.

Marble Tops

Used in Queen Anne and Chippendale periods, early and middle eighteenth century; popularity revived in Victorian period.

Mirrors

BEVELED GLASS: made in England before 1700 by hand; beveling about one inch wide, angle so slight it can barely be felt. Glass was thin and irregular; silvering by mercury process, uneven, causing blotched appearance of old mirrors. Early mirrors usually small; large mirrors were made up of small sections until late eighteenth century, when large glasses became practical because of improved manufacturing methods.

FRAMES: William and Mary period: veneer over pine, wide, rectangular. Queen Anne: walnut, curved tops, crestings. Chippendale: mahogany, rectangular, with elaborate scrolled crestings and side panels, or with carved ornaments such as bird figures, and so forth. Late eighteenth century: gilded; rectangular, oval or round, with elaborate carved top ornaments, such as urns, birds, and so forth. Early nineteenth century: gilded, rectangular, with heavy carved cornices, reverse paintings on glass panel above mirror.

Ornamentation

BOULLE: Inlay of tortoise shell and brass. Popular in France under Louis XIV, late seventeenth century, and later; never widely used in England or America.

BRASS INLAY: Often seen on English clocks of 1800–1810.

CARVING: Used from ancient times. All-over patterns in relief on flat surfaces popular on oak furniture of Jacobean period and earlier. Fine carving of individual designs, such as shells, birds, and so forth, used on furniture in Queen Anne period and later, with greatest popularity during Chippendale period, when mahogany became available in quantity. Mahogany, best wood for fine carving, was first brought to England from South America during reign of Queen Elizabeth; first imported to American colonies about 1700, but not used extensively until near middle of eighteenth century.

GILDING: gold leaf or gold dust used in England by Adam Brothers and later; in America, used chiefly on mirrors. Early gilding is distinct from gilt paint or gilt stencil popular in Empire period.

INLAY: used by Greek and Roman artists: ivory and precious metals. Contrasting wood inlay used on furniture as chief ornamentation by Hepplewhite and Sheraton, also used by Adam Brothers: chiefly "banding" one-half inch to two inches wide, "herringbone," bellflower husk, and other designs.

LACQUER, also called JAPANNING: early work was raised figures of plaster or paste, painted; popular in Queen Anne period. After 1790, flat surface designs painted on varnish.

MARQUETRY: Inlay with shaped pieces of contrasting woods forming elaborate pattern. Popular in France from early seventeenth century on; popular in England in William and Mary period.

ORMOLU: properly, an alloy of copper and zinc; term is also used to describe gilded brass or copper decorations mounted on furniture, used chiefly in France during eighteenth century.

PAINTED DESIGNS: Used from ancient times. Ceased in England during Chippendale period, revived by Adam Brothers, also used by Hepplewhite and Sheraton. Late Empire period used painting as well as stenciling.

SHAPED WOOD: shaping of furniture parts and ornaments, moldings, and so forth. Cyma curve and ogee (reversed cyma) popular in all periods. Scroll, C curves most popular in Chippendale period. Lyre used by Adam, Hepplewhite, Sheraton, Duncan Phyfe; also French clocks and American "lyre" clocks. Ribbon shapes, Chippendale; shield, interlacing hearts, Hepplewhite. See also Turning, Legs, Feet, Finials and Drops.

STENCILING: cheaper than painting, used on less valuable articles. Very popular in Empire period.

TURNING: one of most ancient woodworking arts. Lathes operated by bowstrings used in ancient Egypt, later lathes operated by treadles, water power, then steam power, finally electricity. Turned legs, posts, spindles, stretchers used in all periods. Split turnings (half-columns) used as ornamentation in Jacobean period, turned and fluted quarter-columns popular in Chippendale period and later. Most popular turned shapes: ball, sausage, melon, seventeenth century; trumpet, inverted cup, spiral, William and Mary; carved turnings, early Jacobean, revived in early Georgian; vase, urn, "bamboo," clustered turnings, straight round tapered legs, late Georgian; spool, nineteenth century. See also Legs, Feet, Finials and Drops.

Upholstery

Loose cushions used in early times. Attached to furniture in Elizabethan period (1558–1603) and later. Satin, silk, damask, velvet, brocade; also Turkey work (coarse canvas or sacking with worsted pattern drawn through and knotted like rugs); chintz (first made in India, later in England and France); *toile de Jouy* (a type of chintz originated at Jouy, France); haircloth (horsehair), favored by Hepplewhite and others in late eighteenth century, very popular in nineteenth century; needlepoint: petit point (over one thread), gros point (over two threads). Upholstery was a prerogative of the rich in early times; woven rush seats or wooden seats were more commonly used.

Veneer

Used in Europe long before it reached England. Early veneer was hand-cut, thicker than modern veneer. In England and America, use of veneer started with reign of William and Mary, was abandoned during Chippendale period, revived by the later Georgians (Hepplewhite, Sheraton, and others). Rich burl veneers highly favored in Empire period.

Wood

Native woods always popular, particularly in country districts and for inexpensive furniture. Fashionable woods used by the rich, in urban centers: oak, up to and including Jacobean period; walnut, William and Mary, Queen Anne; mahogany, Chippendale and all later periods; rosewood, satinwood, tulipwood, and other fancy woods used for inlay and veneering by Adam Brothers, Hepplewhite, Sheraton, and others. Ebony popular in France. Maple rare in Europe, common in America; used for furniture chiefly in country districts, but some very fine pieces were made of maple, particularly of the curly and tiger varieties. Cherry, fruit woods, pine, poplar, birch, used chiefly in country and inexpensive furniture; pine and poplar used also in elaborate pieces under veneer or gilding. Bent wood, such as Windsor chair bows, usually of yew in England, hickory in America.

SUPPLEMENT

For the sake of brevity, the historical notes in each chapter are confined to general style development. Two subjects merit somewhat fuller treatment than could be included there or in the Subject Key, which is designed for quick reference rather than full discussion. One of these is decorative hardware which, while not involved in the actual construction of furniture, should be carefully chosen for appropriate style. The other is the subject of finials, which also are decorative rather than structural. These two subjects are discussed briefly in the following paragraphs.

Ornamental Furniture Hardware

An important part of the decoration of early bureaus, desks, and chests of drawers was the hardware. Brass was used on all fine furniture from 1690 to 1825. Drawer pulls and escutcheons were made of cast brass in many designs, and the good housewife did not neglect to keep the brasses well polished. It is unfortunate that the original brasses are missing from many old pieces of furniture. Complete sets of antique brasses are now so rare that such a set may, in many cases, be worth more than the piece of furniture on which it is found.

The earliest brasses were attached by wires clinched on the inside. The insecurity of this method partially accounts for the rarity mentioned above, as handles were easily broken off and lost. A little later, posts were used, secured by handmade nuts of irregular shape on the inside. Threads were cut by hand until about 1820, when thread-cutting machines were invented.

In the seventeenth and early eighteenth centuries (William and Mary, Queen Anne), drawer pulls were usually small but decorative. The brass tear-drop pull, suspended from a small rosette, was popular. Pearl drops, solid or hollow, also were used. Small hand-tooled bails attached to a single knob came slightly later. The rosettes of drawer pulls and the escutcheons covering keyholes were worked in various designs with small tools. Stamping of the entire design with a single die was not developed until the nineteenth century (Empire period).

In the latter half of the eighteenth century, brasses were larger and more elaborate. A popular type was the Chippendale scroll, or "willow" pattern. These brasses were of varied and intricate designs, some solid, some pierced with elaborate openwork scrolls inside the scrolled outline. They were cast, not stamped, and the edges were always beveled and hand-filed. Old brasses were very thin (about $\frac{1}{32}''$). Thick brasses are modern, as are those with rounded or square edges. The escutcheons usually matched the plates of the drawer pulls. Surfaces were smooth and polished.

In the Hepplewhite and Sheraton periods, bails on solid oval plates were used, usually worked with conventional designs. Occasionally pictorial designs were used, and some of these were very fine. One, for example, shows a bee-hive and the legend, "Nothing Without Labor." Another bears a head of Thomas Jefferson; various patriotic designs were used. Most brasses of this period, however, bore simple floral, rope, or geometric designs. Octagonal or round plates also were used, with rings instead of bails, and on some Sheraton pieces the plate is a lion head holding a ring in its mouth. Some drawers had simple brass knobs. Bails on oval plates, however, were most popular.

In the nineteenth century brasses were stamped with dies, and the patterns were more elaborate. The lion's head was a popular decoration. Clusters of grapes, cornucopias, detailed star and floral patterns, urns, and even complete human figures were used. Knobs of brass, pressed or cut glass, and wood were popular on the massive bureaus of the Empire period.

Most early brasses used in America were imported, but good reproductions of old brasses can now be obtained in this country.

Our discussion of brasses would be incomplete without mention of mirror knobs. In the late eighteenth and early nineteenth centuries, wall mirrors were often supported by two small round or oval knobs, with a screw at the back. These were attached in such a way as to tilt the mirrors slightly forward. The faces of these knobs usually were of enamel in a brass frame, or of pressed brass. They were decorated with portraits of American statesmen, ladies in the costumes of the period, and other patriotic and pictorial designs. "Battersea" enamel knobs, named after the section of London where they originated, were most popular.

Hinges were concealed on most furniture, but on certain types such as chests, Welsh dressers, cupboards, and so forth, ornamental hinges were used. These were of brass on fine pieces, otherwise of wrought iron. Popular designs were: H, HL, rat-tail, butterfly, and strap hinges.

Finials

Finials have been used from ancient times. They are, in general, of three main types: those representing birds, animal heads or human busts; urns, with or without a flame; and the elaborate fanciful shapes known as cartouches.

The size of a finial must be determined by the piece on which it is to be mounted. Proportions must be carefully studied to avoid either the top-heavy effect of an overlarge finial, or the incomplete appearance given by one too small. Likewise the wood used, and the degree of ornamentation on a finial, should be in keeping with those of the whole piece. Although, generally speaking, finials were placed at the tops of articles, there is also a class of similarly turned pieces which were used at the intersections of cross-stretchers on tables or highboys. Reverse finials, or drops, were often used on the skirts of early lowboys and highboys. Brass finials were used on mirrors by Hepplewhite and Sheraton, on clocks of the Willard and Terry types, and on some tall clocks. Most finials, however, were of wood. Many of these were simple turned shapes; others were carved, particularly in the Chippendale period. As in other forms of decoration, the richest carving and most realistic effects are found on finials of Philadelphia origin. Those of John Goddard (Newport), while slightly less naturalistic, were also very fine. Wood finials were sometimes gilded, but were usually finished to match the piece of furniture.

Busts of famous political or literary characters were used frequently in England, but rarely in America. Bird finials are found chiefly on old mirrors and on banjo clocks.

Urn shapes are of infinite variation, ranging from the simplest turned shape to richly carved forms. Some have been found with bouquets of flowers carved in great detail. Many have flames rising from the tops, either suggested by a plain spiral or carved with varying degrees of realism. Some are classic shapes, fluted, with lids topped by a graceful subfinial.

Cartouches are found on some of the more elaborate Philadelphia Chippendale pieces, such as highboys.

Acorns and pineapples were also frequently used as inspiration for finials, and here again we find all degrees of elaboration, from the simplest conventional turned form to the most detailed carving.

Brass balls topped with slender spires were used on many tall clocks.

Finials were used on almost every variety of furniture. Bedposts were topped with them; highboys, chests of drawers and desks, particularly those with scroll or broken-arch tops, had from one to three finials, as did clocks. Newel posts of stairways often had massive finials, and in some cases, though more rarely, early settees and chairs were adorned with small finials.

Finials were sometimes made in two or three pieces when expensive wood was used. This was a matter of economy, and today the saving would not be worth the extra effort involved. It is often convenient, however, to make the base separately. Most finials require a base in order to look their best. This base may be a square block, perhaps beaded or fluted, or it may be a turned shape. A wood or steel dowel is used to mount the finial on the article of furniture.

Glossary

Glossary

ACANTHUS: Conventionalized leaf design used extensively in wood carving.

ACORN: Turned shape resembling an acorn; used chiefly as finial or drop.

ANCHOR BLOCK: Wooden block attached to inside of table skirting; the top is then screwed to the block.

APPLIQUÉ: Ornamentation made separately and attached to a plain surface; in furniture, attached carvings or moldings as distinguished from those cut into the solid wood.

APRON: In furniture, a piece used to connect the legs and give a finished appearance: in tables, just below the top; in chairs, just below the seat; in chests, cupboards, and so forth, below the base molding. The lower edge is often curved or scrolled. Also called Skirt.
Special Meaning: In tall clockcases the apron is the flaring top of the waist, on which the hood rests.

ARM BOW: Continuous arm of a Windsor chair, one piece of bent wood extending around the back, its ends forming the arms.

ASTRAGAL: Small half-round molding. Also called Bead.

BAIL: Metal loop, half-loop, or ring forming a drawer or door handle.

BALL AND CLAW: Furniture foot carved to represent bird claws holding a ball; also rat claws or other variants.

BALL FOOT: Round turned foot.

BAMBOO TURNING: Furniture part shaped to suggest bamboo; sometimes used as spindles on Windsor chairs of Sheraton period.

BANDING INLAY: Band of contrasting inlay, usually composed of two or more woods forming a design; wider than line inlay.

BANJO CLOCK: American wall clock invented by Simon Willard; the movement is enclosed in a round drum, below which is a narrow waist and rectangular base, suggesting a banjo in shape.

BAROQUE: Highly ornamented style popular in seventeenth century: exaggeration in size and decoration.

BASE: Lower piece of two-piece furniture, as the stand of a highboy. In one-piece furniture, the lowest part of the case, from and including the base molding, to the floor. Also, the pedestal of a table; the lower end of a column.

BASE MOLDING: Lowest horizontal molding on a piece of furniture.

BATTEN: Strip of wood used as a crosspiece for strength or support.

BATTERSEA ENAMEL: Type of decorative enamelwork developed at Battersea, England, in 1750. White enamel on copper, with painted or transfer design in colors. Used on mirror knobs and other ornamental hardware.

BEAD: Half-round molding, usually small, used for decoration and/or to conceal a joining; also, in turning, a disk-like bulge at the end of a contour unit.

BED BOLT: Special bolt five or six inches long, with tapered square head, used in assembling some types of bedsteads.

BELLFLOWER: Carved, painted, or inlaid design resembling drooping bell-shaped flowers or husks arranged vertically as on a stem.

BELL TOP: Shaped dome rising above a flat top, as on late William and Mary tall clocks.

BENDING WOOD: Process of forming wood into continuous structural shapes; the wood is first softened, if necessary, by soaking, then clamped on a form.

BEVEL: Sloping edge, used decoratively on mirrors and outside surfaces of furniture, and so forth; also used on structural pieces to fit a thicker board into a narrow groove.

BEZEL: In clocks, the brass or wood rim which holds the glass covering the dial. The term usually refers to a round rim, as on a banjo clock; a square frame is called a door.

BLOCK FOOT: Square end of leg without a shaped foot.

BLOCK FRONT: Style of furniture front having recessed center, with each end section consisting of a vertical flattened bulge or "block" protruding from a narrow flat border. The "blocks" are often rounded at top, with shell carving. Also a narrow case, such as that of a tall clock, having a single "block" on front.

BOBTAIL: Tongue projecting from back of some Windsor chair seats, in which two bracing spindles are set.

BONNET TOP: Unbroken arched top used on some tall clocks, highboys, and so forth. Also called Hooded Top, Arched Top.

BOSS: Round or oval ornament attached to a flat surface; also a turned disk used as mounting for a turned or carved rosette, as on the scrolls of a highboy top.

BRACKET: 1. Small ornamental shelf. 2. Triangular piece, usually carved or pierced, placed between leg and skirting for support and/or decoration. 3. Any angle support.

BRACKET CLOCK: English clock designed to stand on a bracket or shelf.

BRACKET FOOT: Furniture foot composed of two roughly triangular blocks joined with a mitered corner. Usually ornamental in shape: profile straight, curved, or ogee; wings cut in scrolls.

BRASSES: In furniture, the term usually refers to ornamental brass handles.

BROCADE: Upholstery fabric woven with raised pattern, often with metallic threads.

BROKEN ARCH: An arch interrupted at the apex, forming ornamental furniture top; also, any variant of this shape, as two opposing gooseneck curves which do not meet. Also called Scroll Top.

BUN FOOT: A ball foot flattened at top and bottom.

BUTT JOINT: Joining of wood squarely across the end grain of both pieces.

BUTTERFLY: Wing-shaped table-leaf support which swings on pivots at top and bottom.

CABRIOLE LEG: Furniture leg shaped in elongated S curve; the diameter is graduated from a bulging knee or hip to a slender ankle. The outward curve at bottom is completed by the foot.

CANOPY BED: Early beds were equipped with a hood or canopy, either of wood or of fabric attached to a wooden frame. The frame was usually supported by the four bedposts. Also called Tester Beds.

CARTOUCHE: Ornamental shape often used as a central decoration or finial; originally, the design represented an unrolled scroll tablet containing a coat of arms, initials, or other symbol, but later forms were often so elaborated that the original design was obscured.

CASE: In cabinetwork, the box-like body of a cabinet, chest, and so forth, as distinguished from the legs and/or other members.

CAVETTO: Concave molding, often the chief feature of a cornice.

CHAMFER: A forty-five-degree cut removing the corner of a post, molding, or leg. Used on outside corners for decoration, on inside corners to reduce undesirable bulkiness.

CHECK: A split or crack running in from the end of a board.

CHINESE: Furniture style combining very simple structural form with intricate surface decoration; "Chinese Chippendale" features simple straight lines, with light fretwork and fluting as decoration.

CLEAT: Strip of wood attached across a flat surface as a brace, or to prevent warping.

CLUB FOOT: A stubby, rounded foot terminating the outward curve of a cabriole leg; frequently has bottom carved to simulate a flat disk or "shoe." Also called Dutch or Queen Anne foot.

CLUSTERED COLUMNS: Three or more slender columns joined to form a single leg or post.

COCK BEADING: Bead projecting above the adjacent surface; not flush.

COLUMN: Pillar or post, usually turned, often fluted or reeded. Used chiefly for decoration: full columns, half-columns, or quarter-columns, the latter set vertically into the corners of furniture cases.

COMB BACK: Style of Windsor chair in which several spindles extend above the main back to a short rail or "comb." In a DOUBLE COMB BACK, the central spindles continue to a secondary comb above the first.

CONTINUOUS FOOT: Similar to bracket feet, but made in one piece with the base molding;

used on low case furniture such as chests, cupboards, and so forth.

CORNER BLOCK: Triangular block set into an inside corner of case work for support.

CORNICE: In furniture, the top horizontal molding across the front and sides of tall pieces.

COUNTERBORED, COUNTERSUNK: Wood surface bored to permit entry of screw head below surface. The hole is then filled with a wooden plug, sanded flat.

COVE: Large concave molding.

CREST: Scrolled, carved, or fretted panel placed upright on top of a clock, mirror, and so forth, for decoration.

CROW'S NEST: In tilt-top tables, the assembled unit by which the top is attached to the pedestal: two squares joined by four corner posts, attached in such a way as to allow the top to tilt and turn.

CYMA: A double curve, also called Ogee. When the upper curve is concave and the lower convex, the technical term is *cyma recta*. When the convex curve is uppermost, it is *cyma reversa*. "Ogee" strictly means *cyma reversa*, but is loosely applied to both.

DADO: Channel cut across a surface to receive inlay, molding, the end of a shelf or frame piece, and so forth.

DENTIL: Molding composed of small blocks regularly spaced, like teeth.

DISHED: Hollowed; also, a flat top surrounded by a raised edge, as on a dish-top table.

DOVETAIL: Method of joining two boards by cutting interlocking shapes on both, wedge-shaped tenons on one member fitting accurately into wedge-shaped cutouts on the other.

DOWEL: Turned straight pin which fits into matching holes in two members, making a joint.

DRAKE FOOT: Variant of the Queen Anne foot: three toes, separated by tapered grooves representing the web.

DRAWBORE: Method of tightening and locking a mortise-and-tenon joint with a wood pin through both members. The pinhole in the tenon is bored 1/32″ nearer the shoulder than the hole through the mortise wall; the joint is drawn tight as the pin is driven in.

DROP: Pendant ornament, usually turned; common in William and Mary and Queen Anne periods.

DRUM: Circular case housing movement of banjo-type clocks.

DUTCH FOOT: Queen Anne foot; a club foot or variant.

EARS: Scrolled ends usually found on top rail of Chippendale chairs.

EGG AND DART: Design often carved on ovolo moldings, resembling alternate eggs and darts.

ESCUTCHEON: Decoration of brass, ivory, or contrasting wood, inlaid or overlaid on a keyhole.

FEATHER EDGE: A wide, smooth bevel, reducing the edge of a board to a thin line.

FIDDLEBACK: Chair back with violin-shaped splat; typical of Queen Anne period.

FINGER JOINT: Joint made by cutting two board ends into alternate finger-like protrusions and matching cutouts; chiefly used in vertical hinge construction for table-leaf supports.

FINIAL: Ornament placed upright to terminate a post or to accent the center or ending of a structural feature. Examples: tops of bedposts; center and corners of broken-arch tops; crossing of curved stretchers in William and Mary furniture. Usually turned or/and carved.

FINIAL BLOCK: Finished block, usually square, sometimes fluted, on which a finial is mounted.

FINISH: Final processing of a wood surface, both for decorative appearance and to preserve the wood. The term applies to any type of surface dressing, from simple polishing and waxing to staining, varnishing, painting, and so forth.

FLAME: Popular finial detail: a point carved to simulate flame, rising from a turned urn shape.

FLAT SWING SUPPORT: Table-leaf support without leg or gate, consisting of a strip of wood hinged or pivoted to understructure of table top.

FLUSH: Joining of two edges on an even plane, forming an unbroken surface.

FLUSH BEADING: Bead set in a groove so that the top of the bead is level with the adjacent surface.

FLUTING: Half-round grooves cut parallel in surface of a column, leg, or pilaster; ridge between grooves one-half width of groove, or less.

FOLIATED: Ornamented with leaf or vine design.

FOLDING LEAF: Table leaf finished on both sides and hinged so as to lie flat on table top when not in use, as in antique card tables.

FRAME: In mirrors, doors, panels, and so forth, the border which holds the glass or wood panel; in case work, the skeleton or framework, as distinguished from the face, or surface.

FRENCH FOOT: Usually, a type of bracket foot favored by Hepplewhite, extending the vertical line of the case downward, with a slight flare at the bottom. Occasionally, the term is applied to a scrolled or spiraled foot with a carved ornament such as a dolphin.

FRET, FRETWORK: Ornamental pattern composed of interlacing lines or curves, either pierced (cut completely through), or carved in low relief on a solid ground. Used in decorative panels, chair backs, brackets, crestings. Also called Latticework.

FRIEZE, FRISE: Heavy upholstery fabric with a nap; may be wool, linen, or cotton.

GATE-LEG: A gate-like assembly used as a leaf support on early drop-leaf tables. Usually composed of four members: a vertical pivot piece with pins turned at each end, a vertical end piece or "leg," and two stretchers connecting the vertical members. The pivot piece was mounted between the understructure of the table top and a low stretcher connecting the fixed table legs. When stretchers went out of style, gates were superseded by swinging legs on vertical hinge supports (about 1720).

GODDARD FOOT: Bracket foot designed by Goddard for block-front furniture: the bulge of the "block" is continued from the case onto the foot, ending in a scroll at the bottom.

GOUGE: Scoop-shaped tool used in wood carving.

GRAIN: Direction or pattern of wood fibers in a board.

GRAINING: Process of painting to imitate the grain of wood.

GRANDFATHER CLOCK: Long-pendulum clock in a tall case, usually seven to nine feet in height. Case is made in two parts: (1) the pendulum case, consisting of base and waist; (2) the hood covering the clock movement and dial.

GRANDMOTHER CLOCK: Long-pendulum clock in a case made like that of a grandfather clock, but usually less than five feet in height.

GROS POINT: *See* Needlepoint.

HAIRCLOTH: Upholstery fabric woven of horsehair, popular in middle nineteenth cen-

tury. A mixture of horsehair and linen was used in the eighteenth century.

HALF-COLUMN: Split half of a turned column, applied as decoration to a flat surface or chamfered corner.

HEART BACK: Heart-shaped chair back used by Hepplewhite. Also called Shield Back.

HERRINGBONE: Joining of two or more pieces of inlay with alternately slanting grain.

H HINGE: Brass or wrought-iron hinge shaped like the letter H.

H STRETCHER: Common stretcher construction: a stretcher at each side joining front to back leg, with a third stretcher connecting the two.

HIGH RELIEF: Deep surface carving, as distinguished from low relief or "flat" carving.

HIGHBOY: Tall chest of drawers made in two sections; the base is a stand on legs, with three or more small drawers; the upper section has several large drawers, usually with three small drawers at top.

HIP: The bulging top of a cabriole leg. Also called Knee.

HITCHCOCK: Chair style originated by Hitchcock in 1826; American version of the "fancy chair," with turned legs and top rail, rush or cane seat, usually painted black with stencil design in gold and colors on back slat.

HOOD: The removable upper section of a grandfather clock case, covering the movement and dial. Also called Bonnet.

HOOP BACK: Windsor chair back having semicircular upper rail formed of bent wood, with both ends mortised into the back bow.

HUSK: Ornamental design resembling drooping wheat husks or cornflowers, arranged vertically as on a stem. Also called Bellflower.

INCISED: Decoration engraved or carved into a surface rather than raised above it.

INLAY: Decorative material, usually wood veneer, laid flush in precut space on a flat surface. Designs are formed by fitting together pieces with contrasting colors and grains.

JIGSAW: Small power saw with detachable blade which can be threaded through a hole to cut interior designs such as pierced fretwork.

JOINERY: Literally, the joining together of two pieces of wood. Generally applied to the whole craft of cabinetmaking and woodworking.

KERF: A saw cut.

KEYSTONE: The center block at the top of an arch.

KNEE: The convex curve or bulge at the top of a cabriole leg. Also called Hip.

KNUCKLE: The scrolled end of a chair arm, as on some Windsor and Chippendale chairs.

LADDER BACK: Chair back with several horizontal slats giving the appearance of a ladder.

LAMINATING: Combining thin layers of wood to form a single thick piece. The layers are usually laid with alternating grain to resist warping.

LANTERN CLOCK: Seventeenth-century English clock resembling a lantern of that period. The top is a dome-shaped bell. Movement and dial are brass, with brass fretwork above dial and at sides; wall or shelf clock.

LAP JOINT: Flush joining of two boards, made by cutting away opposite halves of the thickness of each board.

LATHE (WOOD): Machine which rapidly revolves a piece of wood so that it can be shaped by holding a cutting tool against the surface. The process is called "turning."

LATTICE: *See* Fret.

LEAF (DESK): Front panel hinged so as to open and form a horizontal surface for writing.

LEAF (TABLE): Part of table top hinged so as to drop or fold over when not in use, to conserve space.

LEAF JOINT: Flush joining of table surface and drop leaf by means of a convex molding cut on one edge, and a corresponding concave molding on the other.

LINE INLAY: Narrow line of contrasting wood (usually ⅟₁₆″ wide), laid flush in a precut channel paralleling the edges of a panel, drawer front, table leg, and so forth.

LIP: Drawer edge which extends slightly over the surrounding surface, common in Queen Anne and early Chippendale furniture. The lip may be formed by the rabbeted edge of the drawer front, or by an applied molding.

LOOP BACK: Windsor chair back with continuous side and top rail of bent wood, forming a loop mortised into the seat at both ends.

LOW RELIEF: Carving raised only slightly from surrounding surface: "flat" carving.

LOWBOY: Low side table or chest on legs, resembling the stand of a highboy; may have three to five small drawers.

LYRE CLOCK: Variant of the banjo clock, with case shaped to resemble a lyre.

LYRE MOTIF: Ornamental shape resembling a lyre, used in table supports, chair backs, and other furniture parts, especially by Duncan Phyfe.

MARQUETRY: Elaborate pattern of inlay covering most or all of a surface. Shaped and fitted pieces of veneer in varying shades of color are combined to form a floral or other design.

MASSACHUSETTS SHELF CLOCK: Mantel or shelf clock with case made in two sections: the base has removable panel front of reverse-painted glass or figured veneer; the hood is slightly narrower, with crested top and reverse-painted glass door having a circle of clear glass over dial.

MEDALLION: Plaque of wood or other material, carved, molded, or painted with decorative design, set into a surface.

MELON FOOT: Large bulbous turned foot, sometimes decorated with incised vertical lines.

MILLING: Cutting or dressing a surface by means of rotary cutters or grinders.

MIRROR CLOCK: There are various types of clocks with mirror decoration, but the term usually refers to a New Hampshire mirror clock: a shallow box-like case designed to hang on wall; hinged front composed of a frame enclosing two panes of glass, the lower a mirror, the upper clear over dial, with reverse-painted spandrels.

MITER, MITRE: An equal angle cut on the ends of two pieces, as of molding, to form a corner joint.

MOHAIR: Upholstery fabric originally made from Angora goat hair.

MOLD, MOLDING: Profile shaping, usually to decorate an edge or an angle between two adjoining planes; it may be cut in the solid wood, or shaped separately and applied.

MORTISE: Hole or slot cut in wood to receive a projecting tenon.

MORTISE AND TENON: Joint made by fitting tenon on one member into matching mortise cut in another member.

NECK: Slender upper portion of a contour unit, as the neck of a turned vase.

NEEDLEPOINT: Upholstery material made by embroidering a coarse-weave fabric. In GROS POINT each stitch covers two threads of the fabric, in PETIT POINT each stitch covers one thread.

NEW HAMPSHIRE MIRROR CLOCK: *See* Mirror Clock.

OFF-CENTER TURNING: Contour shaping at an angle, performed by placing workpiece in lathe with lathe centers a calculated distance from the end centers of the piece in opposite directions, as: left of center on one end, right of center on the other end.

OGEE: Double or S curve: technically, *cyma reversa,* convex at top, concave at bottom; chiefly used in profile shaping of moldings, bracket feet, mirror frames, and so forth.

ONION FOOT: Small turned ball, slightly oval in shape.

OVOLO: Quarter-circle convex molding.

OXBOW: Furniture-front contour, concave center, convex ends; reverse of serpentine.

PAD FOOT: Another name for club, Dutch, or Queen Anne foot.

PANEL: Board enclosed in a framework of stiles and rails; also, an entire surface, as the side or front of a chest.

PAW FOOT: Brass or carved wood foot resembling the paw of an animal.

PEAR DROP: Small brass pendant used as drawer pull on late seventeenth-century furniture.

PEDESTAL TABLE: Small table supported on a single central column, or pedestal, to which spreading feet are attached.

PEDIMENT: Triangular top or crest, used on tall furniture. BROKEN PEDIMENT: two sides of a pediment which do not meet at the center; also Broken Arch.

PEMBROKE TABLE: Small drop-leaf table with drawer; the leaves when raised are supported by flat swing supports rather than gates or swing legs.

PENDANT: Hanging ornament. Also called Drop.

PENDULUM: Rod with weight at lower end, suspended from a clock movement to regulate the clock by the speed of its swing.

PETIT POINT: *See* Needlepoint.

PHILADELPHIA CHIPPENDALE: Style and quality of furniture craftsmanship typical of Philadelphia in eighteenth century, when the city was a center of Colonial wealth. Chief characteristics are Chippendale, with emphasis on rich carving. Best known examples are chairs, highboys, and lowboys.

PIE-CRUST TABLE: Round pedestal table with raised scalloped edge.

PIERCED: Ornamental designs cut completely through the material, as in some decorative hardware, fretwork, and so forth.

PIGEONHOLES: Small open compartments in the upper interior of a desk.

PILASTER: Rectangular column attached vertically to a surface. On furniture it is usually purely decorative, and its thickness may be only a fraction of its surface width. Often fluted or carved, with flaring base and top.

PILLAR AND SCROLL: Shelf clock developed by Eli Terry in the early nineteenth century; rectangular case with slender turned pillars at front corners, scrolled cresting, three brass or turned wood finials. The door is a frame enclosing clear glass over dial, reverse-painted glass below; wooden movement.

PIN: Thin turned peg. *See* Drawbore.

PIVOT PIN: Smooth round peg fitting its hole loosely to permit turning; may be made separately or turned on the end of the swinging member.

PLUG: Peg shaped to fill a hole; cover for countersunk screw.

PROFILE: Contour or outline, as seen in cross section.

QUARTER-COLUMN: One-fourth section of a turned column, usually fluted: set vertically in a prepared right-angled channel on front corners of casework, as decoration.

QUEEN ANNE FOOT: *See* Club Foot.

RABBET: Right-angled recess cut along the edge of a board, leaving one surface intact.

RAILS: Horizontal members of furniture framework.

RAKE: Angle of furniture leg which is not exactly vertical.

RAMP: The quickly rising portion of a curve.

RECESS: Opening, niche, cavity; also, any part set back from the surface line.

REEDING: Parallel half-round ridges on the surface of a column, leg, and so forth, resembling a bundle of reeds. Reverse of fluting.

RELIEF: Protrusion of carved design from the surrounding surface. Carving which appears nearly flat is in low relief; prominently raised carving is in high relief.

RETURN: In decorative work, the continuation of a molding at an angle, as in a mitered picture frame, or the mitered horizontal molding on case furniture; also, cutting the end profile of a molding to match the face.

REVERSE PAINTING: Pictures painted on glass were used extensively for decoration on clocks and mirrors in early nineteenth century. Such pictures are painted on the back of the glass, in reverse; that is, surface details first, background last.

ROCOCO: Eighteenth-century style featuring elaborate decoration, but emphasizing grace and delicacy rather than the massive splendor of Baroque.

ROPE MOLDING: Quarter- or half-round molding carved spirally to resemble rope. Also called Cable Molding.

ROSETTE: Flat round ornament usually turned and/or carved; used to terminate a scroll, or as decoration on mirror frames, and so forth.

ROUTING: Cutting a groove with a scoop-shaped plane or with revolving blades.

RUB BLOCK: Triangular block used in right angles for strength and support; the block is coated with glue and rubbed into place until it adheres.

RULE JOINT. *See* Leaf Joint.

RUNNER: Strip of wood in case framework, placed so as to support and guide a drawer.

RUSH: Long narrow leaves cured and twisted together to form a continuous rope for weaving chair seats, and so forth.

SADDLE SEAT: Chair seat made of thick wood, hollowed on both sides of a central ridge which rises from center to front, like the pommel of a saddle.

SANDING: Rubbing with sandpaper to achieve a smooth surface.

SCALLOP: A series of curves cut on the edge of a skirting, and so forth; also, a carved shell ornament resembling the scallop shell.

SCHOOL: Characteristic style associated with a group rather than with an individual, as the Philadelphia School, the Newport School, and so forth; also, the Chippendale School, meaning "Chippendale and his imitators," and so forth.

SCROLL: Spiral or convolute design, resembling the end of a rolled-up scroll tablet. In furniture the term is commonly applied to any C curve.

SERPENTINE: Undulating contour. In furniture, the term specifically applies to a piece with convex center and concave ends, the center swell usually longer than either concave section.

SHAPED: Any contour other than flat; any edge other than straight.

SHELL: Popular carved or inlaid design with many variations; the scallop shell is most

common, but various other seashells also are imitated.

SHIELD BACK: Chair back typical of Hepplewhite; a shield-shaped outline, with large openwork center designs such as three feathers, festoons, vase shapes, and so forth.

SHOE: The flat pad or disk under a Dutch foot, carved as part of the foot. All variants of the Dutch foot were used with or without the shoe, according to individual preference.

SHOULDER: Sudden widening from a narrow neck, as the shoulder of a tenon.

SIDE CHAIR: Chair without arms, usually small.

SKIRT, SKIRTING: *See* Apron.

SLAT: Cross-member of chair back.

SLAT BACK: Early American chair having a number of arched or scrolled slats, turned stiles and legs, rush seat.

SLIDING DOVETAIL: Long dovetail joint used to attach tripod legs to pedestal.

SLIP SEAT: Loose seat, made separately and upholstered before placing in the seat frame of the chair.

SNAKE FOOT: Elongated Dutch foot, pointed, flattened on each side of top, leaving a central ridge from point to ankle.

SOCKETING: Fitting an end of one member into a prepared cavity in another, as a chair leg into a solid seat.

SPACER: Strip of wood fitted to fill a gap between adjoining members.

SPADE FOOT: Square tapered foot cut on a square tapered leg. The leg flares out from the ankle to full top dimension, from which the foot tapers sharply to the floor. A bead is cut at the top of the foot.

SPANDREL: The roughly triangular area resulting in each corner when an arc or circle is enclosed in a square; the corners of a square clock dial, outside the circle of numerals.

SPINDLE: Slender round and tapered rod used in Windsor chair backs, and so forth.

SPLAT: Vertical center panel of a chair back.

SPLAY: Outward slant, as of furniture legs. Also called Rake.

SPLINE: Thin piece of wood set into grooves cut in two adjoining edges, as in a miter joint. The spline is placed with grain at right angles or diagonal to that of the joined members.

SPOOL TURNING: Pattern of successive bulges resembling a row of spools; popular in

America in nineteenth century, as in spool beds.

SQUIRREL CAGE: Another name for Crow's Nest.

STANDARD: Uprights supporting a looking-glass frame.

STENCIL: Design pierced through paper or metal which is then laid on a surface and painted over, transferring the design to the surface.

STILE: Vertical member of furniture frame; also, back chair leg which continues above seat line to form part of back.

STIPPLE: Tiny dots or indentations closely spaced on a surface.

STOP FLUTING: Flute outlined with grooves but not routed out, leaving a bead in each flute; also, flutes filled with brass rods. Usually used at lower end of a column, with plain fluting above.

STRETCHER: Crosspiece or rung connecting the legs of a chair or table.

SUNBURST: Carved rays radiating from a central circle or arc.

SWELL FRONT: Chest front with single long convex curve.

SWING LEG: Drop-leaf support formed by extra leg which swings out from a vertical hinge.

SWIVEL: Pivot.

TAILPIECE: *See* Bobtail.

TEMPLATE: Pattern cut to accurate size and shape, for marking.

TENON: Tongue cut on the end of one member to fit a mortise in another.

TENON PIN: Thin wood pin glued and driven into a hole bored through both members of a mortise-and-tenon joint, for added strength.

TERRY CLOCK: *See* Pillar and Scroll.

TESTER: *See* Canopy.

THREE FEATHERS: Design taken from royal coat of arms, used chiefly by Hepplewhite.

TILT TOP: Pedestal table with top attached so as to hang vertically when not in use.

TIP AND TURN: Pedestal table with top which both tilts and turns.

TOILE DE JOUY: Popular upholstery fabric in eighteenth century; fine cotton printed with floral and other designs; originated at Jouy, France.

TONGUE AND GROOVE: Joining of two boards by means of a continuous projection along the edge of one, and a corresponding groove in the edge of the other.

TORCH: Finial carved to represent flame.

TORUS: Bulging convex molding, larger than astragal or bead.

TRACERY: Delicate latticework of metal, often backed with glass or cloth.

TRANSITIONAL: Overlapping of period styles. Before modern transportation and communication, styles changed slowly, particularly in rural areas. Many authentic antiques show mixed characteristics.

TRIPOD: Three-legged pedestal used for most pedestal tables, candlestands, and fire screens.

TRUCKLE BED: Low bed designed to slide under large bed when not in use. Also called Trundle Bed.

TRUMPET: Turned contour popular in William and Mary period, resembling a trumpet with bell turned upward.

TRUNDLE BED: *see* Truckle Bed.

TRUSS: Bar or rail running between the ends of a table; a brace or support, as on a trestle table.

TURKEY WORK: Embroidered upholstery fabric popular in seventeenth century; pattern of worsted drawn through canvas and knotted, as in Turkey rugs.

TURNING: Process of shaping wood by the application of cutting tools to a rapidly revolving surface. The machine which rotates the wood is called a lathe.

UNDERBRACING: Arrangement of stretchers to brace the legs of chairs, tables, and so forth. Also Underframe.

UNDERCUT: Groove cut inward at the base of a carved design, to sharpen the outline.

UNDERSLUNG: Drawer supported at the top edges of its sides, instead of at the bottom.

URN: Classical design commonly used in turning, especially finials; also as carved, inlaid, or painted decoration.

VALANCE: In furniture, a shaped strip extending across the top of an opening, for decoration.

VASE: Ornamental design used in carving, inlay, painting; also as contour design in chair splats and in turning.

VENEER: Thin layer of decorative wood covering a surface.

WAG-ON-THE-WALL: Pendulum clock without case, designed to hang on wall.

WAIST: Narrow section of tall clockcase, between base and hood.

WARPING: Bending of boards due to changes in moisture content of the wood fibers.

WATER LEAF: Long laurel-like leaf design used in carving and other decorative work.

WHEAT EAR: Carved ornament representing several ears of wheat.

WILLOW PATTERN: Scrolled brass plates, solid or pierced, to which bails are attached: typical drawer handles of Chippendale period.

WINDSOR: Type of chair with bent-wood back frame and spindles, solid wood or rush seat with legs socketed in seat; made in various styles.

WING BLOCKS: Shaped blocks attached at both sides of cabriole leg top, to complete the flare where the leg joins the skirting.

WING CHAIR: Large upholstered chair with high back and side pieces.

WRITING ARM: Wide flat arm found on many Windsor chairs, on right side; sometimes hinged.